THE FRESCOES OF CONRAD ALBRIZIO

THE FRESCOES OF

PUBLIC MURALS IN

CONRAD ALBRIZIO

THE MIDCENTURY SOUTH

CAROLYN A. BERCIER

Introduction by **ELISE GRENIER**

Louisiana State University Press ▌▌ Baton Rouge

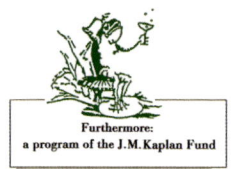

Furthermore:
a program of the J.M.Kaplan Fund

Grateful acknowledgment is made to Furthermore: A Program of the
J. M. Kaplan Fund for its generous assistance in publishing this book.

Published by Louisiana State University Press
Copyright © 2019 by Louisiana State University Press
All rights reserved
Manufactured in China
First printing

DESIGNER: Mandy McDonald Scallan
TYPEFACES: Text: Bulmer MT; Display: Rhode, Bodoni Poster, & Franklin Gothic
PRINTER AND BINDER: Shenzhen Caimei Printing through
    Four Colour Print Group, Louisville, Kentucky

Library of Congress Cataloging-in-Publication Data
Names: Bercier, Carolyn A., 1953– author.
Title: The frescoes of Conrad Albrizio : public murals in the midcentury
    South / Carolyn A. Bercier ; Introduction by Elise Grenier.
Description: Baton Rouge : Louisiana State University Press, 2019. | Includes
    bibliographical references and index.
Identifiers: LCCN 2018046165 | ISBN 978-0-8071-7102-8 (cloth : alk. paper)
Subjects: LCSH: Albrizio, Conrad A. (Conrad Alfred), 1894–1973—Criticism and
    interpretation. | Mural painting and decoration,
    American—Louisiana—History—20th century. | Mural painting and
    decoration, American—Alabama—History—20th century. | Public
    art—Louisiana—History—20th century. | Public
    art—Alabama—History—20th century. | Southern States—In art.
Classification: LCC ND237.A335 B47 2019 | DDC 759.13—dc23
LC record available at https://lccn.loc.gov/2018046165

The paper in this book meets the guidelines for permanence and durability of the
Committee on Production Guidelines for Book Longevity of the Council on Library
Resources. ∞

Contents

Preface

THIS BOOK WAS BORN IN THE mid-1970s when I was an art history student at Louisiana State University. I asked the director of the Anglo-American Art Museum on the LSU campus to suggest a regional artist who I might use as a research subject. It seemed a more useful project to write about someone close to home than one of the many artists who had been examined by eminent scholars. I chose Conrad Albrizio based on the dearth of information surrounding his work and the public nature of much of his art. After graduate school, the information on this artist followed me. I wrote several articles, co-curated an exhibit, gave multiple lectures, made two trips to New York to retrieve sketches and mural studies generously donated to area museums and repositories by the Albrizio family, and now I'm writing this book.

I never knew Conrad Albrizio. He died in 1973 before I began my research. Those who did know him described him as short in stature with a pipe usually held between his teeth.[1] He was seemingly well liked by students, but not always favorably remembered by his peers. He was said to be quiet by some, but others talked about his "raucous" humor.

When I lived in the New Orleans French Quarter from 1980 to 1999, I knew many of the artist's friends and neighbors. They imparted little personal information but did spill some entertaining stories about the man. His neighbor, Dorothy, in whose home I lived, loved to tell the story of when Albrizio invited her for dinner and served her wine in a glass without a base. She spent all evening holding the glass with one hand and trying to eat with the other.[2]

Perhaps the most honest assessment was given by his painting assistant Jack Hastings, who worked with him during the 1940s and 1950s. Jack recalls him as a complicated man who was difficult to comprehend. "Gene [his wife] probably more than any other human gave all to Conrad. Not trying to be overly modest, I feel I made the second greatest effort to understand the man. For several years I listened to him with respect because he knew so much and I knew so little."[3]

My purpose in this book is to examine Albrizio's fresco murals, which cover a significant span of time (1932–1954) and represent a singular and masterly technique. Because these murals cover so much of his career, I also include a good deal of biographical information. The primary aim, however, is to explore a largely public and very accessible art form that deserves to be documented, researched, and cataloged as part of the collective knowledge of southern art history.

Albrizio was wildly prolific and an excellent salesperson of his own talent. He persuaded patrons to award him mural commissions long after the national popularity for fresco murals had passed. Both his audacity and his unwavering belief in the need for public art aided him. As a result, we are left today with many examples of the ancient art of true fresco right here in the South. Never taking shortcuts, Albrizio performed the arduous task of painting on wet plaster, creating a link to antiquity and his own Italian heritage. Because of the permanence of the medium, his fresco murals will endure for generations as a record of southern history, culture, and art. And that is one of the most important purposes of art, after all—to make permanent those fleeting emotions and passing moments of our past.

Introduction   Conrad Albrizio and the Rare Technique of Fresco Painting

MOST STUDENTS ENROLLED AT Louisiana State University in Baton Rouge will attend an English class in one of the oldest buildings on campus, Allen Hall. Allen Hall is part of the original nucleus of the campus, designed in northern Italian Renaissance style and flanked by arcades appropriate for a Mediterranean climate. Today Allen Hall is home to the English Department, but in the early 1930s its classrooms were art studios, and students of painting, drawing, and sculpture walked its halls. There Professor Conrad Albrizio taught an Italian art form he specialized in and that was becoming popular in the United States: large-scale wall paintings executed in the fresco technique. When LSU's Department of Fine Arts was founded in 1936, Albrizio had recently completed several important commissions funded by the Work Projects Administration that had gained him a reputation as a fresco artist. He and his students made Allen Hall into a fresco laboratory. The university and the state of Louisiana are home to a set of rare murals painted in fresco, of which only a handful exist in the United States.

As technically challenging as fresco painting is, Albrizio preferred it to ordinary mural painting, just as artists during the Italian Renaissance and Mexican muralists of the twentieth century did, placing their work on highly visible external walls. Fresco is particularly appropriate for outdoors due to its resistant nature. Albrizio's use of the technique was influenced by his early contact with European traditions. The son of Italian immigrants, he traveled to Italy for training and for materials, and he must have felt a strong connection to his roots. The medium of fresco is highly prevalent in ancient wall paintings in Egyptian, Greek, and Roman cultures, culminating in the Italian Renaissance, and was used by artists from Cimabue and Giotto's time to that of Michelangelo. Albrizio's frescoes share technique and materials with those of his ancient predecessors; the only difference is that of style.

An artist working in fresco is well aware of the permanent nature of his creation; fresco paintings that are many centuries old survive intact today. The term *fresco* means "fresh" in Italian. The method involves the layering of lime and sand mortars; the artist paints in sections on fresh plaster, working quickly before it dries, normally one section each day. A chemical reaction takes place during the drying phase, binding the pigments permanently to the wall. It is essential to distinguish between mural paintings that are not fresco and

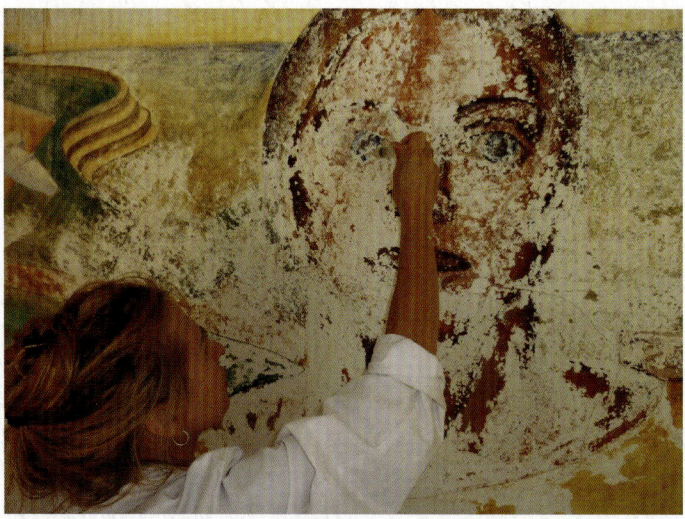

Elise Grenier restoring the Shreveport frescoes after extensive water damage. Courtesy Elise Grenier.

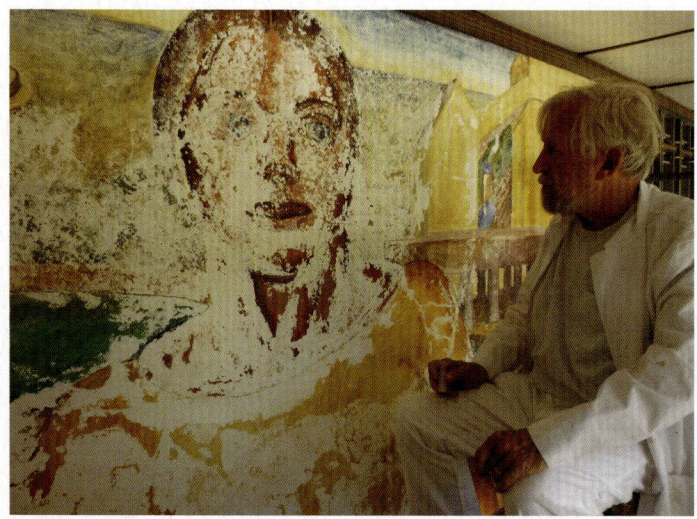

Charles Grenier working on the Shreveport frescoes. Courtesy Elise Grenier.

those that are executed in fresco. In a true fresco, the artist applies his pigments to the damp or fresh plaster as soon as it has been troweled on the wall. Carbon dioxide from the air combines with calcium hydroxide in the wet plaster, forming calcium carbonate. As the wet plaster dries and hardens, the pigments solidify and become as one. When, on the other hand, an artist paints a mural on dry plaster, a binding medium is required to make the pigments adhere to the wall. Pigments of a true fresco cannot peel, and will last as long as the plaster does. A mural painting that is not a fresco is by nature more delicate as it is not a part of the wall but, rather, lies only on the surface.

Conservation treatments have recovered or preserved several of the Albrizio murals in Louisiana, including the monumental fresco cycle at the Louisiana State Exhibit Building in Shreveport, the Capitol Annex frescoes, the Union Passenger Train Station murals in New Orleans, and the Allen Hall frescoes. During assessments and restoration, it was possible to study the working process of the artist. Both chemical and visual analysis of the frescoes revealed evidence of traditional *giornata* and *spolvero* techniques, confirming the preparatory drawing method used in classical fresco painting. Italian terms are universally used for description of frescoes, since the golden age of fresco was the Italian Renaissance. The joins, or *giornata,* in the plaster are distinguishable on close inspection, confirming the correct execution of the fresco technique—that is, the completion of one small section at a time as the plaster dries.

A day's work, or *giornata,* reveals details about the working process of the artist. Joins in each day's work were never meant to be distinguished by the viewer; in fact, most frescoes are large-scale and not meant to be viewed up close. However, a conservator can use clues left by the artist to determine how many days it took to complete a fresco, and even the order in which the sections were painted. We can penetrate the artist's secrets with analysis of pigments and materials, and learn whether he was working slowly or was in a hurry. We can also see up close which areas were belabored or revised, and which areas were spontaneous or added as an afterthought.

There are as many varieties of paint and mortar application techniques as there are artists. Albrizio typically was a perfectionist in both technique and application, and fortunately he left much information in his writings as well. He preferred to use an extremely smooth plaster as his canvas, troweled to a fine finish, much like Michelangelo's Sistine Chapel frescoes in this respect. Artists of the Italian Renaissance liked to use several layers of mortar, each layer worked to an increasingly smooth finish by varying the ingredients, the proportions of materials, and troweling techniques. Albrizio, taking his cue from Italian Renaissance artists, used imported marble dust for his finished coat to achieve this highly desired effect. The materials—the pigments, and the lime and sand that Albrizio used to create his artwork—were as carefully selected, measured, mixed, and applied, with the same criteria, as those of the best fresco artists of hundreds of years prior.

Artists often left traces of their planning and execution method for their paintings. The composition and subject matter were decided first and often required revisions or formal approval from the sponsor or client. Just as in the Italian Renaissance, this was true for WPA artists, and Albrizio was no exception. Sketches could be executed in situ—directly on the wall or on the preparatory plaster layer—or on paper, with small- or large-scale drawings. The creative process is often most evident in the preparatory phase of a mural, rather than in the final product, and with fresco, much planning was done ahead of time, since, unlike other methods of painting, there was little possibility of correction once the fresco had dried. The life-size drawings, called cartoons, that were pinned up to trace onto the wall did not often survive. These fascinating preparatory drawings were considered only working drawings, and although some were kept on file by the artist for use in other projects, few survive today due to their transient nature. Fortunately, a large number of Albrizio's sketches and full-scale drawings were preserved and are housed in museums around the state. During extensive research, art historian and curator Carolyn Bercier secured from his family in New York City in the 1980s 132 drawings that Albrizio had done on a visit to Italy in the 1920s and '30s. They were donated in 1987 to the Southeastern Architectural Archive at Tulane University, where they are cataloged and available for research. The cartoons used to paint the New Orleans Union Passenger Terminal murals were also given to Bercier by Albrizio's family, and she in turn donated them to the Louisiana State Museum in New Orleans, where they are available for research and exhibition.

On close examination, tiny dots of gray pigment are ubiquitous throughout the Albrizio frescoes. They are of ephemeral charcoal, evidence of the process of transferring the drawings to the wall, yet they are indelible, as are the pigments applied by brush, because they are chemically bound to the plaster. These fascinating and minute details offer a glimpse into the artist's creative process.

Louisiana is a repository for Albrizio's work, and his monumental architectural paintings will remain in good condition well into the decades—and even centuries—to come, thanks to his technique of execution. Preservation efforts have allowed us to study, document, and appreciate at close hand the techniques and methods used. Two areas of the Allen Hall fresco cycle were covered by several layers of latex paint and accretions years after their creation. Their presence was discovered during explorative investigation, and preliminary testing revealed that the paintings had not been destroyed during later construction as had been previously assumed. A full recovery was possible thanks to their inherently stable nature, and they will remain in excellent condition indefinitely. In 2001 the massive Shreveport frescoes required attention; although they were well preserved out-of-doors, a freak hailstorm blew golf-ball-sized hail into the portico of the Louisiana State Exhibit Building, damaging portions of the plaster. All considered, the frescoes remain in good condition. The State Capitol murals were recovered during renovations in the 1980s, and others, such as *Rural Free Delivery* in the WPA post office of DeRidder, require no maintenance and are in mint condition, a testimony to the enduring technique used.

The fresco medium, because of its chemical and physical stability, is virtually indestructible and forgiving, even if painted over, obscured by walls, or exposed to the elements in an outdoor portico. Albrizio, like Michelangelo and other old masters, made a conscious choice to express himself in this exacting and complex medium, aware of the significance of the murals he made and intending his unique contribution to endure through time.

—ELISE GRENIER
Grenier Conservation

Timeline of the Artist's Life

1894 October 20—born in New York City of Italian immigrant parents.

1914 Enters the Beaux Arts Institute in New York to study architecture.

1919 Moves to New Orleans, Louisiana, to work as an architectural designer.

1920 Becomes affiliated with the New Orleans Arts and Crafts Club.

1923 Returns to New York to study at the Art Students League.

1924 First trip to Europe; studies at L'Académie de la Grande Chaumière in Paris, travels the continent.

1925 Returns to America; New Orleans Arts and Crafts Club features an exhibit of the Majorcan landscapes.

1929 Second trip to Europe; enrolls in La Scuola Nazionale di Arte e Mestieri to study encaustic, fresco, and oil painting.

1930 Studies fresco painting at the American School of Arts in Fontainebleau, France; executes first fresco in the school foyer.

December—returns to New Orleans.

1932 Paints the frescoes in the Louisiana State Capitol, Baton Rouge.

Travels again to Rome to study fresco painting.

Establishes the Fresco Guild with the help of Alma Reed and the Delphic Studios, New York City.

1935–1937 Completes the painting *Jordan,* depicting an African American baptism. This tempera-on-board work becomes one of the most monumental of his career.

Works as an instructor in fresco painting, Leonardo da Vinci Art School, New York City; executes a fresco for the school auditorium illustrating Roosevelt and the New Deal.

1936 Appointed as an art instructor, Louisiana State University, Baton Rouge.

Paints first fresco under the auspices of the federal government at the DeRidder, Louisiana, post office.

1938 Paints a second federally sponsored fresco at the Russellville, Alabama, post office.

Paints a fresco program contrasting north and south Louisiana at the Louisiana State Exhibit Building in Shreveport.

Executes a fresco program in the State Capitol Annex Building, Baton Rouge.

1939 Becomes active in a confraternity of artists known as the New Southern Group; exhibits his easel paintings depicting the life of African Americans in the South during the years of the Depression.

1940 Paints his last federally sponsored fresco in the Iberia Parish Courthouse, New Iberia, Louisiana.

1943 Takes a one-year sabbatical leave in New York City, begins painting in a surrealist and expressionist style.

1944 Resumes teaching at Louisiana State University in Baton Rouge.

1945 Awarded a Rosenwald fellowship; returns to New York City to paint; paintings become rhythmical and undulating in style, expressing feelings of rebirth, survival, and cosmic order.

1946 Exhibits his works of the 1940s at the Passedoit Gallery, New York City.

1947 Rosenwald fellowship extended.

1948 Returns to the South; solo show at the Delgado Museum of Art, New Orleans.

1949 Begins the epic fresco cycle in the Waterman Steamship Building, Mobile, Alabama.

1951 Paints a fresco panel for the Pan-Am Southern Corporation, New Orleans.

1954 Completes his last and most monumental fresco program in the New Orleans Union Passenger Terminal.
Resigns from his teaching position at Louisiana State University.

1955 Travels to Mexico to study the art of mosaic.
Begins a mosaic mural for the Louisiana Supreme Court Building, New Orleans.

1957 Constructs a mosaic panel for the First National Bank of Houma, Louisiana.
Constructs a mosaic panel for the courthouse in Gretna, Louisiana.
Returns to Mexico for further study in mosaic.

1958 Executes a mosaic mural for the courthouse in Mobile.
Executes a small mosaic panel of a mother and child for the YWCA of Mobile.
Last trip to Europe; travels to Venice to study mosaic.

1963-1964 Executes a mosaic program for the Algiers (Louisiana) Mental Health Center.

1965 Constructs a major mosaic mural for the Mobile General Hospital.
Constructs two mosaic panels for the Mobile Municipal Auditorium.

1973 January—after successive strokes and ill health, dies in Baton Rouge at the age of 78.

THE FRESCOES OF CONRAD ALBRIZIO

1.

Education of the Artist

THE SON OF ITALIAN IMMIGRANTS Alfonso Albrizio and Angelina Raimondo Albrizio, Conrad Alfred Albrizio was born in New York City in 1894.[1] The Albrizio family was part of the great Italian influx of the late nineteenth and early twentieth centuries, residing in one of the many Italian neighborhoods on the lower east side of Manhattan.[2] Typical housing was a tenement or a subdivided single-family dwelling. Alfonso worked as a shoemaker and for many years practiced his trade alongside the famed maker of theatrical and ballet shoes, Salvatore Capezio.[3] He had little formal schooling but worked hard to see that his seven children were well educated. In 1914, Conrad enrolled at the Beaux Arts Institute to study architecture and soon launched a professional career as an architectural designer with the well-known New York firm of La Large and Morris.[4] Two of Conrad's brothers also pursued careers in art: Joseph was a sculptor and architect who worked mainly in Puerto Rico, and Humbert, an abstract sculptor, was associated with the University of Iowa. Humbert's works are featured in museums and galleries across the United States.[5]

During World War I while in the Navy, Conrad visited New Orleans, where, according to his family, he was drawn to the quaint and peaceful niches of the French Quarter.[6] He jumped at the chance to return to the city in 1919 as an architectural designer on the Hibernia Bank building. That opportunity arose on the heels of a very brief marriage to a young Italian-American woman in New York that no doubt also motivated the twenty-five-year-old to seek new horizons.[7] The picturesque landscape of south Louisiana and the burgeoning art scene in the French Quarter of the 1920s were very alluring to the young romantic. He quickly found an apartment and

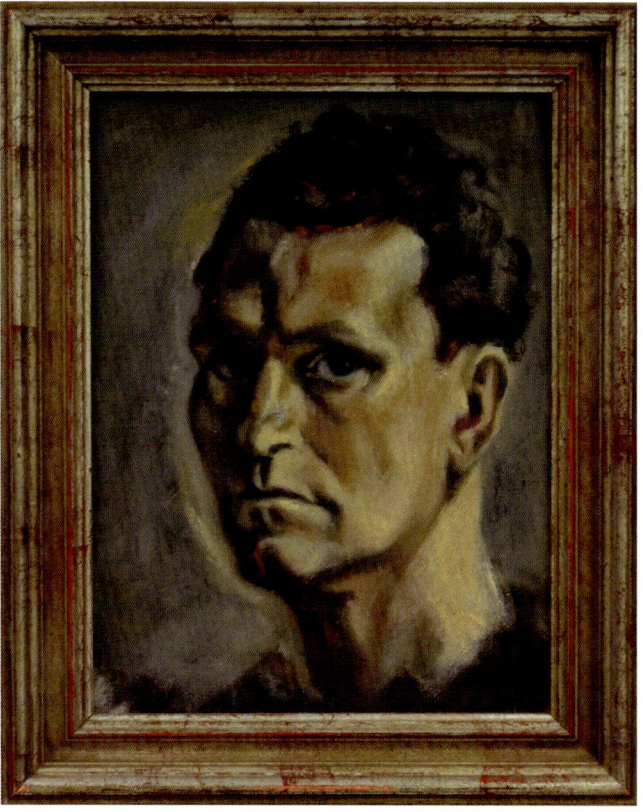

Plate 1.

Portrait of Conrad A. Albrizio [Self-Portrait], 1930, oil on canvas, 16¼ × 12 inches, LSU Museum of Art, 71.21.2, Gift of the Artist.

studio near Jackson Square amid a mix of writers and painters, and in his spare time he began to paint (plate 1).

In the French Quarter, Albrizio encountered a world of creative, free-spirited, often party-loving bohemians who included such notables as William Faulkner, Sherwood Ander-

son, Lyle Saxon, Bill Spratling, Alberta Kinsey, and Caroline Durieux. In fact, Albrizio's studio was next door to the garret of Faulkner and his roommate, Spratling.[8] Many of them eventually became part of the well-known New Orleans Arts and Crafts Club, a group that organized classes in drawing, painting, and sculpture and arranged exhibits for local artists. Albrizio was a founding member of the organization and remained active until its demise in 1951.[9] His association with this circle cannot be overplayed. It secured his place in the prominent and active art scene in New Orleans and nurtured his fledgling talent. New Orleans's answer to the Rive Gauche in Paris was a fertile field for a variety of occupations; journalists (Lyle Saxon), university professors (Frans Blom and William Spratling), visual artists (Alberta Kinsey and Caroline Durieux), writers, and historians thrived there. This rich assembly of Vieux Carré neighbors shared a love of the history and exotic culture of New Orleans and the desire to preserve the unique quality of the old city.

Albrizio's desire to foster his creative expression took him briefly back to New York in 1923 where he enrolled in the Art Students League, a school founded by artists for artists. He took classes with the painter George Luks, an American realist who was a member of the loose gathering of artists known as the Ashcan School. These early twentieth-century painters depicted scenes of daily urban life, especially in poorer neighborhoods. Albrizio mingled with experienced artists at the Art Students League as well as beginners like himself. He earned money working on architectural projects in New York, and when finances allowed, he made his first trip to Europe in 1924.[10]

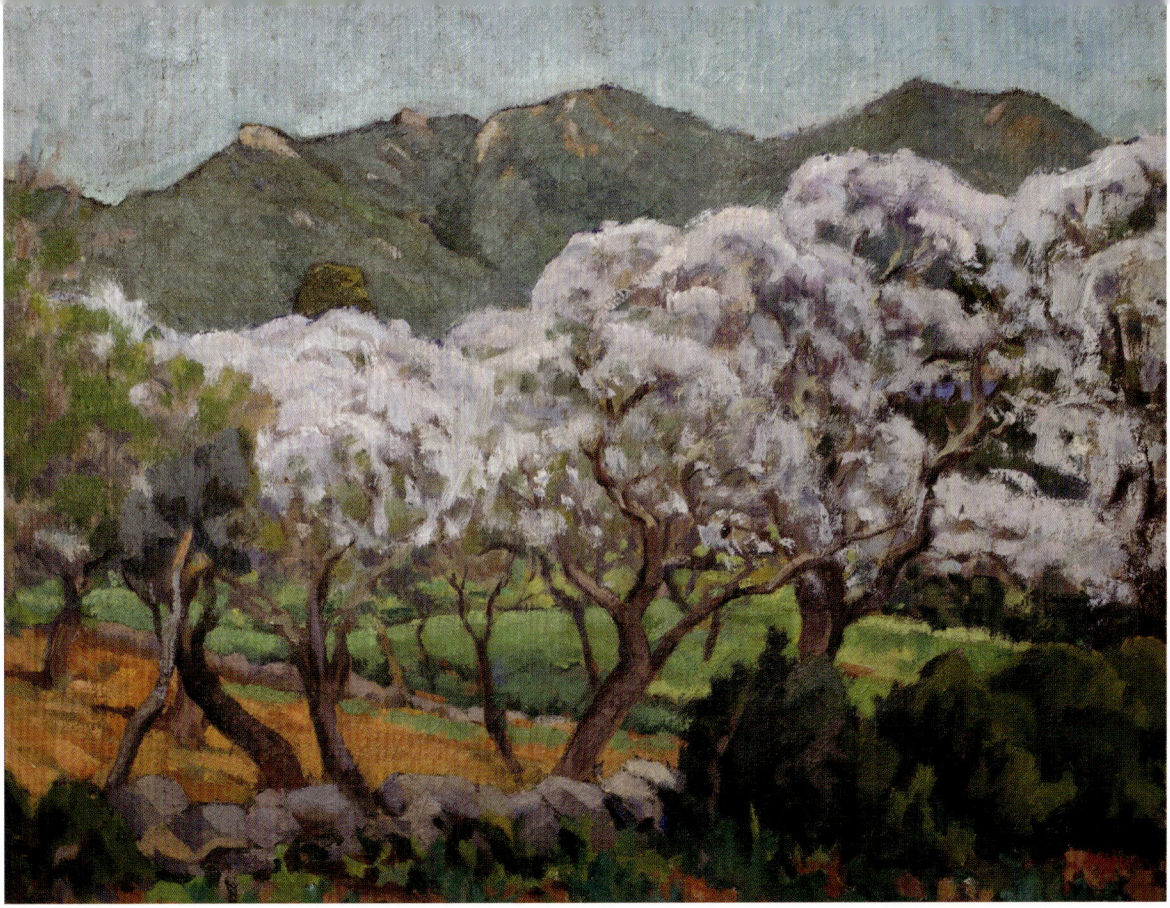

Plate 2.
Blooming Almond Trees, c. 1931, oil on canvas, 18½ × 22½ inches, Collection of Dorian M. Bennett, New Orleans, LA.
Photo by Partick Barnes.

Like most young artists traveling abroad for the first time, Albrizio was filled with excitement, anxious to experience the wonders of the art world firsthand. Paris was his initial stop. He enrolled at L'Académie de la Grande Chaumière, an independent art academy where he studied for six months. Located in the artsy district of Montparnasse, the school provided few amenities, but its low fees attracted struggling students. Paris, an inspiration for so many artists throughout history, did not inflame the young Albrizio. "Paris was a tre-

mendous disappointment for me," he lamented, "for her people were so cold and brusque, and completely apart from the ageless art and beauty of their surroundings. It was as though they were overripe and their art were dead."[11] With youthful enthusiasm he continued his travels through Europe, "visiting museums and doing historical research on matters of art."[12]

When he reached Rome, he found it quite different. "She [Rome], in all her glory and grandeur, was alive. Art was a part of the people . . . and they with it."[13] It's worth noting that at

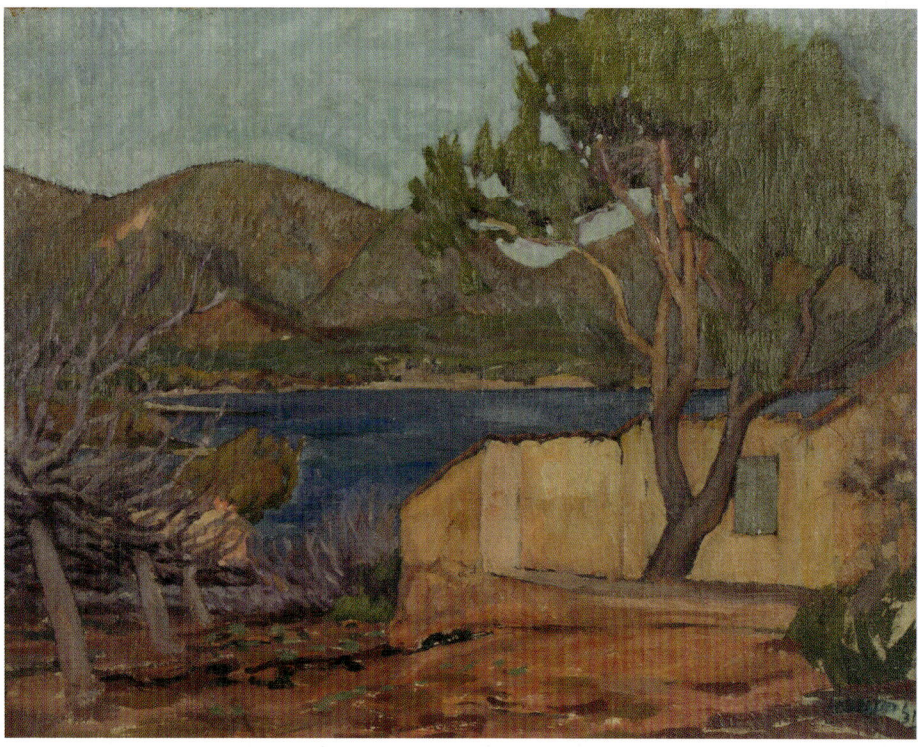

Plate 3.
Landscape, c. 1931, oil on canvas. The New Orleans Museum of Art: Gift of Mr. and Mrs. Eugene B. French, 74.252.

this time the great heritage of Italian art was resurfacing after the excitement of the modern art movement of the Italian Futurists before World War I. The advancements of the Renaissance and even classical art were once more remembered as an important part of the history of art. Albrizio must have felt a tie with this rich artistic heritage of his ancestral country.

After traveling across the southern coasts of France and Spain, Albrizio ended his voyage with an excursion to the island of Majorca to visit his New Orleans friend Ronald Hargrave, also a member of the Arts and Crafts Club as well as an artist. Hargrave had a home on Majorca, where Albrizio settled into a comfortable routine. The two painted about three canvases per day, inspired by the "varying light of the changing seasons." These works constituted a major exhibit sponsored by the Arts and Crafts Club when Albrizio returned to New Orleans in 1925. One oil painting, *The Enchanted Pool,* caught the attention of the *New Orleans States*'s art critic, marking the first public recognition of Albrizio as an artist:

Cliffs of the Majorcan coast are shown with rippling water breaking gently against them. It is the thoughtfulness with which the composition and color are worked out and the toil with heart and soul as well as brush, that the artist put into this picture; the skillful application of the paint and the inspiring handling of the subject that lifts it above the other pictures in the exhibit, and gives it that something back of the mere painted rocks and water that makes them live and seem to have soul behind the paint.[14]

That painting is now lost, but Albrizio's landscapes from the early part of his career are among his best. They are done freely and with a genuine response to his environment (plates 2 and 3).

Albrizio returned to New York in the summer of 1925 due to his mother's death.[15] Soon after, he went back to New Orleans, where he continued his study of painting while supporting himself with architectural jobs. "I realized that what takes place in the painter's mind must find form," he said. "This is the whole problem of painting."[16] Form, style, technique—some of the most basic elements of painting were slowly taking shape for the young artist at this time.

In 1929 Albrizio again traveled to Europe, this time more certain of his interests and direction. He headed for Rome and enrolled in La Scuola Nazionale di Arti e Mestieri (the National School of Arts and Trades), where he studied fresco, encaustic, and oil painting. His teacher was Venturini Papari, described by Albrizio as the "outstanding technician in Italy today and retained by the Italian government to maintain and restore the old masters."[17] Albrizio's study of these techniques under the tutelage of this honored professor was certainly instrumental in advancing his love of the medium of fresco. Moreover, he was in the heart of Rome, where frescoes from ancient civilizations through the Renaissance graced the walls of public buildings.

By 1930, he had arrived in France, where he studied fresco at the American School of the Arts in Fontainebleau.[18] Albrizio learned what he always called the "French technique" of fresco painting, which he described as applying many layers of light pigment wash onto wet plaster. Each layer is carefully superimposed, one over the other, until the desired hue is achieved. "In general," Albrizio said, "this type of painting in fresco results in a luminous, transparent quality but is limited in scope and cramped in style."[19] In contrast, the Italian method was more robust and vigorous, yielding a vibrant and bolder surface. While studying at the American School, Albrizio was chosen to execute a small fresco in a foyer there. This was his first solo fresco panel. The school still exists, but the fresco is gone. It was either destroyed or covered by paint or other building material.[20]

Contemporary muralists are not familiar with the term "French technique," nor is it recorded in art manuals or handbooks. Evidently that moniker was Albrizio's own. The precise method and style of painting that young Conrad learned in France was much more delicate than what he observed in Italy, Mexico, and, later, the United States. It is a technique in handling the medium as practiced by the French muralists. Although Albrizio found it restrictive and very time consuming, it did produce a unique result desirable to some artists.

2.

The Louisiana State Capitol Frescoes

ALBRIZIO RETURNED FROM FRANCE in December of 1930 and settled in New Orleans.[1] In 1931, he married Imogene (Jean) Inge from Greensboro, Alabama. A year older than Conrad and married twice before, she was a writer by profession but devoted to her new husband and his career.[2] Albrizio painted her portrait around the time of their marriage (plate 4).

Huey Long was governor of Louisiana when Albrizio arrived in New Orleans. Determined to make good on his campaign promise of accessible education for all, Long had channeled $1.5 million into Louisiana State University.[3] He championed other programs as well, such as the building of a new state capitol that was to be a monument not only to the state, but also to Long himself. The state legislature allocated $5 million from the state liquidation committee for the construction of the new capitol, a sum that allowed more than enough money for artwork for the building.[4] Long approached the New Orleans firm of Weiss, Dreyfous & Seiferth to design the building, and construction started in December of 1930. Albrizio was chosen along with three other artists from New Orleans and approximately ten artists from across the United States to execute the ornamental details of the structure.

Sculptor Lorado Taft led the group of out-of-state sculptors in the building decoration. Taft did the sculptures that flank the entrance, one representing patriotism and the other the pioneer spirit. Lee Lawrie, who also worked on the Nebraska State Capitol, carved the frame around the grand entrance, while Adolph Weinman cut the horizontal panels on either side—the left panel standing for government, the right for peace and liberty. Atop the first level of the tower is a sculptural frieze of the history of Louisiana fashioned by

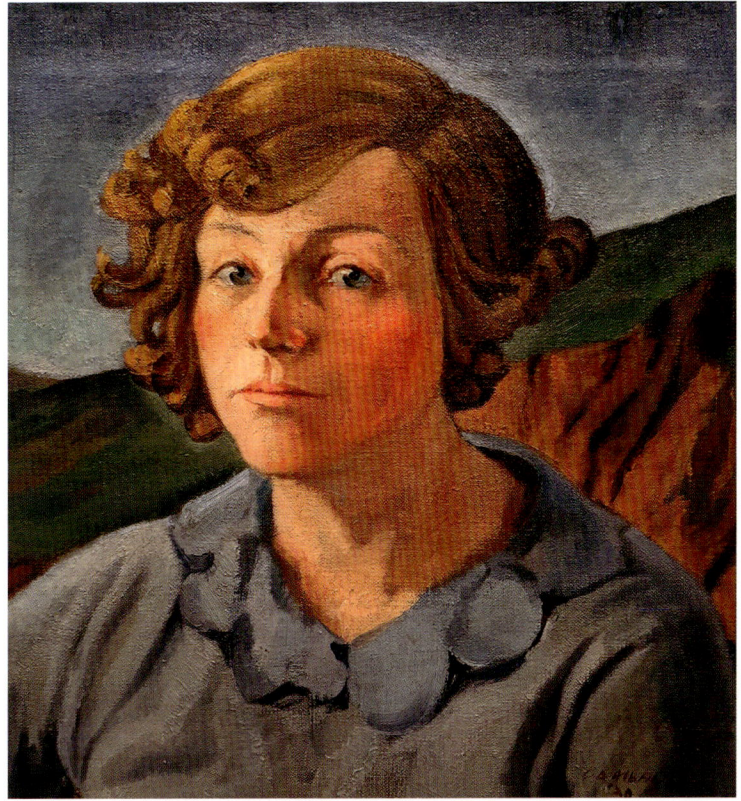

Plate 4.

Portrait of Mrs. Conrad A. Albrizio, born Jean Inge of Alabama, 1930, oil on canvas, 16⅛ × 14¼ inches, LSU Museum of Art, 71.21.1, Gift of the Artist.

Ulric Ellerhusen, who also carved four allegorical relief figures on the twenty-second floor representing science, law, philosophy, and art. The Piccirilli Brothers of New York City produced all of the bronzework inside the building, and Jules Guerin painted wall murals above the legislative chambers.[5] New Orleans sculp-

tor Albert Rieker was commissioned to do a large sculpture of Bienville on the exterior, and the head of Newcomb College's pottery department, Juanita Gonzales, created plaques of past Louisiana governors and generals. Sculptor Angela Gregory worked in her uptown New Orleans studio to create eight portrait relief panels for the interior.[6] Albrizio was asked to create interior murals. He proposed six fresco panels—four located in the governor's reception room and one in each of the two courtrooms.[7] This commission of almost 900 square feet was Albrizio's first major fresco assignment. In fact, it was one of the first major fresco efforts undertaken in the United States by an American artist.

Unfortunately, the murals in the first-floor governor's reception room were destroyed during a renovation of the capitol in 1955. Now only sketches and a few rare photographs and prints remain (plate 5).[8] One can see from this rendering that the room provided a fanciful and flourishing vision for visitors. Four panels enveloped the 21-foot-by-13-foot space with an idealized image of Louisiana for those who visited the governor's private office. A gentle and languid scene of antebellum plantation life and the current-day growing industrial wealth born from state resources surrounded agitated politicians and callers as they waited (plates 6, 7, and 8). A beautiful personification of Louisiana herself sat above the doorway, protecting this abundant kingdom (plate 9). There was no depiction of the Civil War, hurricanes, the ravages of yellow fever, the Great Flood of 1927, or any other tragedies that had befallen the state; even the enslaved workers seem peaceful in their daily tasks. The reassuring and dreamlike images that Albrizio produced not

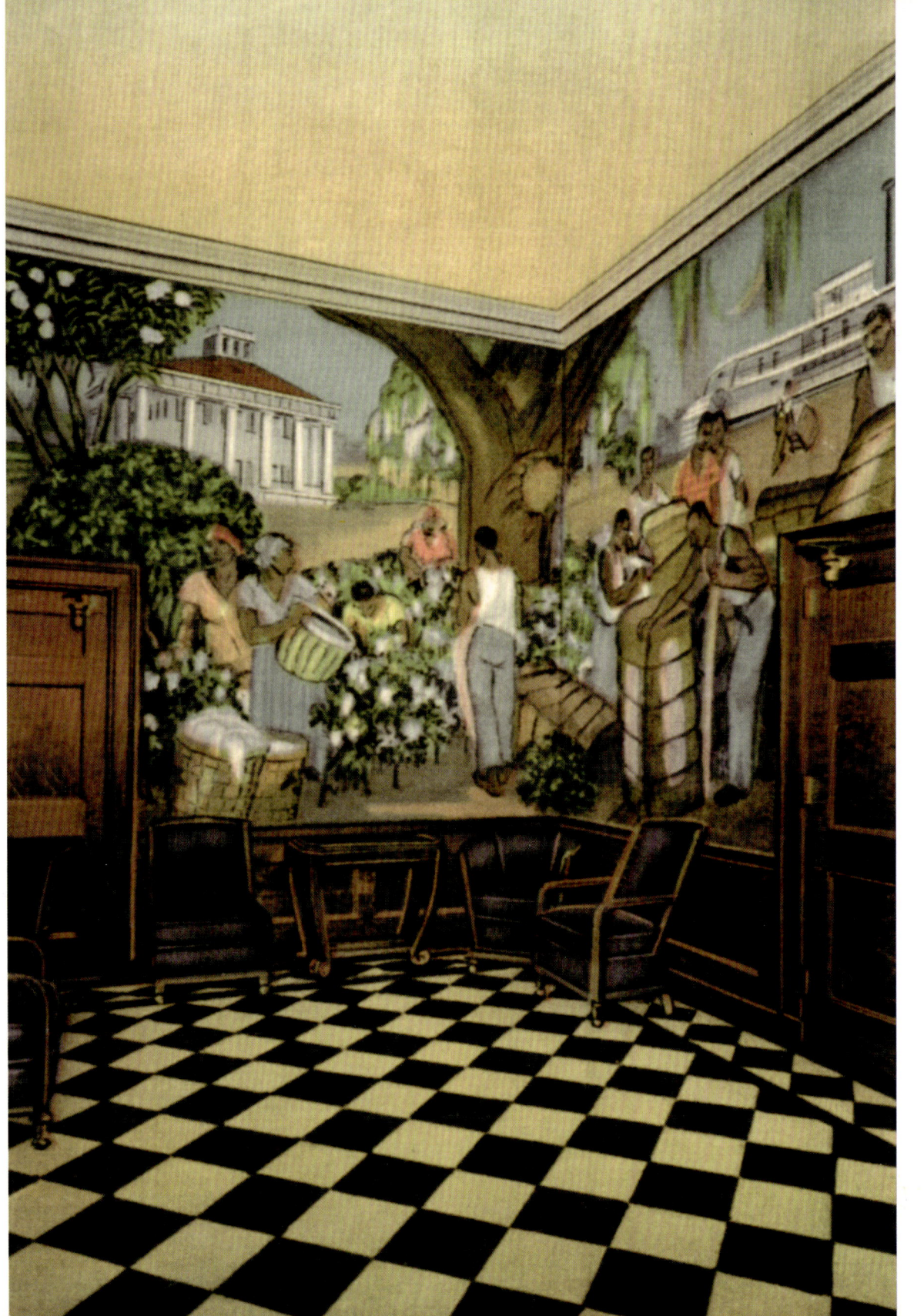

Plate 5.

Governor's Reception Room, c. 1932, poster.

Author's collection.

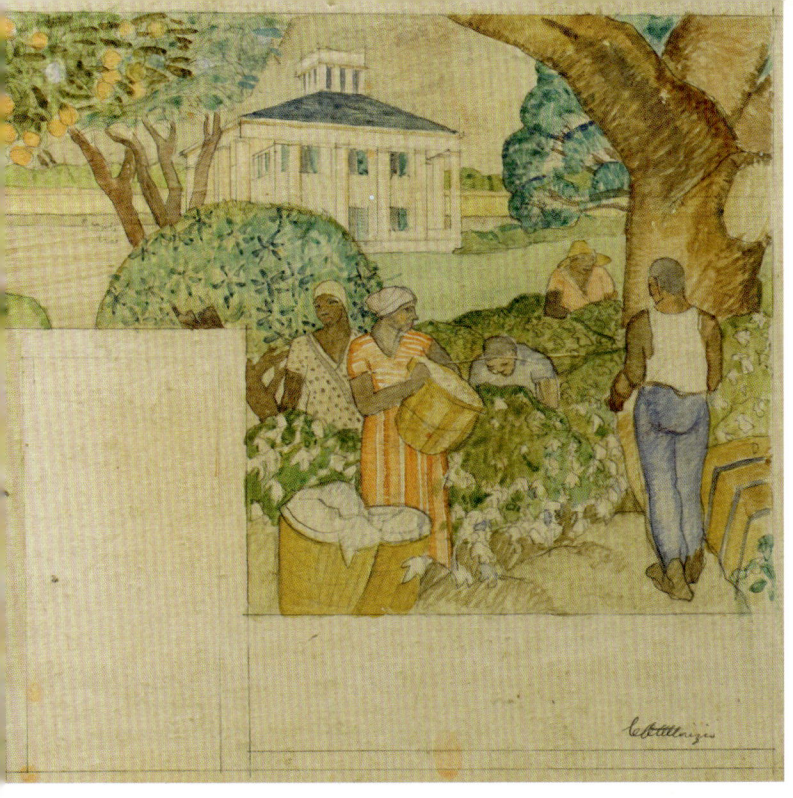

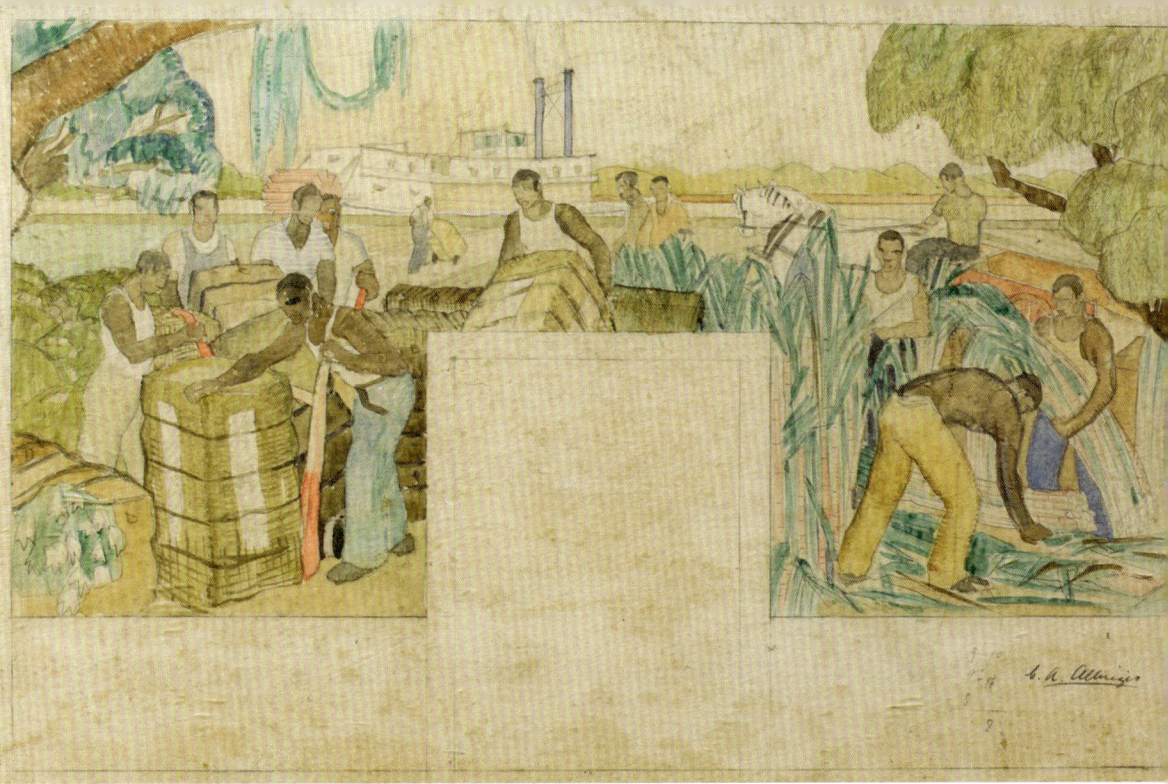

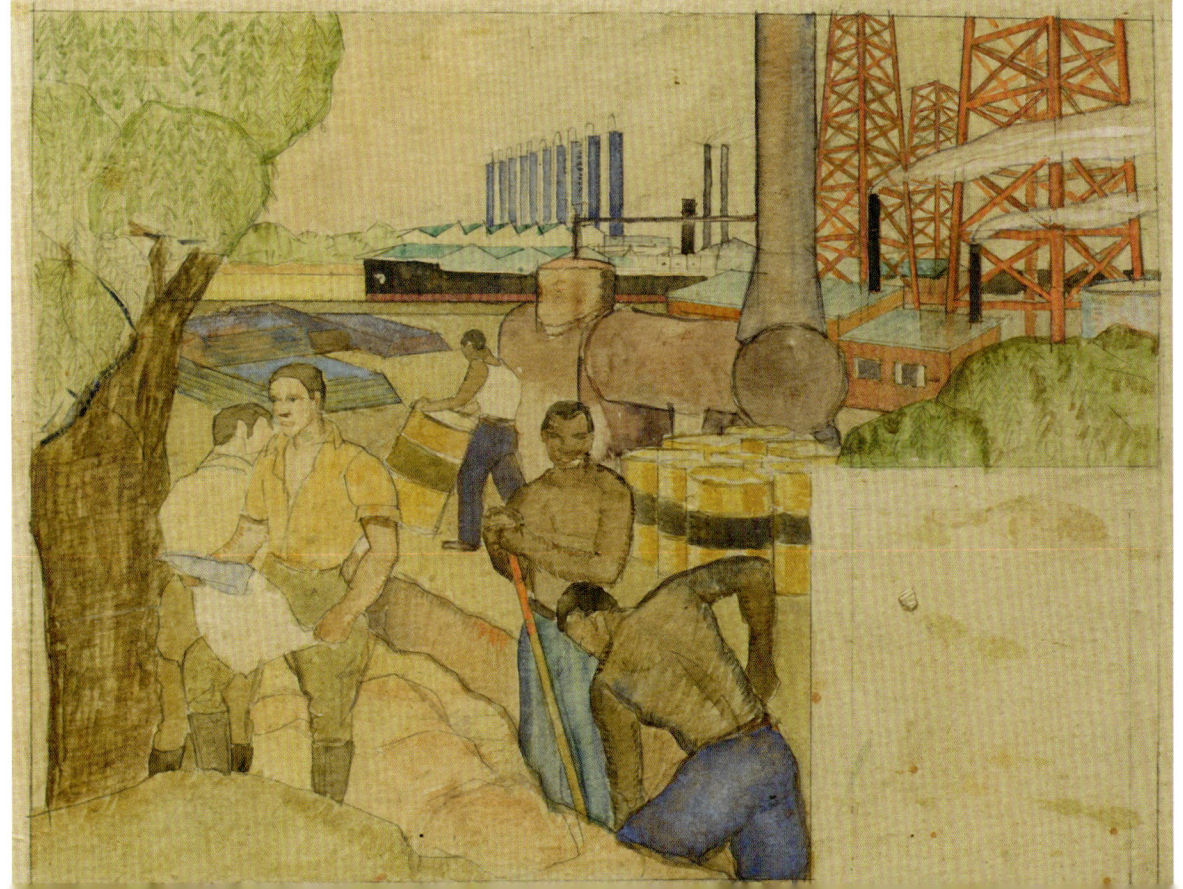

Plate 6.

Old Plantation Life in Louisiana, East Wall of the Governor's Reception Room, Louisiana State Capitol, Baton Touge, 1930, watercolor on paper/cartoon for fresco, 14⅜ × 21¾ inches, LSU Museum of Art, 71.18.2, Gift of the Friends of LSU Museum of Art. Photography: Malarie Zaunbrecher.

Plate 7.

Trucking Cotton and Cutting Sugar Cane, South Wall of the Governor's Reception Room, Louisiana State Capitol, Baton Rouge, 1930, watercolor on paper/cartoon for fresco, 14⅜ × 21¾ inches, LSU Museum of Art, 71.18.3, Gift of the Friends of LSU Museum of Art. Photography: Malarie Zaunbrecher.

Plate 8.

Industrial Louisiana, 1930, watercolor on paper/cartoon for fresco, 14¼ × 14¼ inches, LSU Museum of Art, 71.18.4, Gift of the Friends of LSU Museum of Art. Photography: Malarie Zaunbrecher.

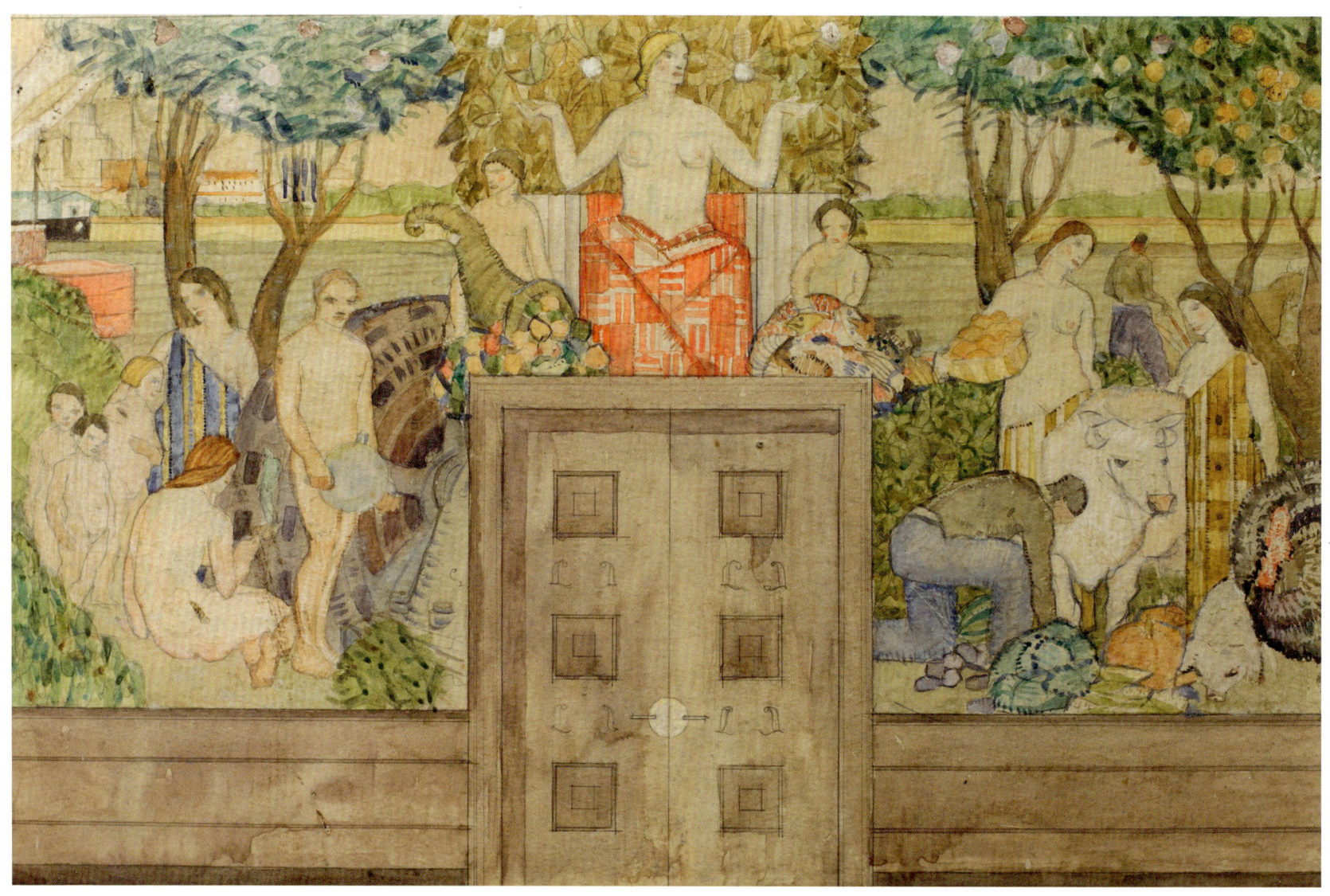

Plate 9.

Allegory of Louisiana, 1930, watercolor on paper/cartoon for fresco, 14 × 21½ inches, LSU Museum of Art, 71.17, Gift of Mr. and Mrs. Victor A. Sachse, Jr. Photography: Malarie Zaunbrecher.

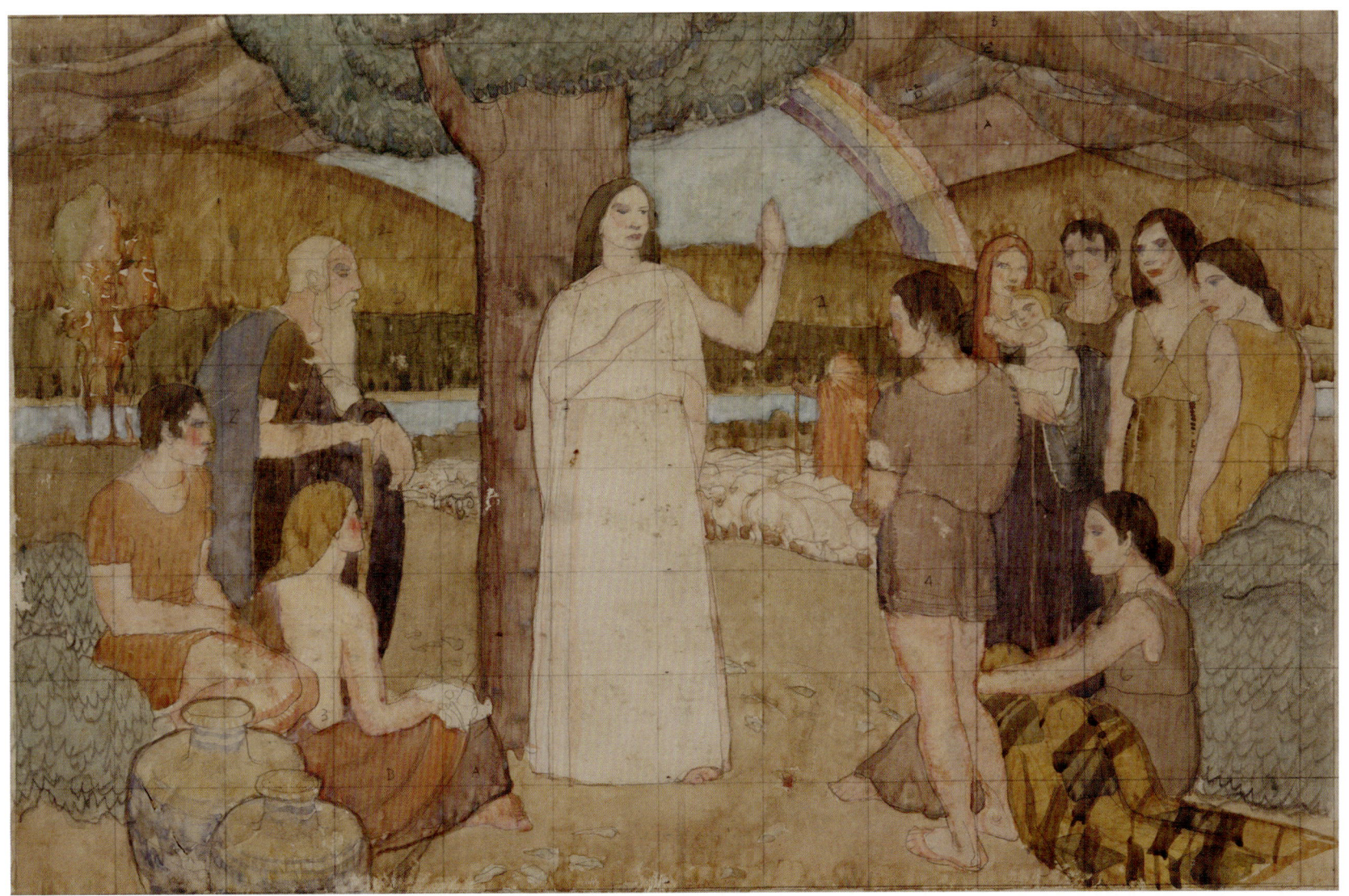

Plate 10.

And the Lord Commanded Me . . . Deuteronomy 4:14: Study for a Mural, State Capitol, Court of Appeals, 4th Floor, 1930, pencil and watercolor on paper, 25 × 20 inches, LSU Museum of Art, 93.7.1, Gift of the estate of Mrs. Ernestine H. Eastland Lowrey. Photography: David Humphreys.

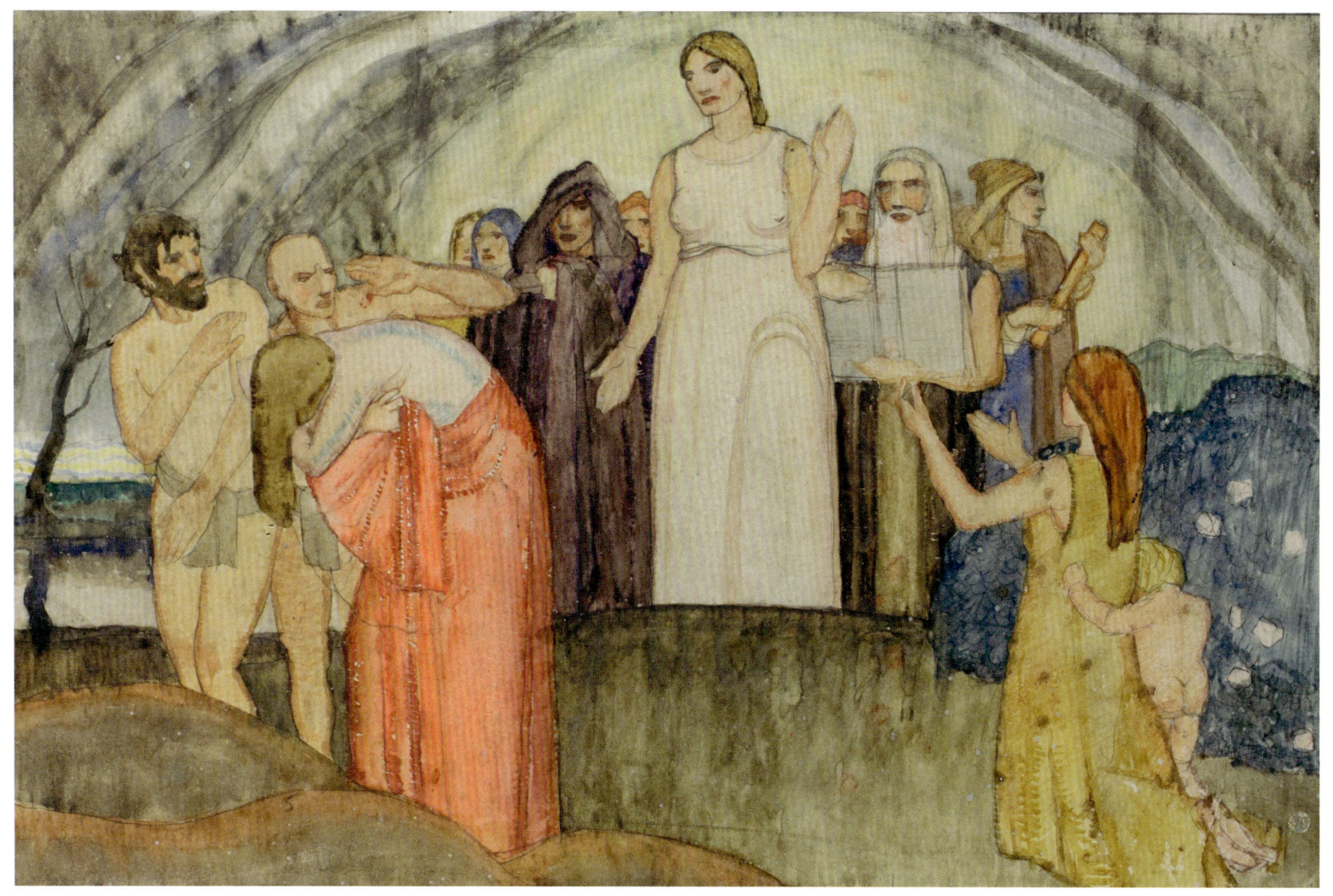

Plate 11.

But the Judgement Shall Return unto . . . Psalms 94:15, Study for a Mural, State Capitol, Supreme Court, 1930, graphite and watercolor on paper, 20 × 25 inches, LSU Museum of Art, 93.7.2, Gift of the estate of Mrs. Ernestine H. Eastland Lowrey. Photography: Malarie Zaunbrecher.

only lauded Long's Louisiana, but also fell squarely within the trend of American art that swept the nation during the 1930s—American Regionalism. Regionalism glorified the unique, usually rural values of different parts of America during the years of the Depression. Albrizio, assisted by artist Ernest Borne of New York, completed the reception room in about five weeks, working each day from morning until almost midnight.[9]

Albrizio wanted the panels for the two courtrooms to be related in subject yet still unique. He ultimately chose biblical quotations as inspiration. For the Court of Appeals panel, he selected Deuteronomy 4:14: "And the Lord commanded me to teach you statutes and judgments that ye might do these."[10] In the center of the panel is the personification of Justice preaching the "statutes and judgments" to the people (plate 10). Gathered around Justice are a shepherd and his flock, suggesting Christ shepherding his people. The rainbow overhead bridges the two groups of attending figures and emphasizes the orbital movement around the central form. The two large jars in the foreground punctuate the movement, and symbolically stand for temperance and justice, also cardinal virtues.

The mural for the Supreme Court chamber was based on Psalm 94:15: "That judgment shall return unto righteousness and all the upright in heart shall follow it."[11] Again, Justice provides the central focus of the composition (plate 11). Her left hand is raised in truth while her right hand admonishes the "children of darkness." Behind Justice are personifications of Fate (to her right) and Law (to her left). This panel is now in the governor's pressroom, and is the only remaining fresco in the capitol.

The courtroom panels seem awkward in their contemporary setting. An old photograph from the 1932 *Baton Rouge State-Times,* which can no longer be located, shows the frescoes in situ. The earth-hued palette of the panels beautifully suited the interior of the 1930s courtrooms, with their rich architectural details and oak furniture.

3.

The Influence of the Mexican Muralists

AFTER COMPLETING HIS COMMISSION for the Louisiana State Capitol, Albrizio returned to New York later in 1932 to continue studying fresco and to teach the technique through the Fresco Guild. Albrizio established the guild under the auspices of the Delphic Studios, a school created in 1927 by journalist and art patron Alma Reed, who promoted the works of Mexican muralist José Clemente Orozco. According to Albrizio, the Fresco Guild was the first fresco school in America.[1] In 1934, Albrizio incorporated the Fresco Guild into the Leonardo da Vinci Art School, where he taught fresco and other studio classes.

Spurred by the works of the Mexican muralists, the enthusiasm for fresco was sweeping across America. Orozco's mural at Pomona College in Claremont, California, had introduced the medium as a major art form in the United States in 1930. Entitled *Prometheus,* it was the first major work of art in fresco by a Mexican muralist outside of Mexico. It was monumental and hailed as "the most living wall in America" (plate 12).[2]

The Mexican muralists, specifically Diego Rivera, José Clemente Orozco, and David Alfaro Siqueiros, had used fresco in Mexico since the early 1920s. When the Mexican Revolution ended, the Mexican government commissioned these artists to educate the often-illiterate populace on the social and political views of the post-revolution government— that is, betterment of the people. The tempera murals that the artists initially created were found to be too fragile for public buildings. Fresco, however, which had a long history in Mexican art, was the ideal medium. Painting on wet plaster created an indelible surface that was virtually permanent.

Orozco followed his California mural with a fresco in

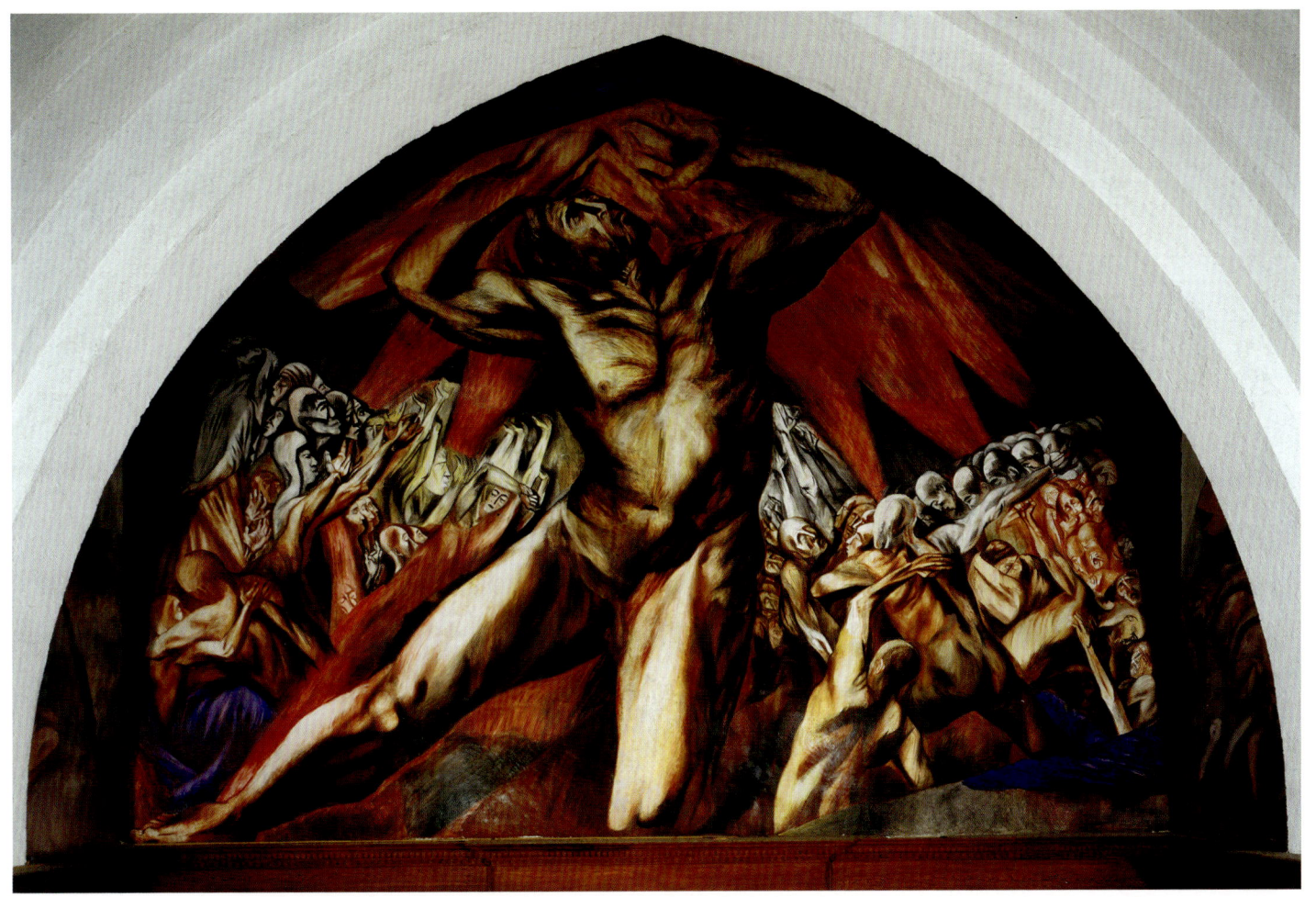

the New School for Social Research in New York City and then with an ambitious series at Dartmouth College's Baker Library, *The Epic of Culture in the New World.* Siqueiros showed his hand in 1932 at the Los Angeles Chouinard Art Institute with a mural depicting the rallying middle class of his native Mexico. Perhaps the most influential of the Mexican muralists for Albrizio was Rivera, who in 1931 painted a mural in the luncheon room of the San Francisco Stock Exchange interpreting the natural and human resources of the state of California. He did a second mural in Detroit in 1932

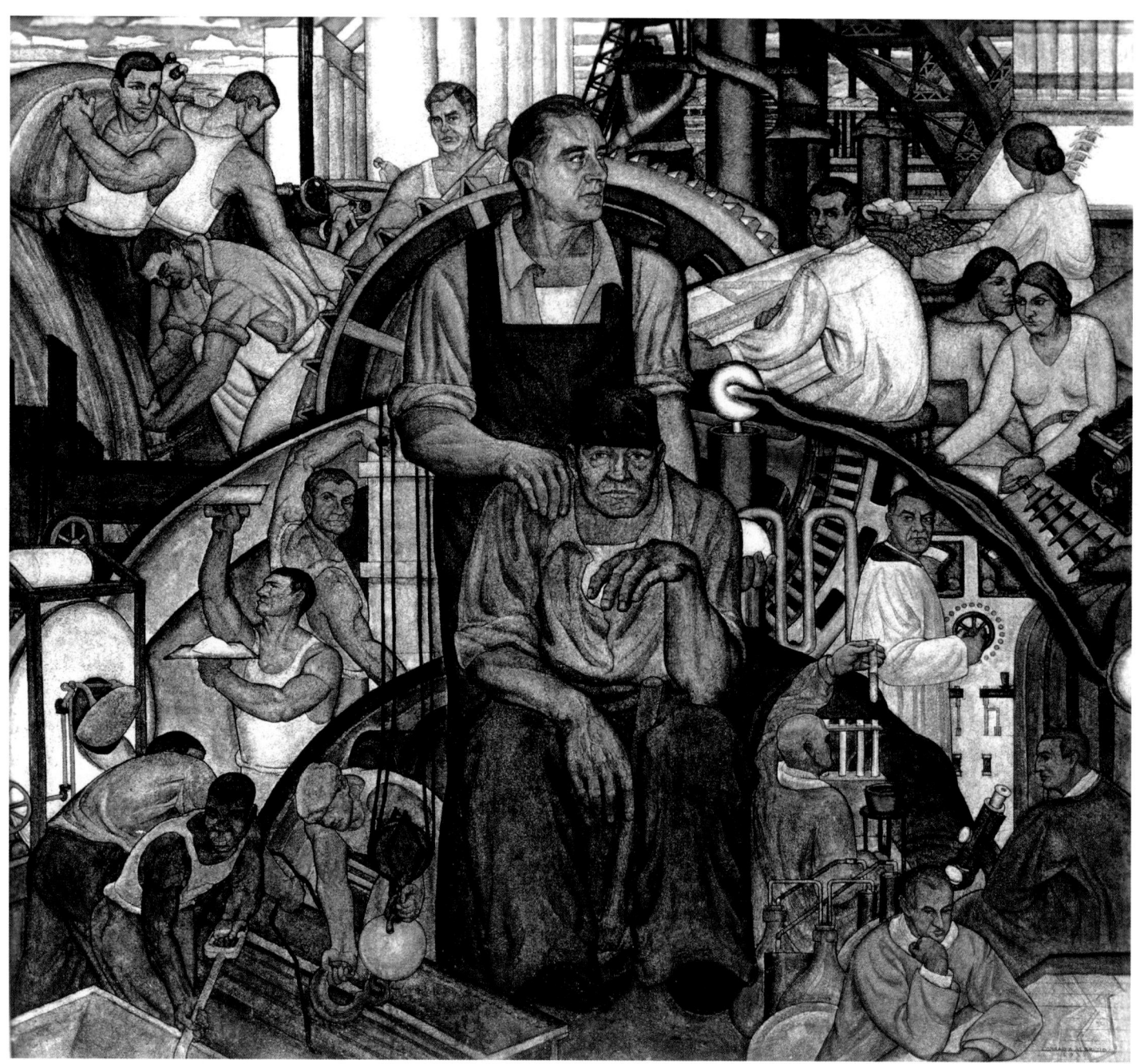

Plate 13.
Study for New Deal fresco at the Leonardo da Vinci Art School, New York City, 1934, charcoal on paper, National Archives, Washington, DC.

at the Art Institute and then later that year a controversial fresco at Rockefeller Center in New York. The controversy involved a portrait of Vladimir Lenin that Rivera inserted among a group of technicians "shown in control of the physical and social world."[3] The Rockefellers, patrons of the work, ordered the mural destroyed in 1934 because of its political implications, and only drawings and photographs remain. Rivera created a similar version for the Palace of Fine Arts in Mexico City and installed it in 1934.[4]

The Mexican muralists arrived in the United States at a time of economic and political crisis. The medium through which these artists had communicated in Mexico might well suit an overwhelmed America. George Biddle, artist and friend of Franklin D. Roosevelt, wrote to him in 1933, the year of Rivera's dismissal from the Rockefeller Center project, suggesting the creation of government-supported art programs. Biddle's idea to offer the public a modern art form that spoke to current issues was revolutionary: "The younger artists of America are conscious as they never have been of the social revolution that our country and civilization are going through: and they would be eager to express these ideals in a permanent art form if they were given the government's cooperation. They would be contributing to and expressing in living monuments the social ideas that you are struggling to achieve."[5]

Inspired by Rivera's fresco at the Rockefeller Center, Albrizio painted a fresco of FDR in the auditorium of the Leonardo da Vinci Art School in New York in 1934. He positioned the president, in overalls, at the center of the composition, honoring the government-funded art projects popular across the country during the 1930s. The fresco also contained portraits of many other notable political figures. Sitting below FDR was the personification of downtrodden America (plate 13).[6]

4.

A New Deal for Albrizio

AMERICA WAS NOW POISED FOR A public art form that would reflect the fervent patriotism of its citizens between World Wars I and II. The country also needed a potent psychological lift during the Great Depression. In October of 1934, the Section of Painting and Sculpture (known as "the Section") was established as one of many art agencies subsidized by the federal government to aid in a better home environment and living standard. Designed differently from other federally sponsored art programs, such as the Public Works of Art Project (PWAP) and the Federal Emergency Relief Administration (FERA) under which Albrizio would also work, the Section was not concerned primarily with relief or the dole. Its main purpose was to acquire quality art for public buildings. It stressed three important points that separated it from other federal programs of the era.

1. The United States government, through this section, was now directly responsible for the art in federal buildings. (This responsibility had been traditionally that of the architect who held the government contract.)
2. The program was national in scope and continuous in operation. (In other programs, art embellishment had been incidental to each government contract.)
3. The emphasis was upon American art and the quality of the product. (Previously, European modes had predominated, and the stress had been upon the professional reputation of the artist.)[1]

Edward Bruce, one of the directors of the PWAP, described the philosophy of the Section:

It was decided that the time had come when the decoration of public buildings with painting and sculpture should be planned in such a way that artists in every portion of the country would feel the stimulating influence of the Government's recognition of quality and of its desire to secure quality. . . .

One of the first steps taken by the Treasury Department Art Projects was to initiate a series of competitions which artists could enter anonymously. . . . Mural designs, sculpture models, all were submitted unsigned. The name of the entrant was not disclosed until after the award was made. . . . For the first time America purchased art on a large scale regardless of the fame of the artists, the purchasing being based entirely on the quality of the work.[2]

The Section attracted artists who were firmly established and financially secure as opposed to those who were unemployed. After negotiating a contract with the artist, the Section was not prepared to provide continuous financial security for the needy painters. This perfectly suited Albrizio's needs. By 1936 he was a college art instructor and not eligible for the dole. Under the auspices of the Section, he painted three fresco programs—two panels in Louisiana and one in Alabama.

APPOINTMENT AT LOUISIANA STATE UNIVERSITY

In February 1936, Albrizio was hired as an instructor of fine arts at Louisiana State University in Baton Rouge. He taught classes in drawing, painting, and fresco—now nationally popular as an art form. He was eager to teach fresco classes at LSU as he had done in New York and began instruction immediately. The opportunity for students to study the technique under the eye of a master was monumental. A good fresco painter could find steady employment in the 1930s and '40s, which encouraged many students to learn the technique. Albrizio was delighted to be in the South again and saw the regional inspiration as a great boost to his work. He noted:

The south should supply a rich nucleus for what will ultimately constitute the true American Art. Art should not be regarded as a luxury or an appendage, but in its proper light as an integral part of national and regional culture. Louisiana's cultural and natural advantages, together with the inherent temperament of her people, should enable the state to play a leading role in the evolution of a distinct and interpretive type of southern art. This goal can be obtained, however, only if a courageous group of men and women from Louisiana and other states are willing to accept the challenge of the future by dedicating their talents to the cause of winning for the South the recognition it deserves.[3]

RURAL FREE DELIVERY
DeRidder, Louisiana, Post Office

In 1936, Albrizio won a competition issued by the Section to paint a mural in the DeRidder, Louisiana, post office. He was asked to submit pencil sketches for a design. If the sketches met the approval of the director of procurement, a contract would be granted and the painting begun.

Albrizio first canvassed citizens of the small town of DeRidder for mural ideas and found that the majority of residents wanted "a panel reminiscent of the town."[4] DeRidder started as a small lumber camp, and timber had remained an

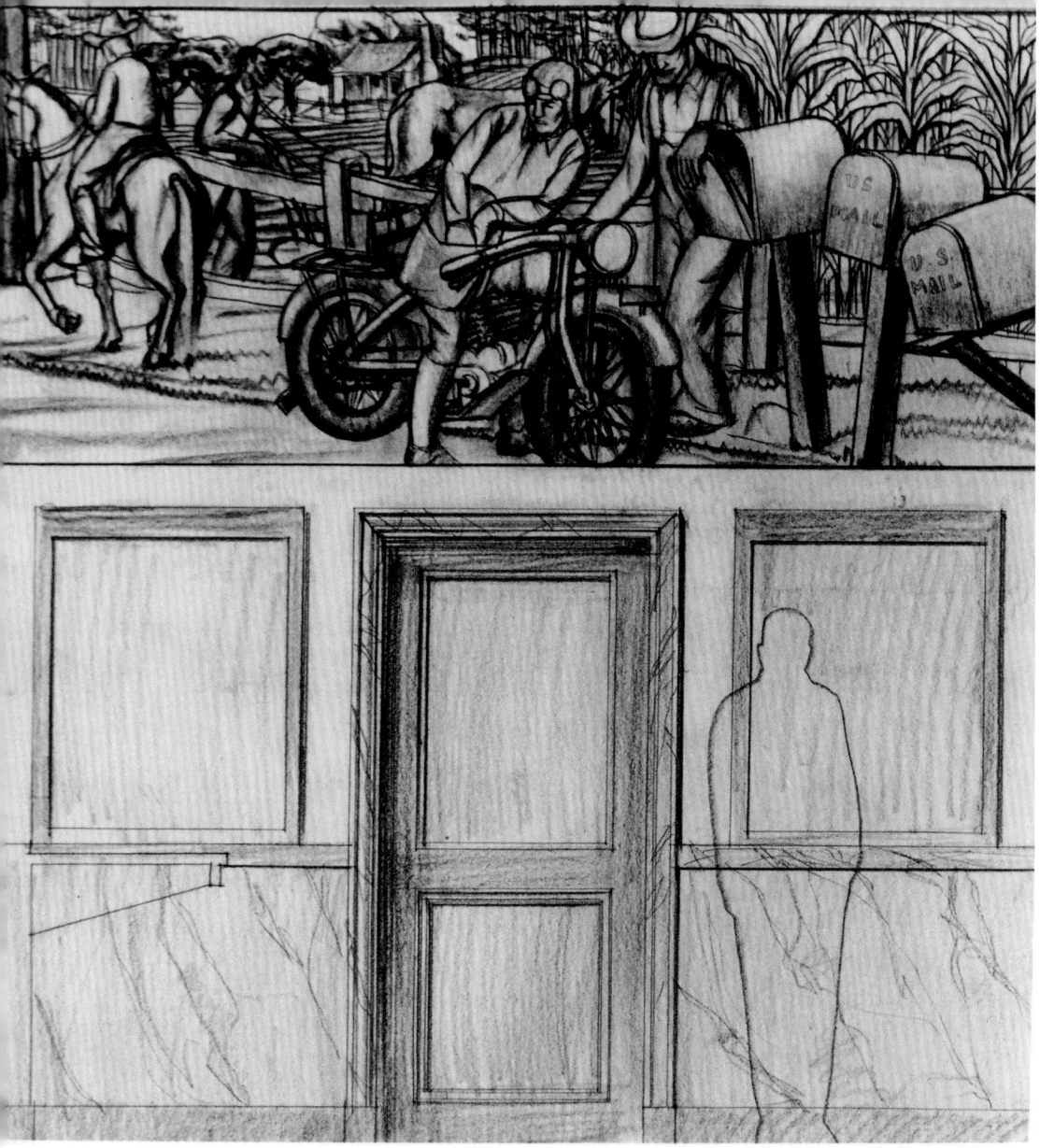

Plate 14.
Sketch for *Rural Free Delivery*, 1936, graphite on paper, National Archives, Washington, DC.

important industry for many years until its recent depletion. Sheep herding and agriculture provided the major means of livelihood in the 1930s. With that in mind, Albrizio sketched a rural setting with a farmer walking to his mailbox. In the background were a herdsman on horseback tending his flock and a "motorcycle mailman," a common aspect of rural mail service at the time (plate 14). In June of 1936, Albrizio submitted his sketches to the review committee. After suggesting that the mailman be replaced by a herdsman and the farmer in the foreground be seated, the committee accepted the design for the post office.[5] The revisions were made, and a contract was issued on July 18, 1936. The mural was to measure 5 feet by 11 feet, and the total payment was $550.[6]

From this fee Albrizio was expected to cover all costs incurred in the execution and installation of the work, including all transportation to and from the site.[7] He was to receive $200 upon completion of the preliminary sketches, $150 when the work was half completed, and the final $200 upon full completion. The Section required photographs from the artist showing each completed stage of work.[8] It's easy to see why these government commissions did not attract starving artists. Most artists barely broke even when carrying out government projects.

Albrizio carefully examined the walls of the new post office before beginning. He found the interior walls to be covered with metal lath and positioned far from the exterior walls, thus providing a suitable base for the fresco.[9] The existing plaster needed to be increased to a uniform thickness before application of the finish coat, which would receive the paint. A small molding was attached to the underside of

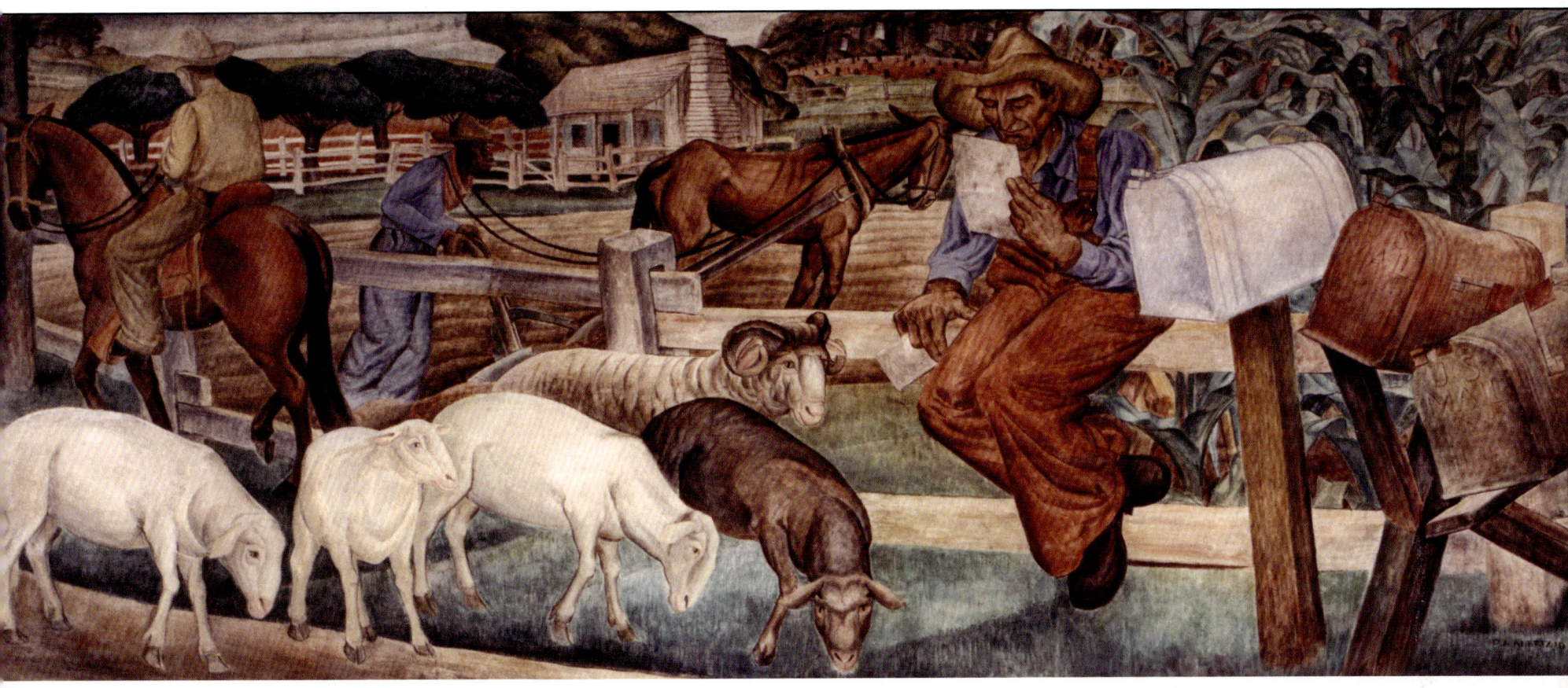

Plate 15. *Rural Free Delivery,* 1936, fresco, DeRidder, Louisiana, post office (now the Beauregard Parish Tourist Commission). Photo by Brad Smith.

the projecting layer to act as a splay between the added layer and the existing wall. Albrizio hired a professional plasterer to prepare the wall surface as the strenuous task often caused his hand to shake excessively while painting.[10] He began painting the fresco in early September of 1936 between his semester obligations at LSU.[11] It was completed on September 10 (plate 15).[12]

This charming scene relies on a very simple division of space to create depth in this small panel. The looming figure in front captures the viewer's attention; it is then led to the middle section, where a plowman tills the soil. The sheep herder on horseback suggests a pathway into the distance, where a small rural farmhouse defines the far ground.

FIRST IRON ORE PRODUCED IN RUSSELLVILLE

Russellville, Alabama, Post Office

The second mural Albrizio painted under the auspices of the Section was done by invitation. In May of 1937 he received a letter from Edward Rowan, superintendent of the Section, asking him to submit designs for a post office mural in Russellville, Alabama.[13] The Section had quickly come to realize that small competitions kept their offices inundated with applications. Therefore, any job under $1,000 was now awarded by invitation instead of competition.[14] Because of his work in DeRidder, Albrizio was asked to design a mural for the post office in the small town of Russellville in northern Alabama.

Albrizio was paid $775 for the mural, issued in the same increments as the DeRidder fresco.[15] As with the DeRidder project, he traveled to Russellville to talk to area residents to form an idea of what was important to them. He was escorted around town by Dr. J. M. Clark, a dentist, local historian, and member of the Natchez Trace Association. They visited the local iron mine, limestone quarry, cotton mill, and other sites of interest. Clark favored the beehive iron furnace, which after one hundred years of neglect lay in ruins outside of the city. Albrizio was apparently not moved by the aesthetic potential of the furnace and submitted to Washington two alternate sketches for consideration. One was of the limestone quarry, and the other the iron mine and cotton mill (plates 16 and 17).[16]

The Section approved the sketch of the limestone quarry and officially sanctioned its placement in the new post office.[17] In the meantime, Clark became furious when he learned that his favored 1817 iron furnace would not be the subject of the mural, and many local organizations agreed with him. He immediately wrote a letter to his congressman, Brockman Bankhead, Speaker of the U.S. House of Representatives, asking that the design be changed. That letter was forwarded to the Section, and Rowan asked Albrizio to respond to Bankhead. The artist complied, thanking Bankhead for his interest, calling Russellville a "lovely" town, and expressing his pleasure to be working in Alabama. "I am especially pleased to have the opportunity of locating some of my work in Alabama since my wife Imogene Inge is a native of the State," said Albrizio, "and some day we plan to return to live on the family plantation near Greensboro."[18]

Albrizio felt pressured to honor the wishes of Clark even though he thought the subject of the quarry would yield a better composition. In a letter to Rowan, Albrizio explained that he feared that the difference in size between the large furnace and any nearby figures would yield an ill-proportioned drawing. Letters volleyed back and forth between Albrizio, Clark, and Rowan. Albrizio described the difficulty of placing the large furnace in the space of the mural but added, "If in your mind, you still believe that subject matter is more important than the result possible under existing physical conditions, I am willing to do the best I can."[19]

His new sketch was enthusiastically received by Russellville's citizens, the Section, and even Clark, who claimed he was going to have it framed. Clark then offered a series of

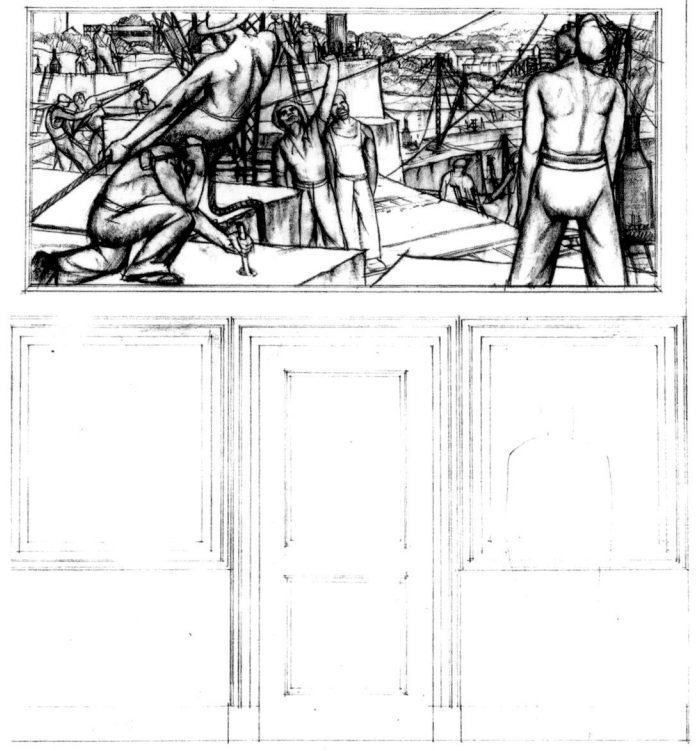

Plate 16.
Sketch for Russellville, AL, post office fresco, 1937, graphite on paper,
National Archives, Washington, DC.

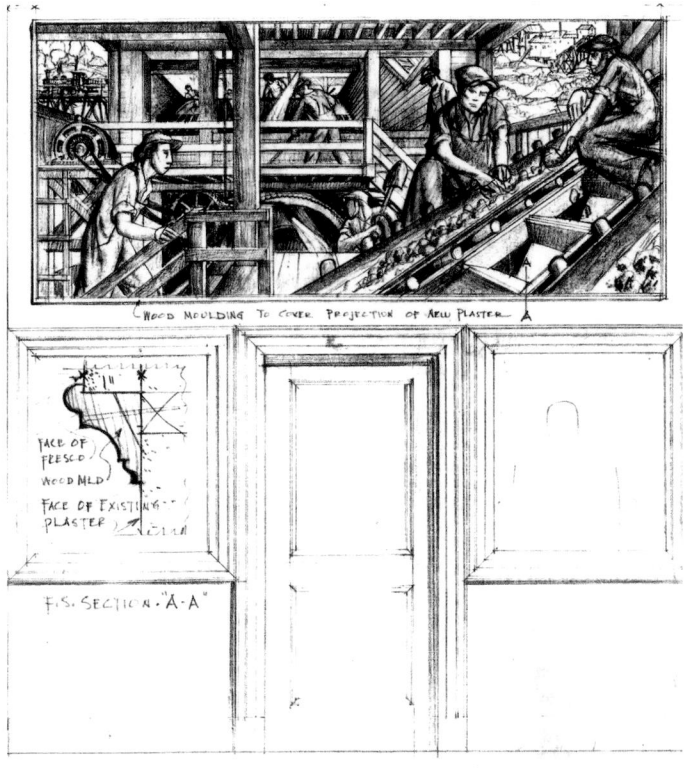

Plate 17.
Sketch for Russellville, AL, post office fresco, 1937, graphite on paper,
National Archives, Washington, DC.

suggestions on how the sketch could be improved.[20] Finally, by June 6, 1938, the fresco was finished, almost a year later than planned (plate 18).[21]

In this fresco, the beehive-shaped furnace, the water wheel that supplied power for the forge, the warehouse, and the suspended 500-pound hammer used for shaping the pig iron draw our attention to the area directly behind the picture plane. The activity wanes as the composition moves into the distance, leaving the only major background feature as Cedar Creek, which supplied the water power and transportation for the operation. The noble worker predominates, especially the slaves whose documented labor was still extant.

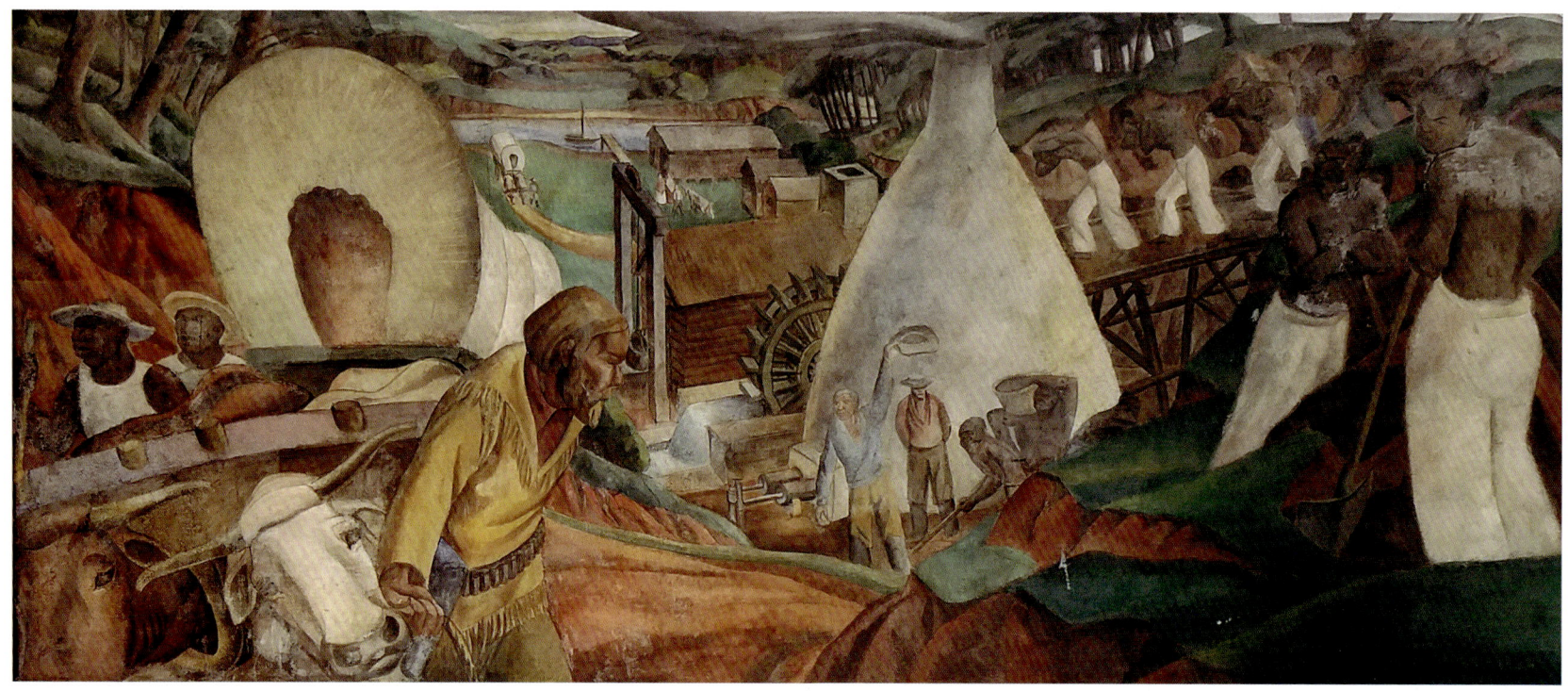

Plate 18.

First Iron Ore Produced in Russellville, 1938, fresco, Russellville, AL, post office. Photograph © 2018 United States Postal Service.

Albrizio's experiences in DeRidder and Russellville demonstrate that the government could be heavy-handed in these federally supported projects. This was not ideal for the artist, but artists have always endured the parameters of working on commission. Although awkward in their organization, the government art programs did accomplish their goal—to provide broadly accessible art and to laud the people and places in every pocket of this country. The frescoes in DeRidder and Russellville still stand, and continue to honor the people and the place, past and present.

5.

Public Works under the Federal Emergency Relief Act

THE SHREVEPORT FRESCOES

IN 1938, ALBRIZIO PAINTED FRESCOES IN the portico of the Louisiana State Exhibit Building in Shreveport. The building was constructed under the Federal Emergency Relief Act of 1933, which provided relief grants, not loans, to states through the Federal Emergency Relief Administration (FERA).[1] The control of the grant was very flexible and left the states with the responsibility of administration, organization, and partial funding.[2] In the case of the Louisiana State Exhibit Building, the commission for the decorative work was probably contracted by the architect, with some control by the state committee instigating the project.

Based in Shreveport, the architectural firm of Neild, Somdal and Neild worked on the Exhibit Building while also engaged with another FERA project, the State Capitol Annex in Baton Rouge. Albrizio had already been assigned the fresco panels in the annex as an adjunct to his work on the state capitol. He was a good salesman of his work and easily collaborated with fellow architects. It's likely that his work in Baton Rouge led to his commission in Shreveport.

The Exhibit Building, constructed between 1934 and 1938, cost the state $550,000 and was touted as the largest circular building in the world.[3] It had a center court and was designed to house exhibits and dioramas during the Louisiana State Fair. Four panels totaling 700 square feet comprised the fresco area. The two main panels each measured 12 feet by 16 feet, and the two accompanying panels each measured 10 feet by 16 feet. Positioned on either side of two 14-ton elliptical granite columns in the portico, the frescoes enhanced the impressive entranceway (plate 19).

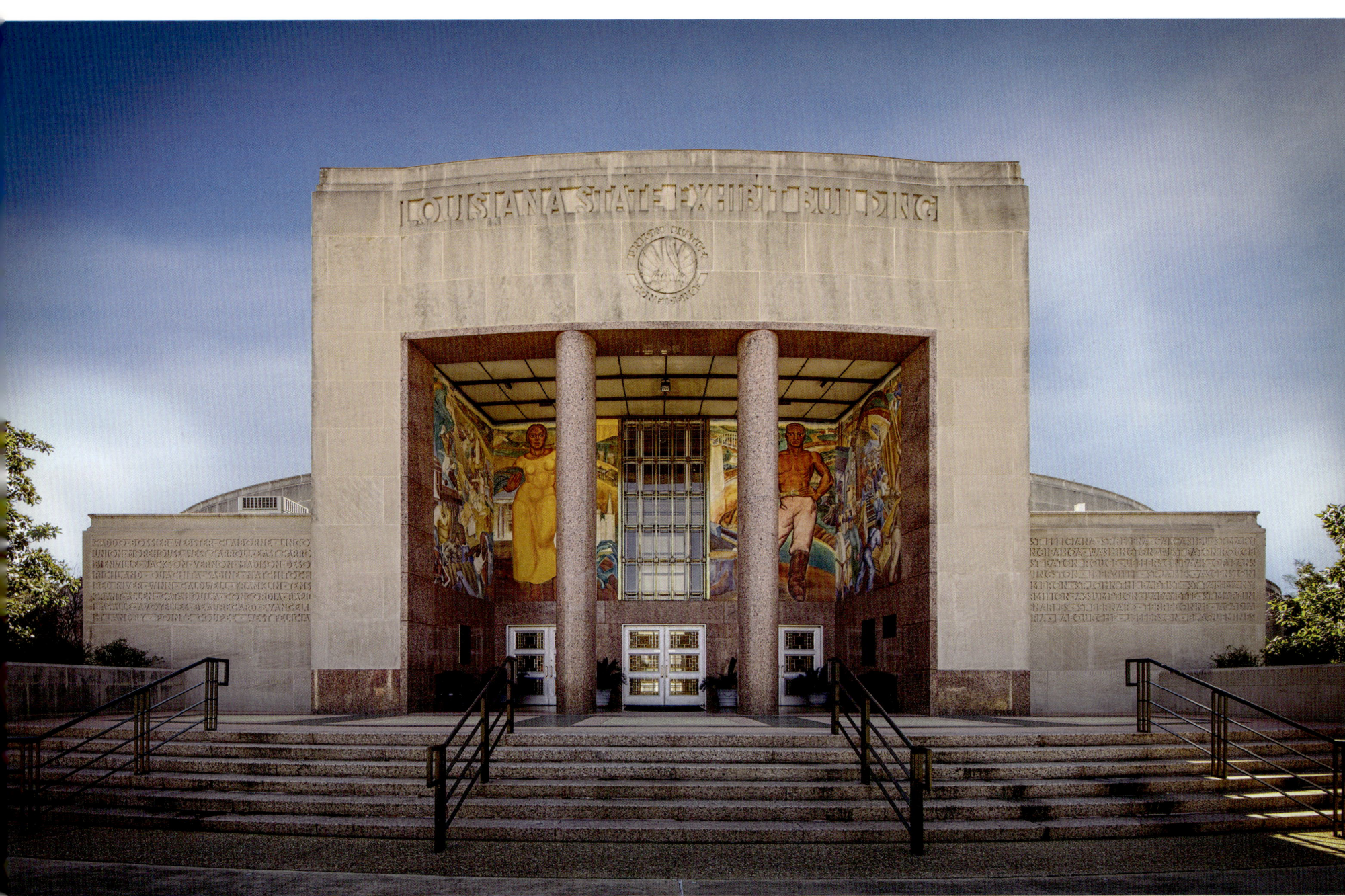

Plate 19.
Exterior, Louisiana State Exhibit Building, Shreveport, LA. Courtesy Louisiana State Exhibit Museum, Shreveport, photo by Brian Lewis.

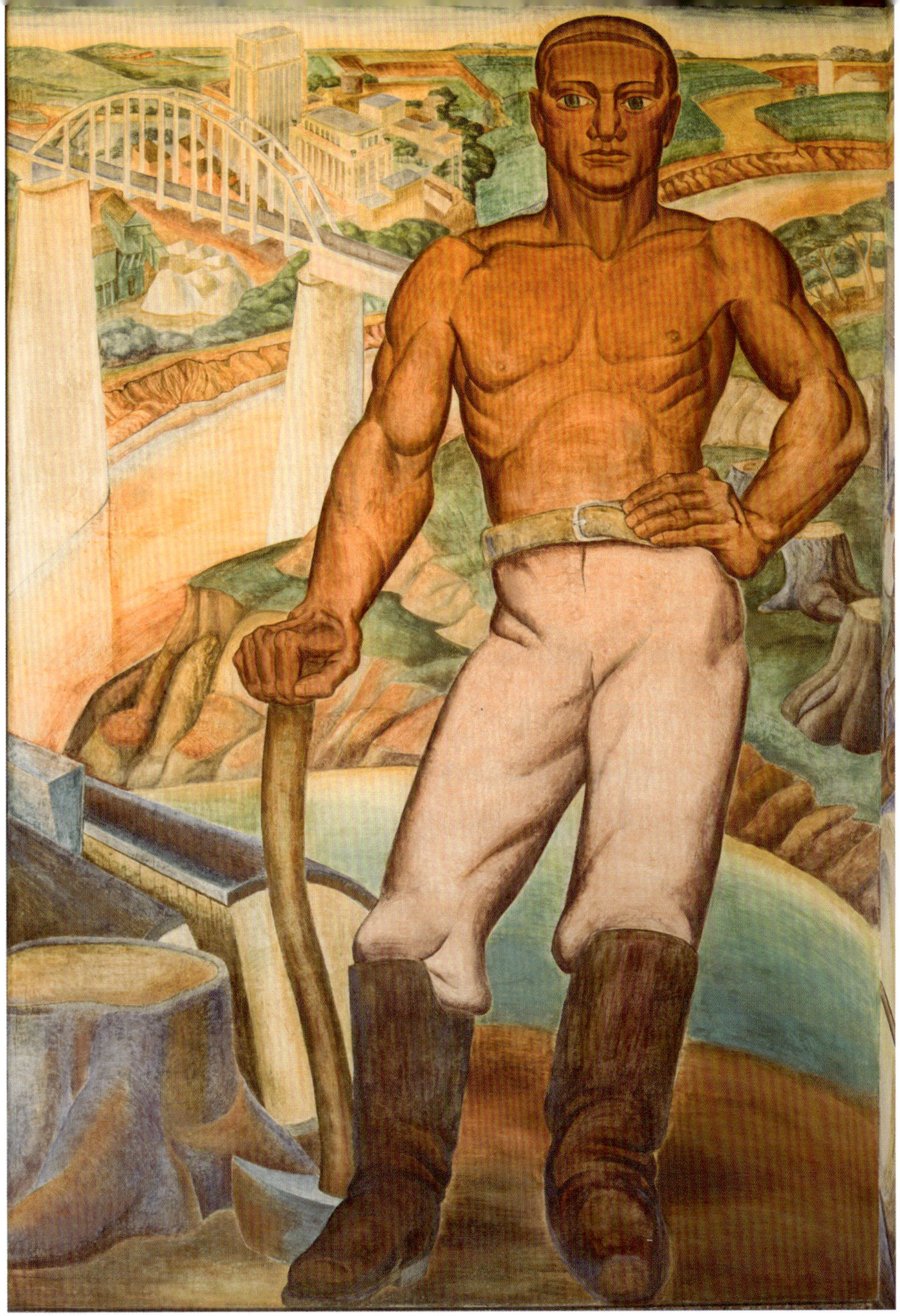

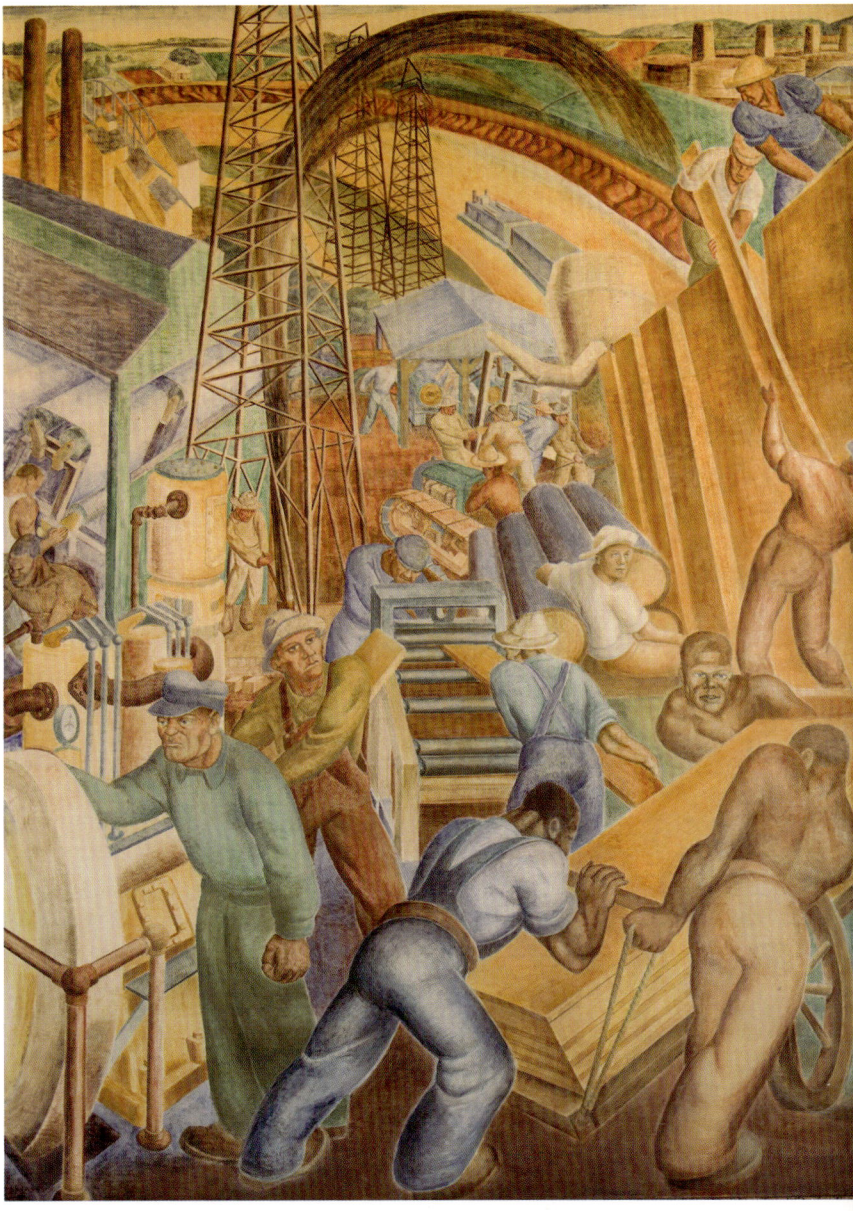

Plate 20.
North Louisiana, 1938, fresco, Louisiana State Exhibit Building, Shreveport.
Courtesy Louisiana State Exhibit Museum, Shreveport, photo by Brian Lewis.

Plate 21.
Activities of North Louisiana, 1938, fresco, Louisiana State Exhibit Building, Shreveport. Courtesy Louisiana State Exhibit Museum, Shreveport, photo by Brian Lewis.

Since the building would draw people from all areas of the state, Albrizio chose north and south Louisiana as subjects for the panels. Flanking the doorway are personifications of the two regions, and at 90-degree angles are partner panels depicting activities unique to each region.

Grenier Conservation performed extensive restoration on the panels in 2001 after a hailstorm caused widespread damage on all four panels. Although the vibrant color looks thick and pasty, conservator Elise Grenier reported that the final application of plaster was very thin. Albrizio did not create the cartoons, or full-size sketches, that normally would have been used to transfer the design onto the working surface. Instead, he painted from a sketch scaled two inches to one foot and drew directly onto the wall surface.[4] Albrizio was likely working far behind schedule after the delays in the Russellville project earlier that year, and he had still before him the Capitol Annex commission as well as his duties at LSU. Although not an inferior project by any means, the Exhibit Building frescoes were probably completed in much less time than Albrizio had originally planned.

The panel to the right of the main entrance depicts a bare-chested lumberjack standing massive and powerful (plate 20). Approximately 16 feet tall, he has a harsh muscular body and severe physiognomy that enhance his colossal appearance. Conventions such as the fallen log in the foreground help to draw the viewer's attention into the distance, giving depth to the exaggerated rectangular shape of the frame. In the background are the Red River and the Long-Allen Bridge. The landscape includes the red clay banks of northern Louisiana dotted with the stumps of hewn trees, representing the rich lumbering industry. In the upper left is the largest city in north Louisiana, Shreveport, recognizable by the Slattery Building, the parish courthouse, and the gravel domes.

The companion panel to this work shows the industrial activities of the northern part of the state (plate 21). As if diagonally cut from the upper right to the lower left, the panel is divided into two parts. The lower area depicts lumber and the upper area shows details of the oil industry.

To the left of the entrance is the personification of south Louisiana (plate 22). A bulky female figure, Michelangelesque in quality, alludes to the fertility and productivity of the largely agricultural region. Her immense form provides a sturdy counterpart to the lumberjack in an almost mirror image. She stands next to a field of sugarcane with a bouquet of stalks in her arms. Directly behind her are New Orleans's St. Louis Cathedral and a nineteenth-century plantation house. In the distance are industrial warehouses, a rice dryer, and the contour of the Shushan Airport in New Orleans (today called Lakefront Airport)—a new and stellar airfield of that time.

The adjacent panel illustrates laborers in south Louisiana (plate 23). Flowing from the upper left corner of the mural, the design pours across the picture plane, just as the Mississippi River pours across the state providing fertile land and a major trade route for the cash crops of sugarcane, rice, and cotton. In the distance, shrimpers await the blessing of the fleet before heading to the Gulf of Mexico.

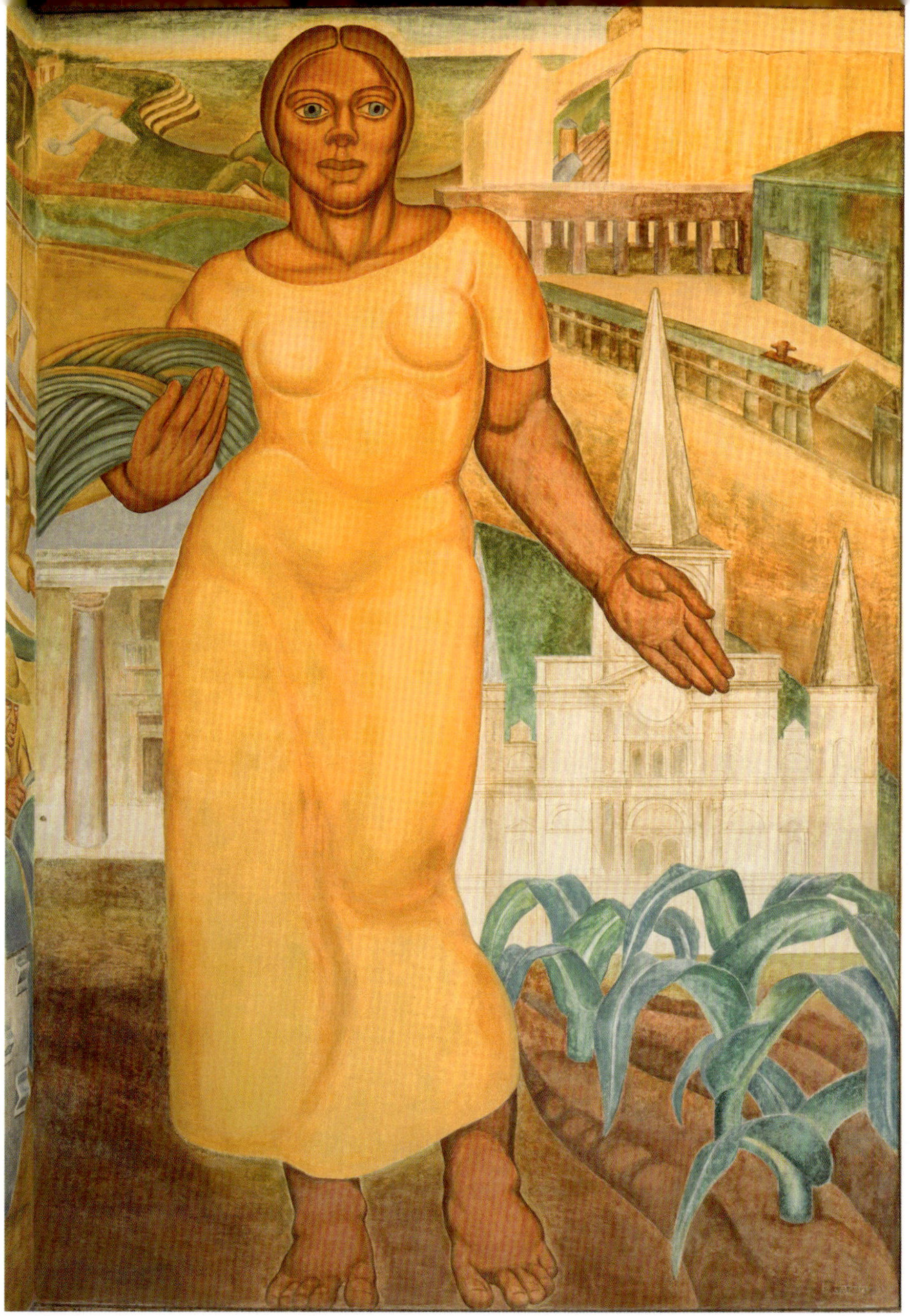

Plate 22.

South Louisiana, 1938, fresco, Louisiana State Exhibit Building, Shreveport. Courtesy Louisiana State Exhibit Museum, Shreveport, photo by Brian Lewis.

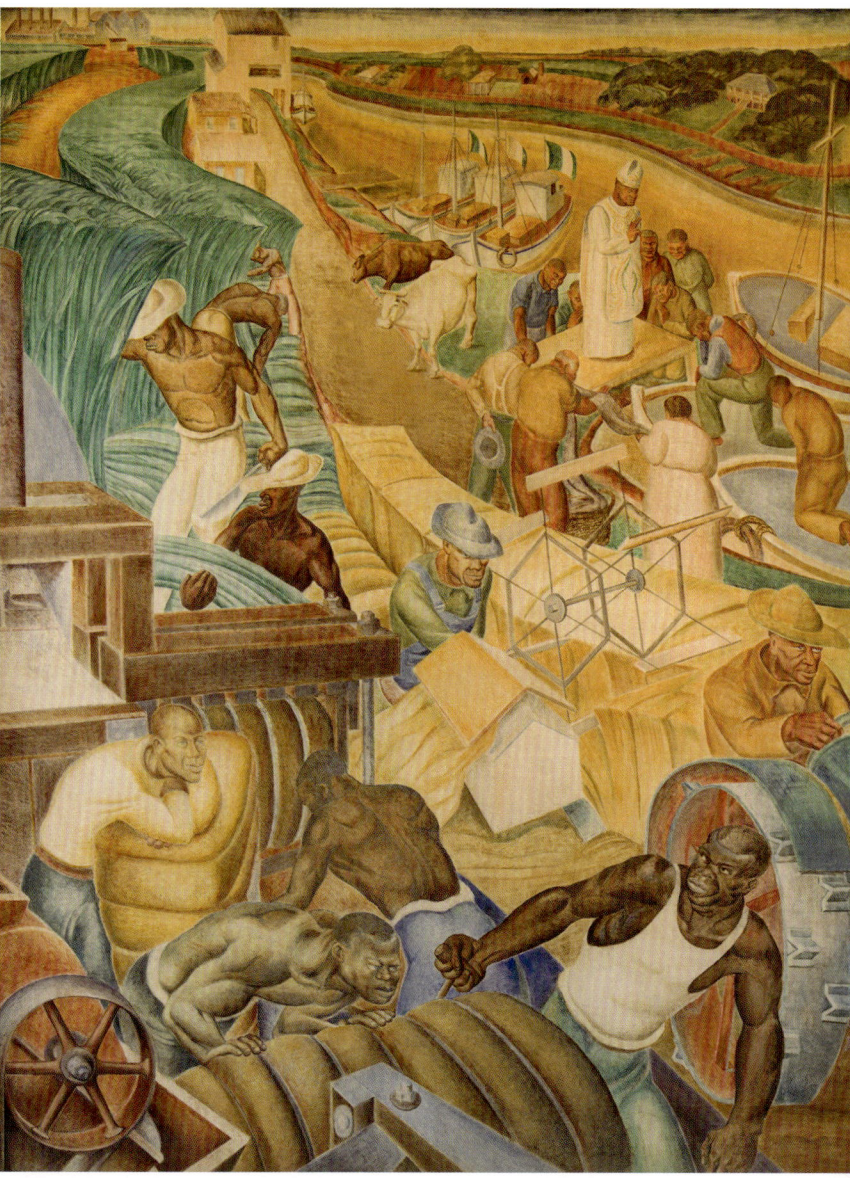

Plate 23.

Activities of South Louisiana, 1938, fresco, Louisiana State Exhibit Building, Shreveport. Courtesy Louisiana State Exhibit Museum, Shreveport, photo by Brian Lewis.

THE CAPITOL ANNEX FRESCOES

In 1937 the State Capitol Annex Building in Baton Rouge was constructed. In the fall of 1938, having completed the Shreveport murals, Albrizio began work on the 36 square feet of mural space located in the annex lobby. Commissioned by the state administration through FERA, this program was Albrizio's third major fresco cycle in Louisiana.[5] He juggled its execution with his teaching duties at LSU and finished the work in approximately two months. The murals were to represent the achievements of the state under Governor Richard W. Leche, who served Louisiana in 1938–1939. They consisted of four panels, two measuring 8 feet by 12 feet and two measuring 8 feet by 9 feet.[6]

The panel *Social Security and Well-Being* illustrates the efforts of the state in providing for its citizens (plate 24).[7] Various welfare activities rotate around a central triangular arrangement. Starting at the lower right corner of the composition and moving diagonally are seen the bestowal of aid to the blind, the provision of a home and family for dependent children, the distribution of pensions to the aged, and the assistance given to minorities and unemployables.[8]

The panel *State Construction* depicts workmen in the diversified duties of surveying, transporting girders, and chiseling stone (plate 25). The panel originally incorporated the portraits of Governor Leche and annex architect Edward F. Neild of Shreveport. The men were shown standing in the center foreground reviewing blueprints for the annex construction. In 1940, the Louisiana House of Representatives approached Governor Sam Jones requesting the removal of the Leche portrait. Leche had been sentenced to a ten-year penitentiary stay for mail fraud.

His portrait in a government building was seen as inappropriate.[9] The request was granted and Albrizio agreed to remove the Leche portrait, along with architect Neild, from the fresco. The portraits were replaced by a workman clothed in brown overalls. Still striving to open the two-dimensional plane of the wall, Albrizio used the massive form of a girder pushing into the space to create depth. To the left extends a graceful upsweep formed by the repetitive figures of white-clad laborers.

The panel *State Industry* (plate 26) has a curvilinear composition. It features various arcs and orbital shapes in contrast to the angular accents of the previous panels. The workings of an oil refinery are the main subject, with mills and warehouses in the background.

Rural Hospitalization reflects state improvements in health care (plate 27).[10] The right foreground is the cutaway interior of a country home. A doctor and nurse have come to the aid of a needy family, whose crude wood-burning stove is located to the right. To the left is one of the state's newest services, the mobile hospital, which catered to individuals in outlying areas who were unable to reach urban health centers and otherwise could never have received proper medical care.

With each mural assignment, Albrizio's technique evolved and his compositions became more sophisticated. As he continued doing mural art, he made a concerted effort to improve his designs, understanding that these public works must attract the attention of onlookers who might not ordinarily be drawn to visual information (plate 28). During Albrizio's frequent visits to New York, he had the opportunity to work and study with popular American painters

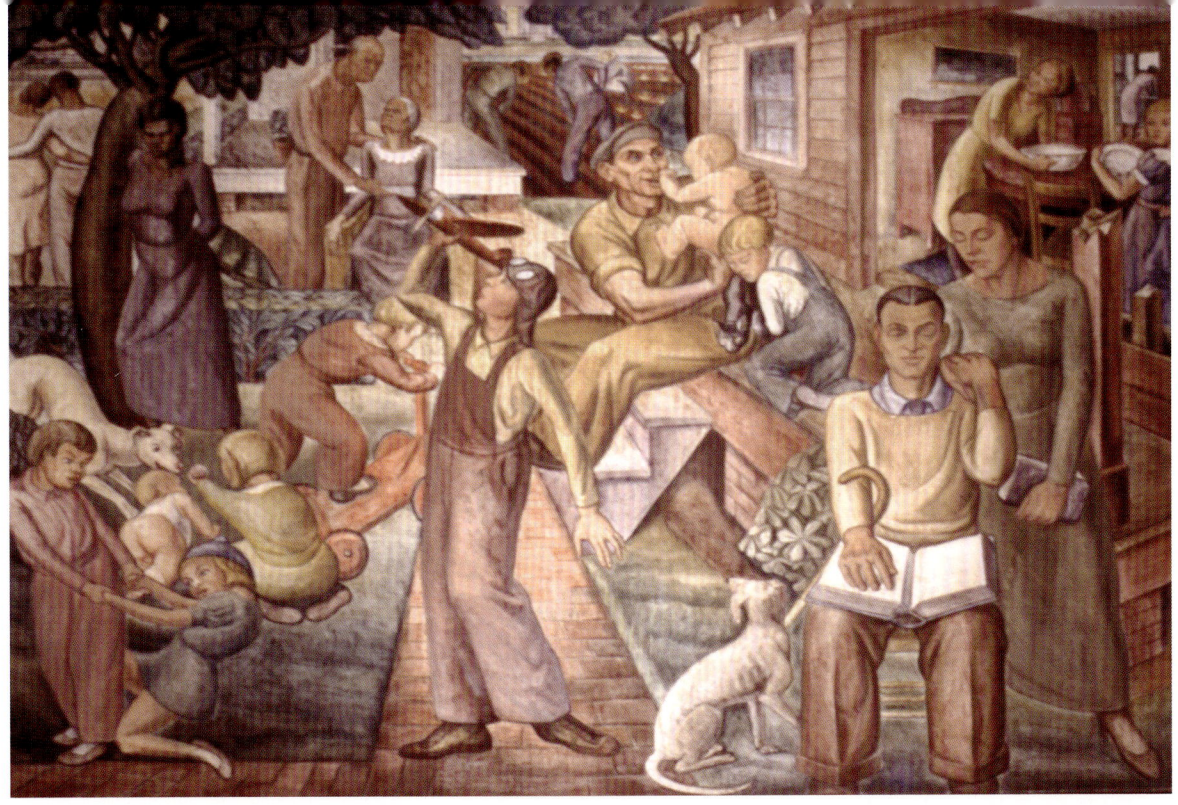

Plate 24.
Social Security and Well-Being, 1936, fresco, Capitol Annex Building, Baton Rouge. Author's collection.

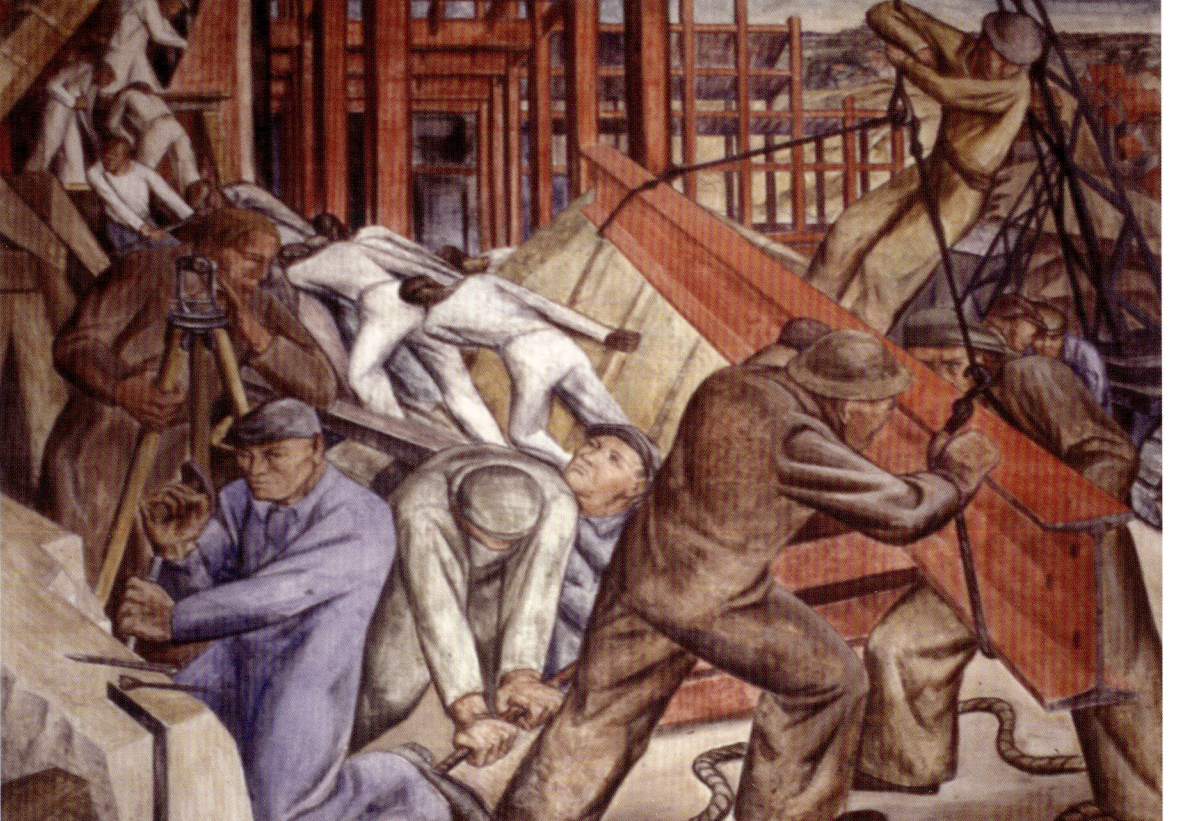

Plate 25.
State Construction, 1936, fresco, Capitol Annex Building, Baton Rouge. Author's collection.

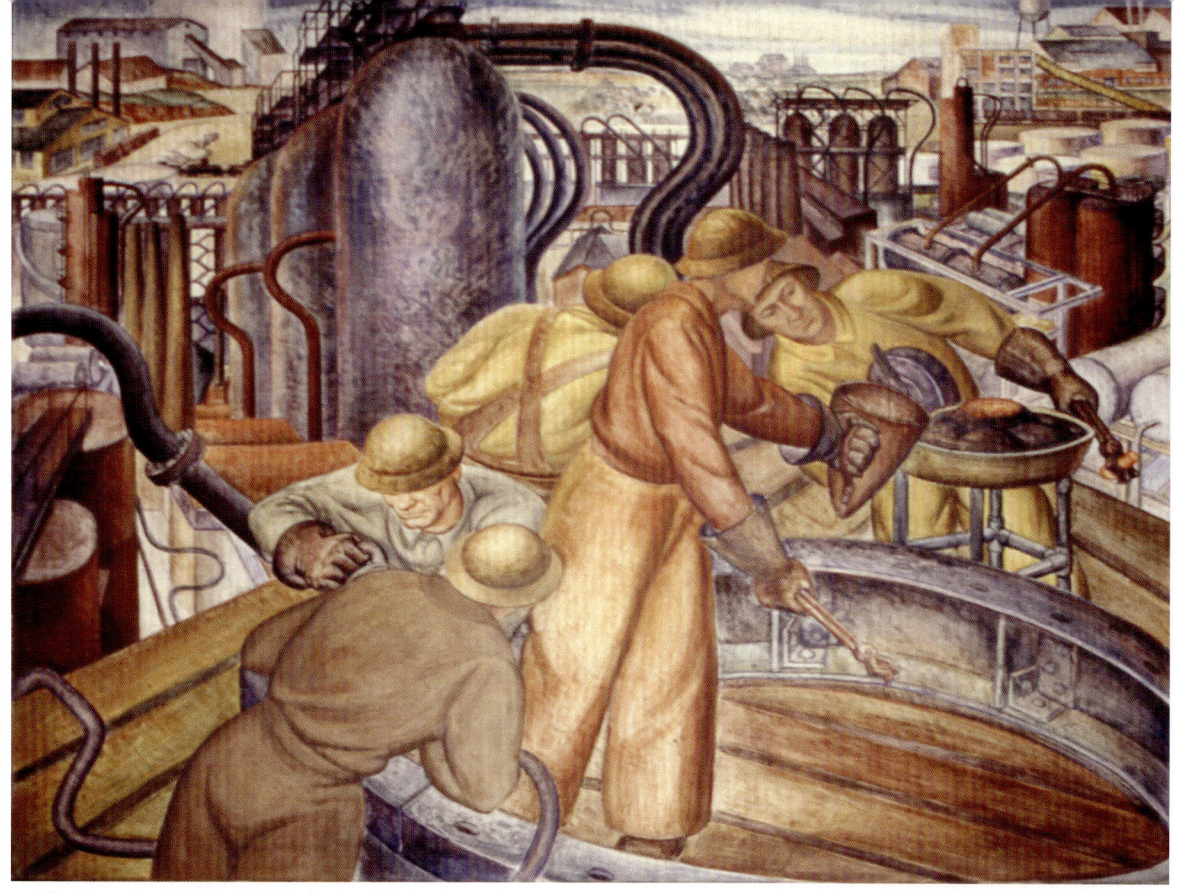

Plate 26.

State Industry, 1936, fresco, Capitol Annex
Building, Baton Rouge. Author's collection.

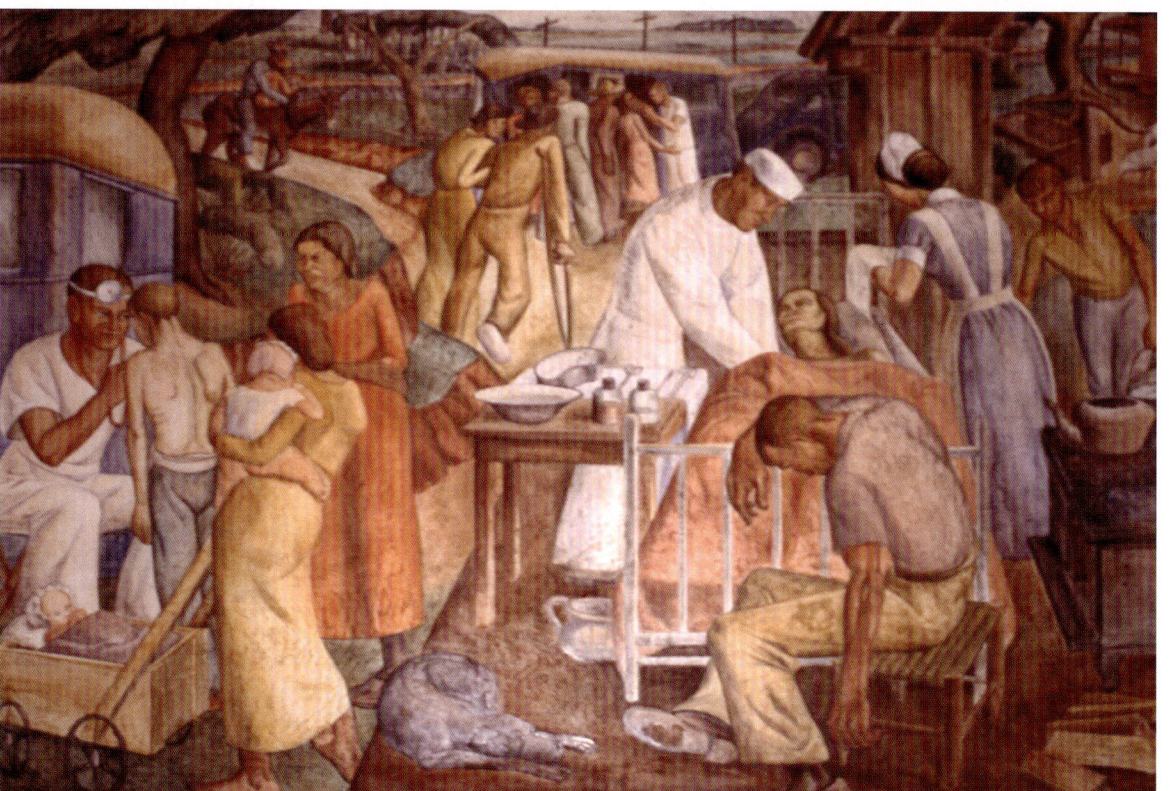

Plate 27.

Rural Hospitalization, 1936, fresco, Capitol Annex
Building, Baton Rouge. Author's collection.

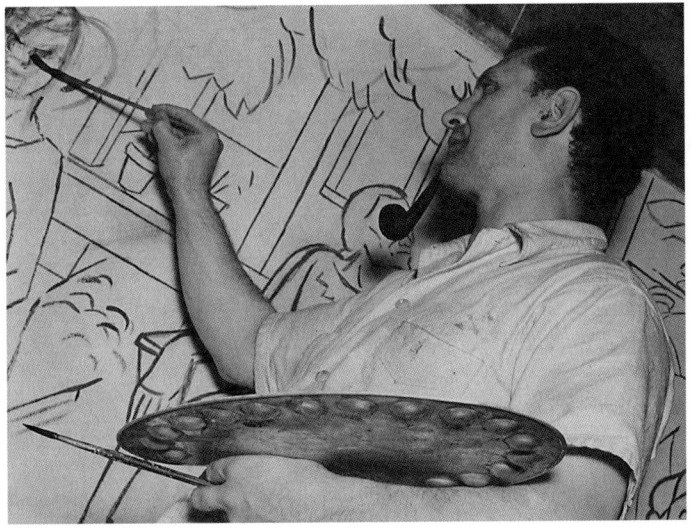

Plate 28.
Albrizio working on a mural (unidentified). State Library of Louisiana.

1. Balance (or equilibrium)—created by shifts and countershifts in relation to the overall pattern within the picture frame.
2. Connection—when one element in a work leads to another.
3. Rhythm—the repetition in a dynamic sequence, at alternating intervals, of similar factors. Rhythm can be created by interlocking edges, centrifugal opposition, or centripetal opposition.[13]

Albrizio became acutely aware of these principles, as shown in his designs. His organization of the Shreveport and Capitol Annex murals demonstrates his attempt to use Benton's elements. They became a hallmark of Albrizio's designs as he developed an increasingly sophisticated visual vocabulary in his later murals of the 1940s and 1950s.

XAVIER GONZALEZ

The Section of Painting and Sculpture supported many other artists in Louisiana besides Albrizio. Approximately two dozen artists, painters, and sculptors decorated federal buildings across the state with murals, sculptures, and reliefs. Albrizio was the only one, however, to work in true fresco and the only one to continue his mural masterpieces after the nationwide enthusiasm for fresco murals began to wane at the end of the 1930s.

As a point of comparison, a local contemporary of Conrad Albrizio was Xavier Gonzalez. Born in Spain in 1898, Gonzalez came to the United States in 1925 with his family and attended the Art Institute of Chicago before moving to New Orleans in 1931 to teach at Newcomb. There he met

from whom he learned a great deal. One of his most important associations was with famed American Regional painter Thomas Hart Benton, who served on the faculty of the Art Students League from 1926 to 1935.[11] Albrizio was in New York around the same time, working with Alma Reed and the Fresco Guild and teaching at the Leonardo da Vinci Art School in 1934. Letters from Albrizio to Benton suggest that they must have had at least a casual acquaintance during their overlapping time in the city.[12] Albrizio's work of the mid- to late 1930s shows evidence of Benton's influence.

Benton set forth a list of design elements for students that he felt would yield an aesthetically pleasing mural composition. These were:

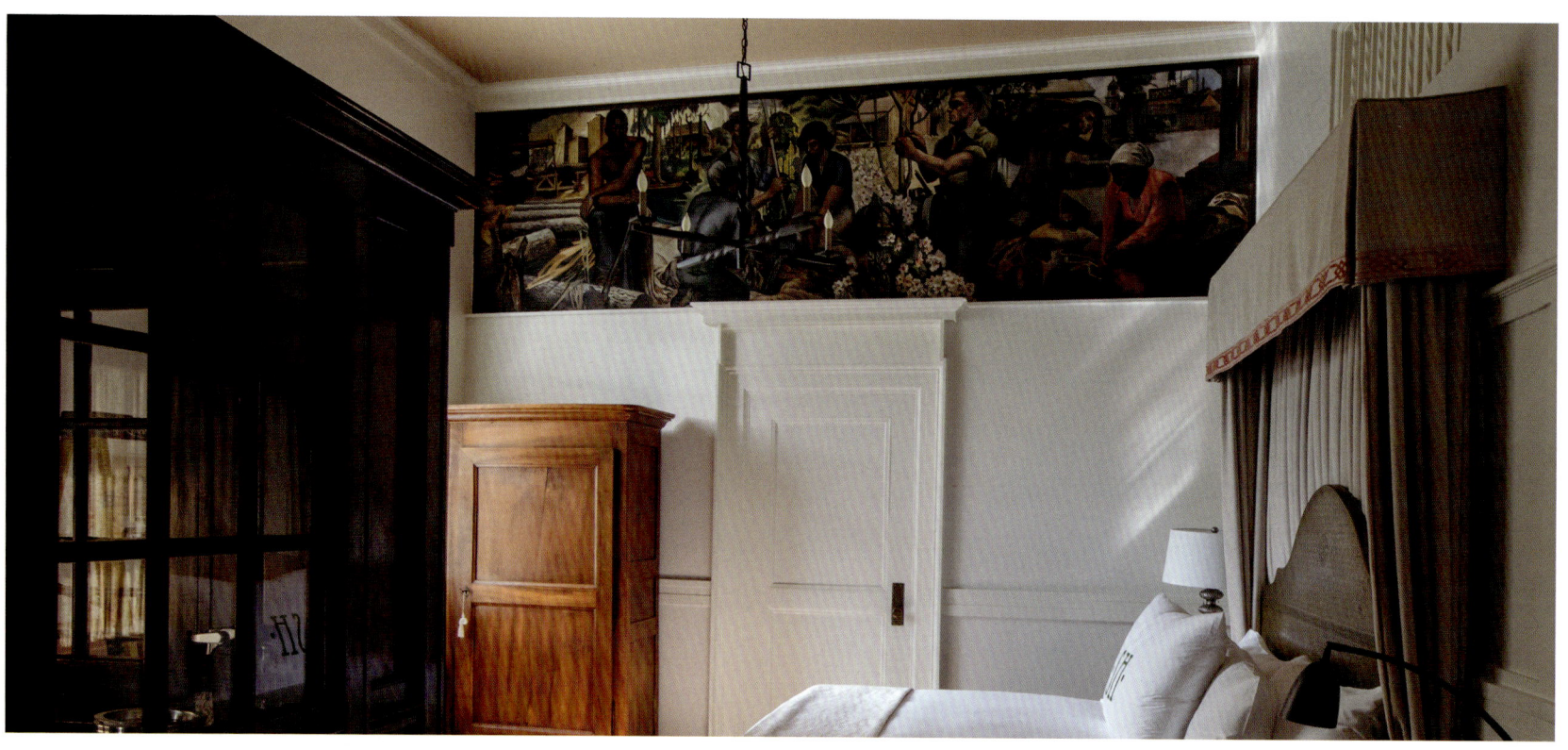

Plate 29.

Xavier Gonzalez, *Tung Oil Industry,* 1939, oil on canvas. Originally in Covington, LA, post office; now located in the Southern Hotel, Covington. Photo by Bevil Knapp.

Ethel Edwards, also an artist, whom he married. The two lived in New Orleans until the mid-1940s, when they moved to New York City, where Gonzalez continued his career until his death in 1993.[14] Gonzalez was a well-respected local artist who produced many sculptural pieces as well as paintings. A nice example of Gonzalez's work for the Section is the 1939 post office mural executed in Covington, Louisiana, called *Tung Oil Industry* (plate 29), now located in a bedroom of the Southern Hotel. The painting celebrated the brief cultivation of tung trees in St. Tammany Parish in the early twentieth century. The mural is oil on canvas, which was secured to the wall after painting. A less challenging medium than fresco, oil on canvas allowed for more subtle modeling in the figures and greater detail.

6.

The End of the 1930s and into the 1940s

ALBRIZIO WAS FORTUNATE TO have had steady work throughout the 1930s. Besides his appointment at LSU, he had completed six major fresco panels in the Louisiana State Capitol, four in the Capitol Annex, two government-sponsored post office murals, and one large fresco program at the Louisiana State Exhibit Building in Shreveport. He was about to embark on a panel for the Iberia Parish Courthouse in New Iberia, Louisiana. He had also completed one of his most important easel paintings, *Jordan* (plate 30), which was shown at the Whitney Museum's Sixth Annual Show of Contemporary Art in New York City in 1937.[1] This painting depicting the religious ecstasy of African Americans was described by a *New Orleans Times-Picayune/States* critic in the 1930s as "a flow of solid shape into solid shape and blending frenzies of line and outline."

THE ALLEN HALL FRESCOES

Despite these notable accomplishments, and many more to come, it is the work of Albrizio's students that is most remembered on the LSU campus. Between 1937 and 1939, the east and west entrances to Allen Hall, which then housed the Art Department, were given over to young muralists to test their skills.

Albrizio chose four students to fresco the space: Sue Brown, Jean Birkland, Anne Woolfolk, and Roy Henderson. Each student later reported total freedom in choosing their subject. Most of them adhered closely to the 1930s' ideal of glorifying the local landscape. (A fifth student, Ben Watkins, painted frescoes on the exterior of Hill Memorial Library that were later destroyed.)[2]

Brown painted the large exterior mural at the northeast entrance (plate 31). She reported that her theme was educa-

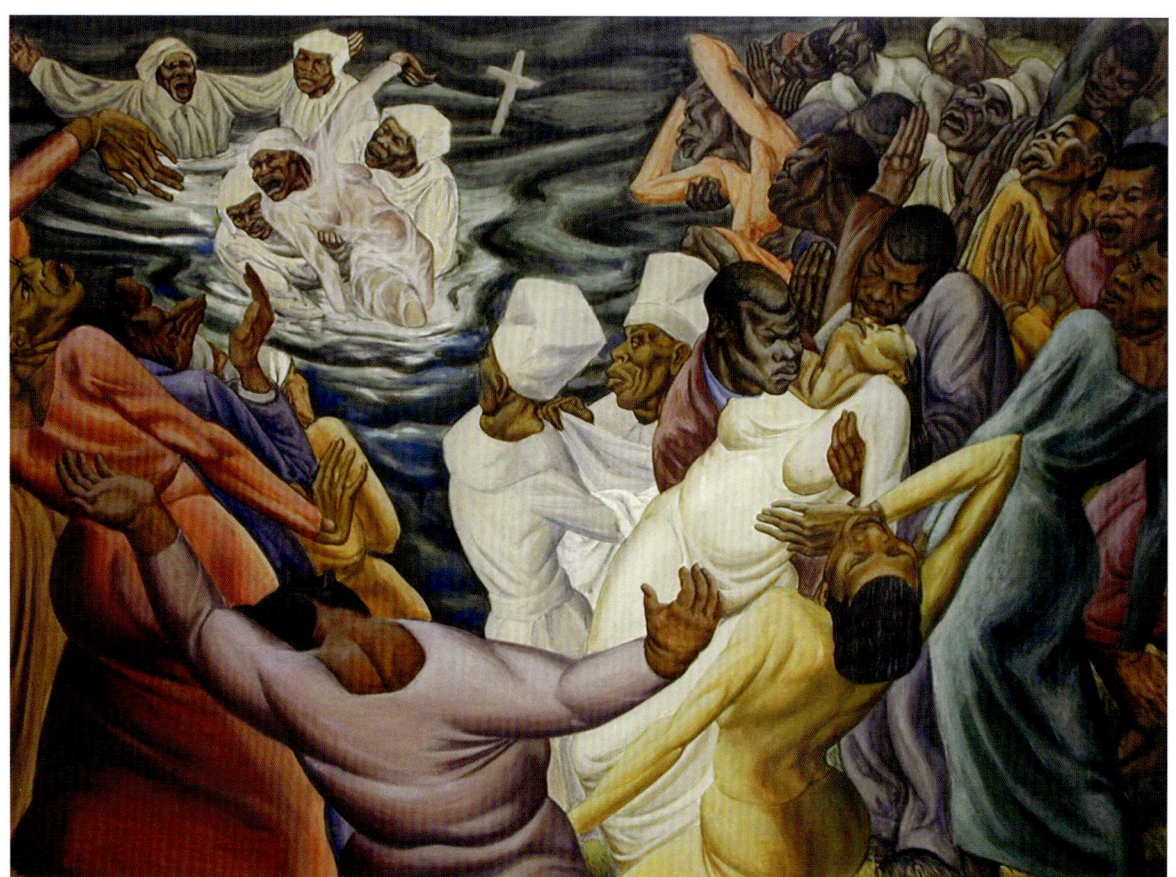

Plate 30.
Jordan, 1935–1937, oil on panel, 40 × 48 inches, Louisiana Art and Science Museum, 1984.006.001.

tion, which she expressed as a woman guiding a child and a man instructing a young boy. They loom over the many people who rush through the entrance, but the scene is also visible from a distance. The view approaching the portico from the east creates an important sight line across the quadrangle. "I was never satisfied with the mural paintings I did," said Brown (now Dietrich) in a 1990 interview with *LSU Magazine,* "but I got great satisfaction out of working on a large scale. Just the size of a mural was very satisfying. It was always on display."[3]

Birkland's and Woolfolk's designs paid tribute to the thriving academics at LSU in the 1930s and to state resources. The student workers in the cane fields chronicle the monumental strides the university made in the 1920s and '30s in

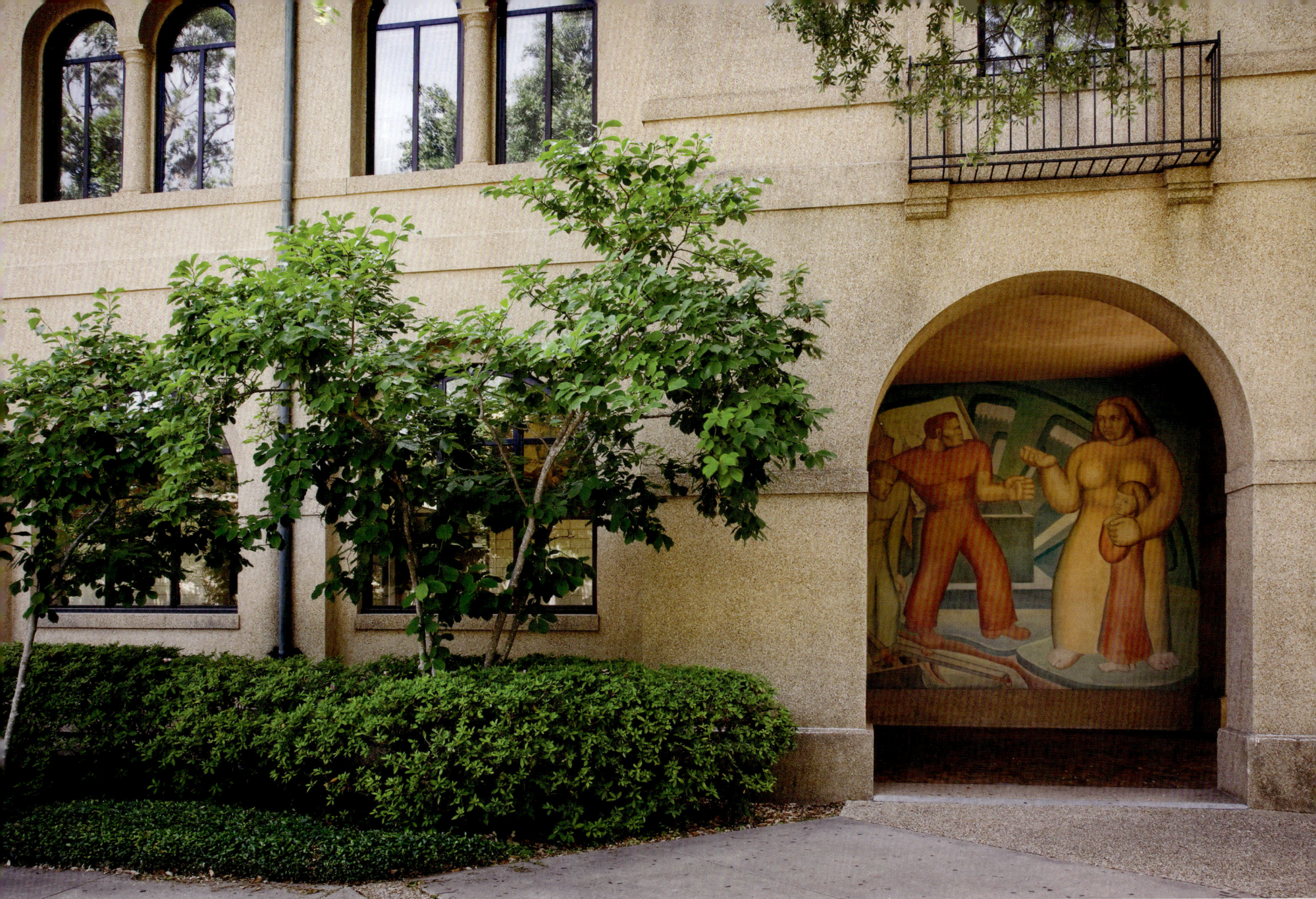

Plate 31.
Sue Brown, *Education,* 1936, fresco, LSU, Baton Rouge. Jim Zietz, LSU.

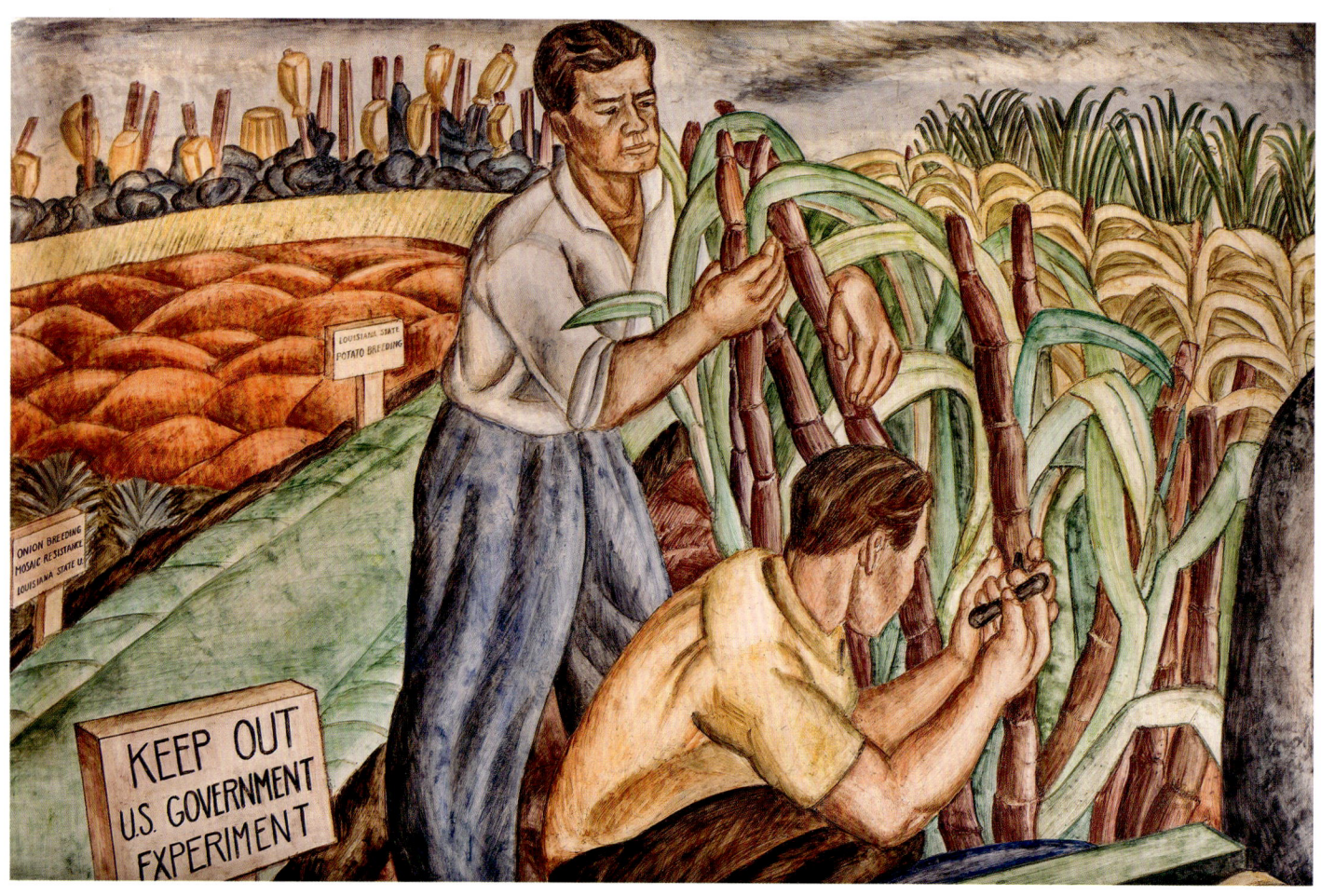

Plate 32.
Jean Birkland, *Louisiana Life,* 1938, fresco, LSU, Baton Rouge. Eddy Perez, LSU.

sugar research and cultivation (plate 32). LSU was a leading center in sugar agriculture and engineering, hosting the International Society of Sugarcane Technologists in 1938. Since the 1920s, the university had produced graduates in top positions in the sugar industry worldwide. "I felt that many of the people who were important in their fields were educated at this university and should be represented," said Woolfolk.[4] Birkland included representation of the many Hispanic students who studied at LSU. It's notable, though, that African Americans are depicted only in manual labor positions, such

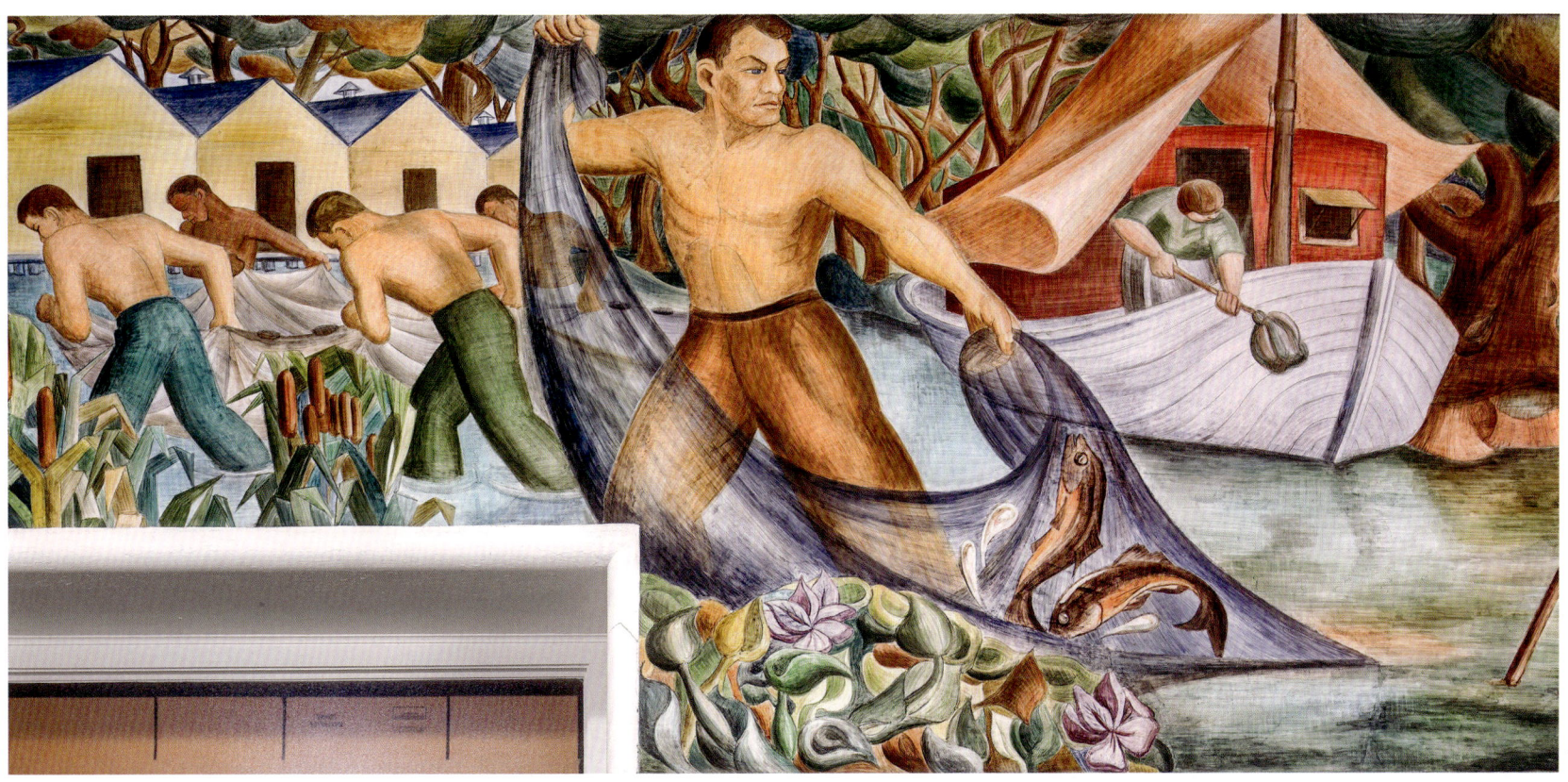

Plate 33.

Anne Woolfolk, *Industries of Louisiana,* 1938, fresco, LSU, Baton Rouge. Eddy Perez, LSU.

as working the fields, driving carts, and dragging fishnets. Full integration at LSU would not happen until 1964.[5]

Woolfolk produced the largest linear footage of fresco painting, completing work for both her undergraduate and graduate requirements. She approached her compositions lyrically. The rhythmic movement of figures and fishnets flowing down the corridor mirrors the ebb and flow of gulf waters (plate 33). Dancing fish and swirling flowers provide engaging interludes. Woolfolk discussed the problem of the considerable length and narrowness of the hall in her thesis and how it affected her composition. "I wanted areas to be seen in fragments," she wrote. "I visually broke the area

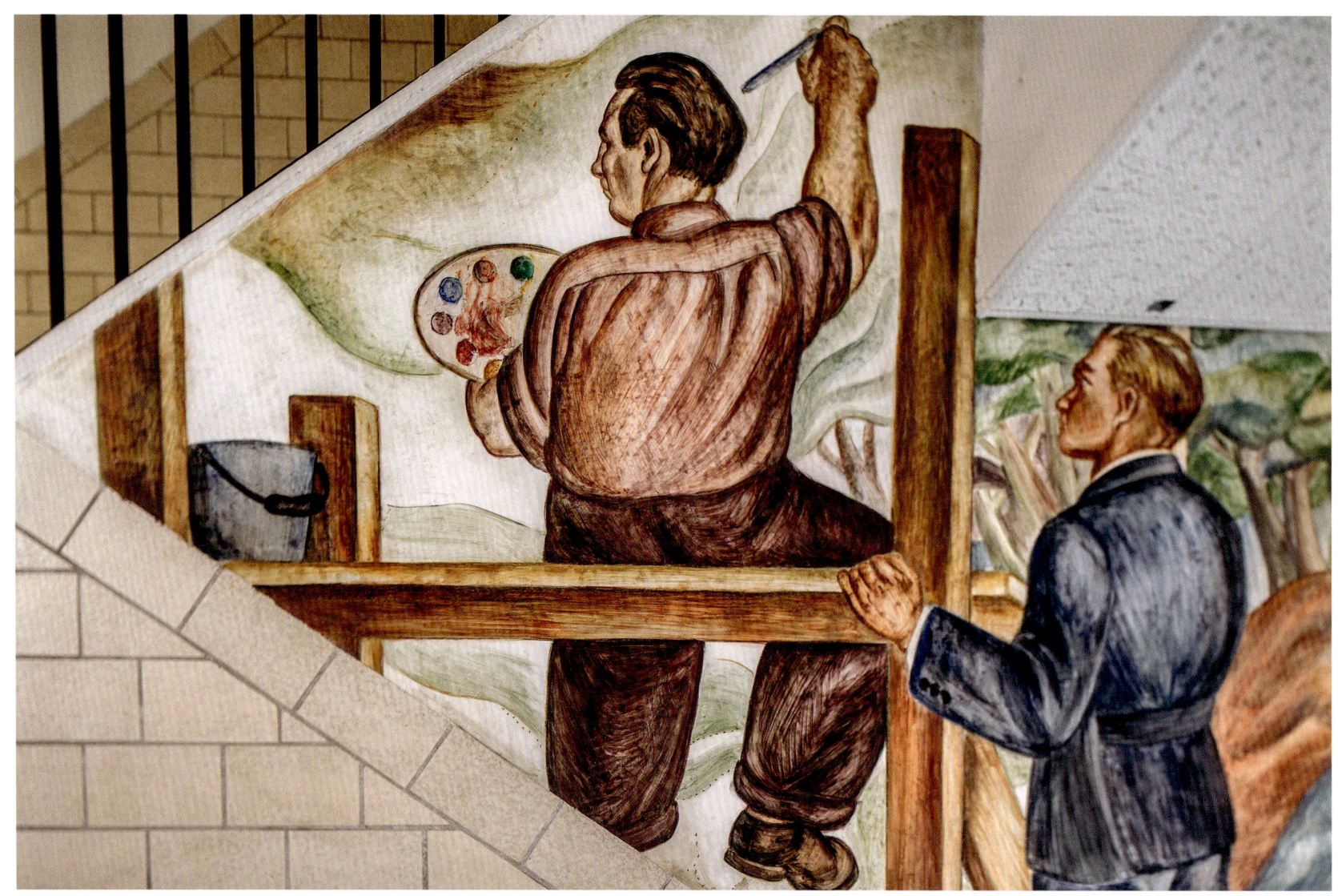

Plate 34.
Anne Woolfolk, *Portrait of Conrad Albrizio,* 1938, fresco, LSU, Baton Rouge. Eddy Perez, LSU.

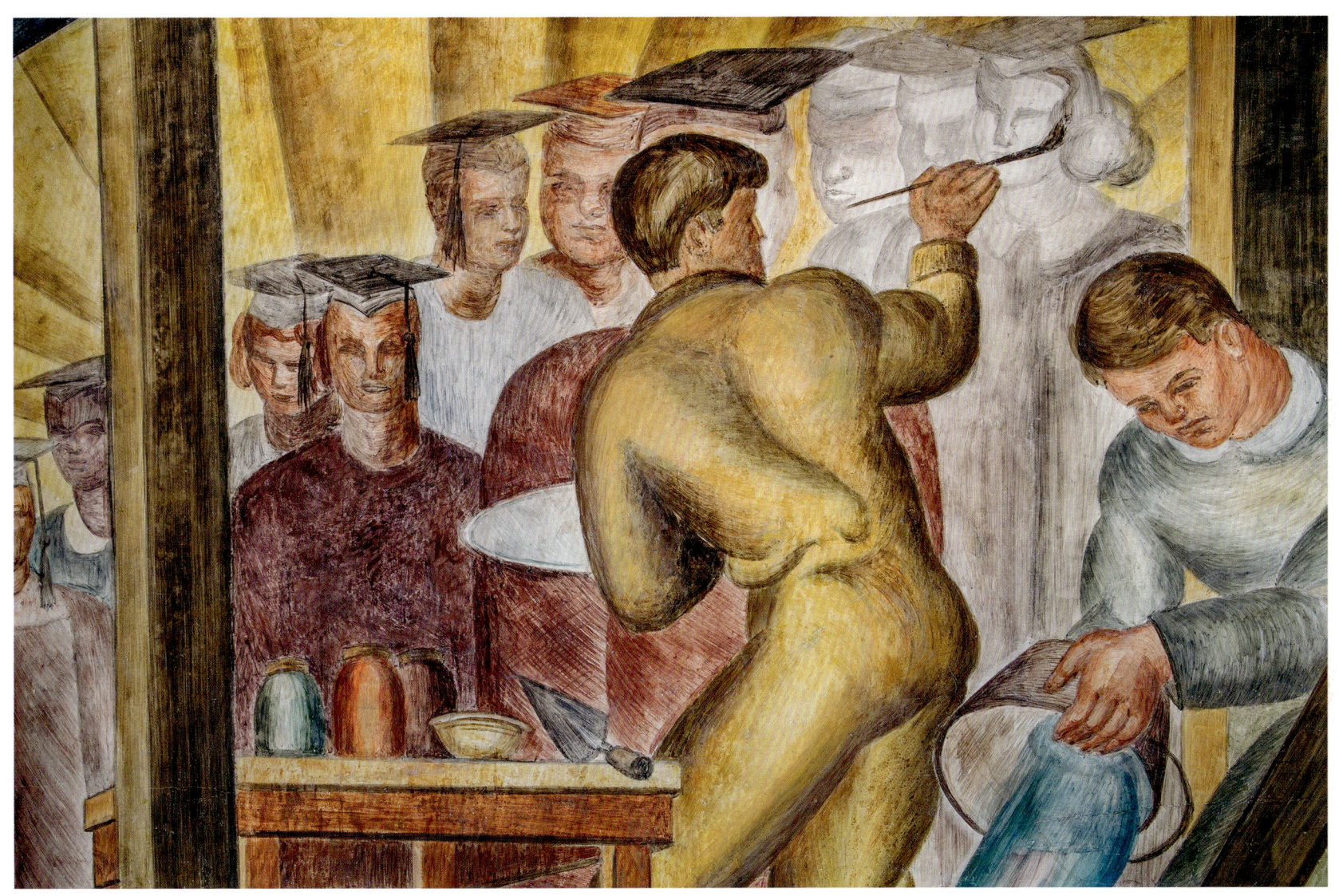

Plate 35.

Roy Henderson, *Graduating Students Including Professor Albrizio,* 1938, fresco, LSU, Baton Rouge, LA. Eddy Perez, LSU.

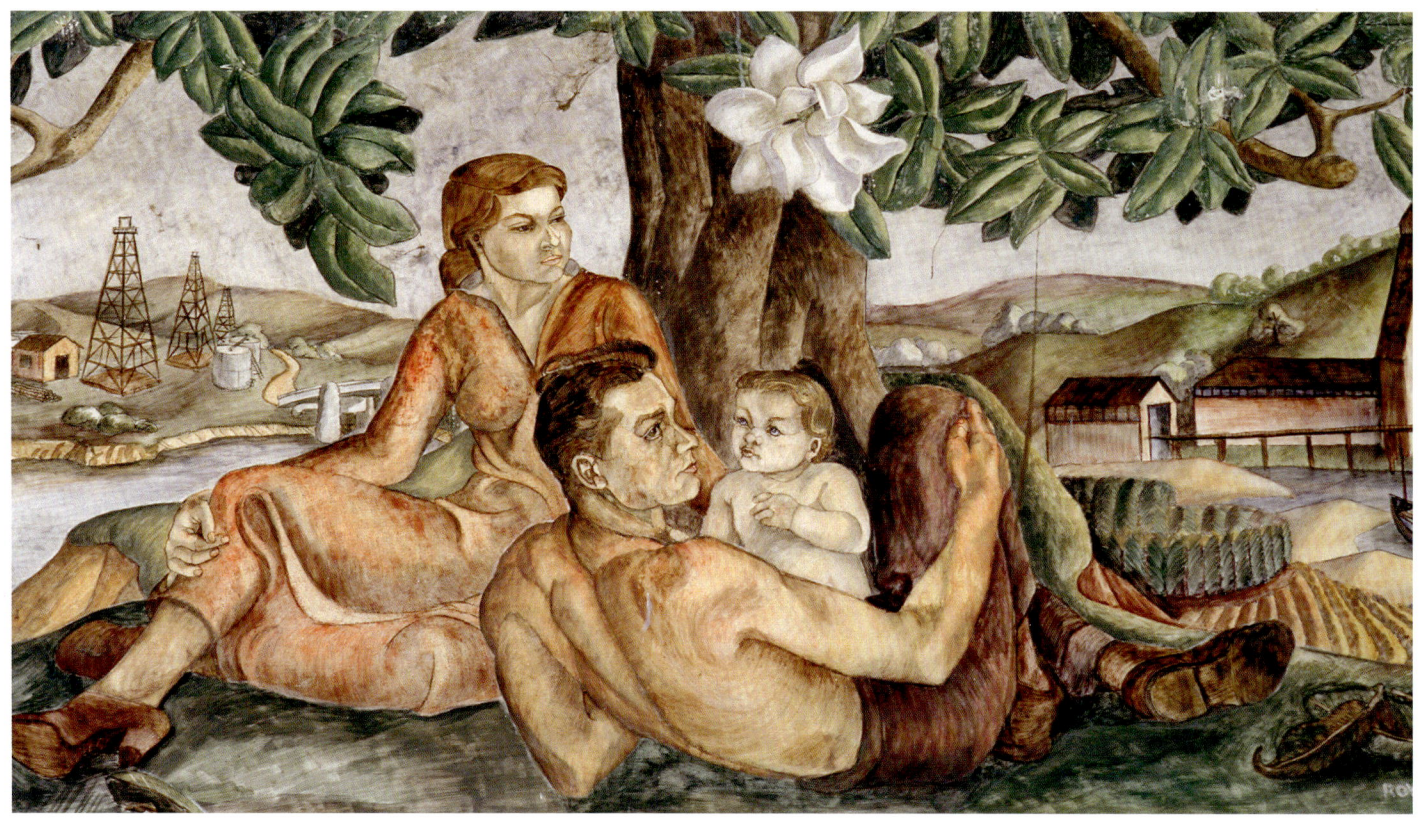

Plate 36.
Roy Henderson,
Louisiana Life, 1938,
fresco, LSU, Baton
Rouge. Jim Zietz, LSU.

into passages by alternating cool color palettes and warm palettes."[6]

Tucked under the stairway on the east end of the building is a portrait of Professor Albrizio. He is shown seated on a scaffold holding an artist's palette while several students watch him work on a mural (plate 34). Woolfolk is not the only student who placed Albrizio in her composition. Henderson included him in a group portrait of graduating stu-

dents on the west-end entrance of Allen Hall (plate 35).

Henderson depicted many iconic aspects of LSU. His most interesting fresco, however, is a large panel over the north door on the east end of the building (plate 36). A family of three—mother, father, and child—lounges beneath a sprawling magnolia tree with a single blossom above their heads. In the background is a Louisiana landscape of oil derricks and rich farmland. The mural shows the security

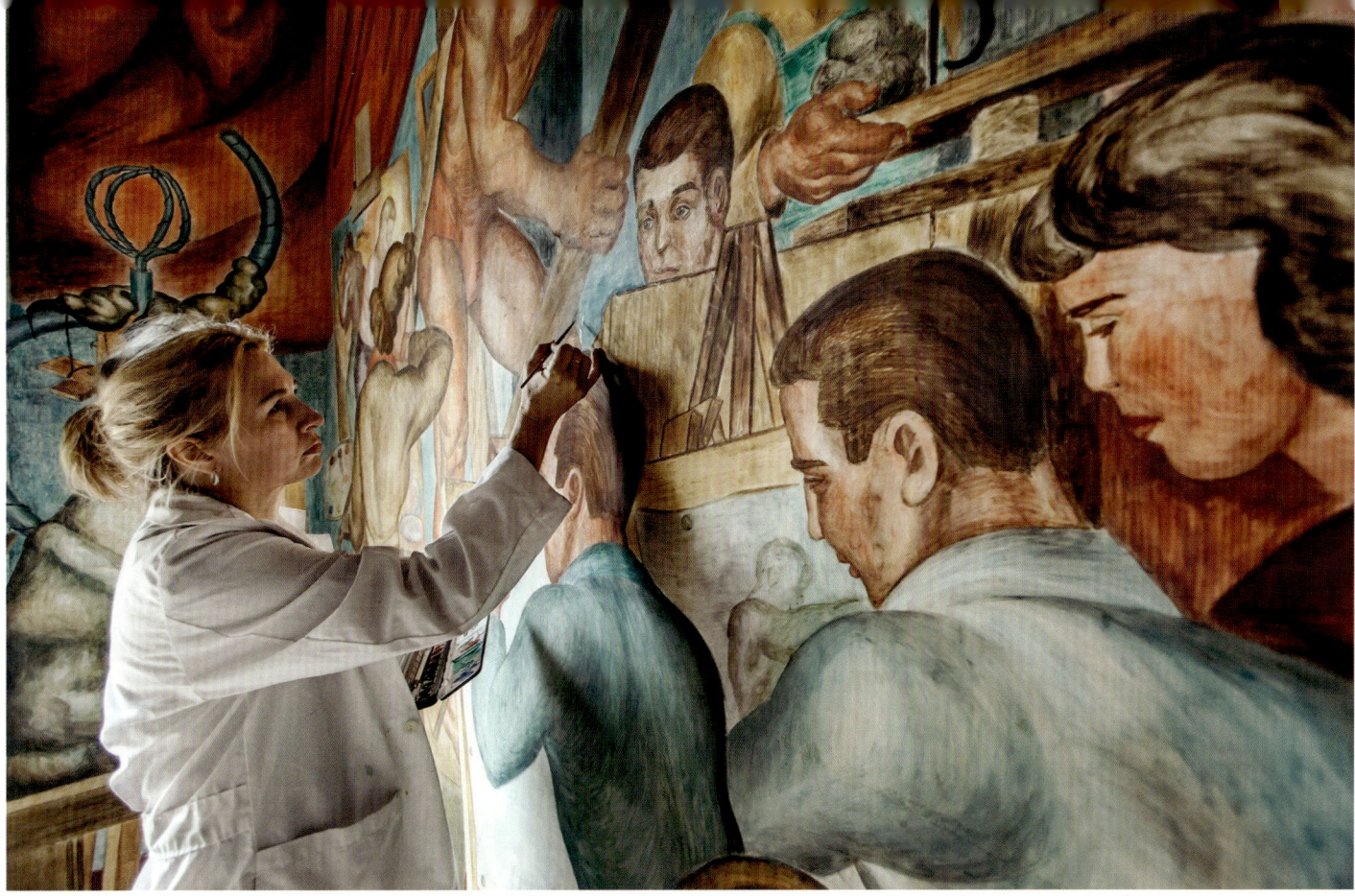

Plate 37.
Conservator Elise Grenier working on Allen Hall fresco, LSU, Baton Rouge. Jim Zietz, LSU.

of family and the riches of the land, but perhaps the symbolism tells us more. Just as the triumvirate of the Holy Family is symbolic of Christian salvation, the family beneath a magnolia-blossom "star" reminds us that all Louisiana citizens were offered prosperity and protection through the fruitfulness of the state.

Although the Allen Hall frescoes were not painted by Albrizio's hand, they were executed under his tutelage. On the art faculty at LSU for eighteen years, Albrizio guided many students through their studies. It is probable that he was well liked, judging from the inclusion of his image in the murals. "He never dictated to us as to what we should think or try to get us to express his ideas. He was interested in getting students to express their own ideas and opinions," said Brown, who worked with Albrizio as a graduate and undergraduate student.[7] Birkland (now McCandless) added, "I think he gave us a pride in the things we accomplished through our own efforts rather than just his approval."[8]

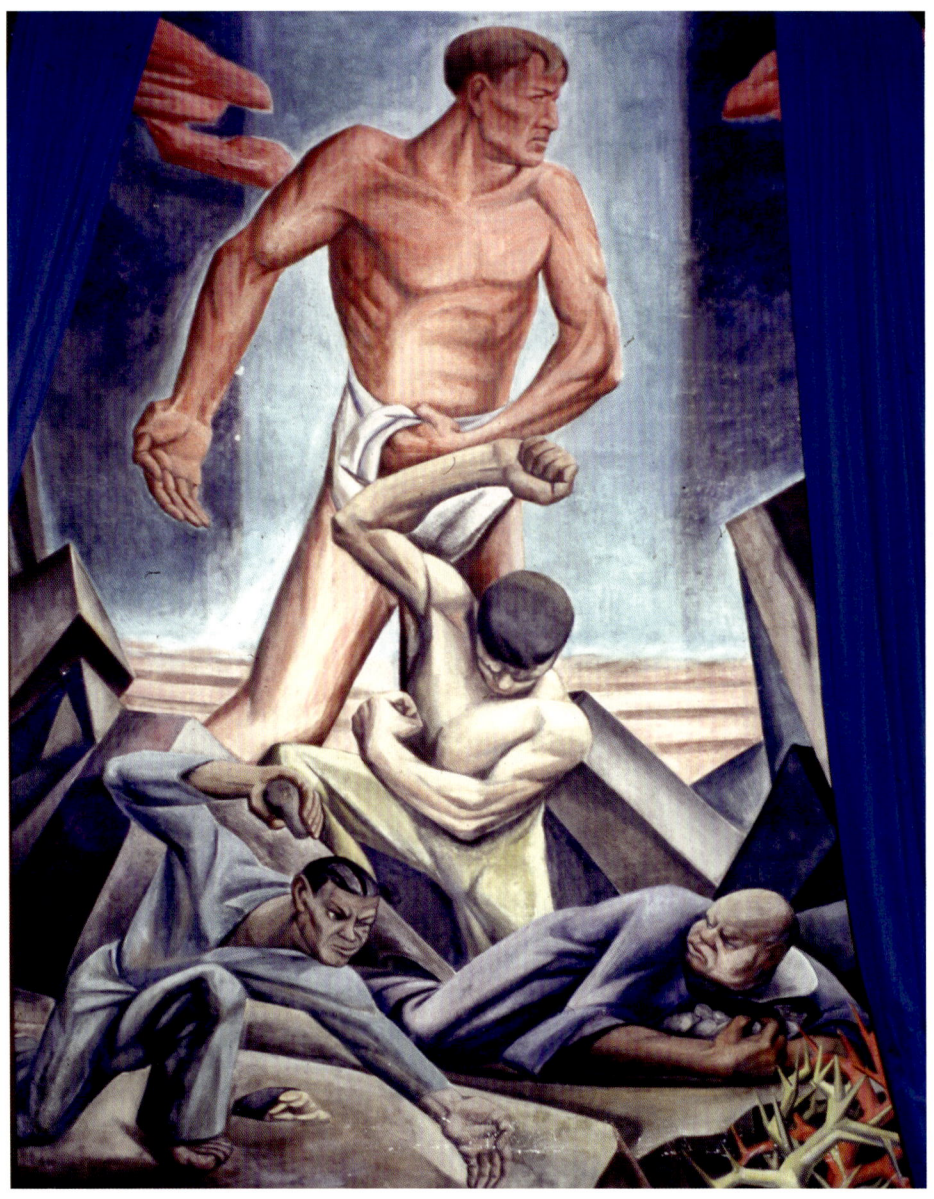

Plate 38.
Struggle of Man, 1940, fresco, Iberia Parish Courthouse, New Iberia, LA. Author's collection.

Many of these murals were covered by paint in the 1960s. In 2001, conservation of the east-end fresco, which had always been visible, began. This was the first cleaning or conservation attempted since the frescoes were painted in the 1930s. After careful research and analysis of the wall surface, conservator Elise Grenier found additional murals on the west end of the building and in the east-end portico. In 2012, she restored all panels to their original appearance (plate 37).

STRUGGLE OF MAN

The Iberia Parish Courthouse

The last government-supported mural that Albrizio painted was for the Iberia Parish Courthouse in New Iberia, Louisiana, in 1940. It was likely done under the auspices of the Section of Painting and Sculpture, because it was won by competition; however, no documents have been found related to the work. The style of this mural, called *Struggle of Man* (plate 38), differs from the realistic genre that guided Albrizio's hand during the 1930s. The figures are symbolic representations of the human condition and the eternal conflict between good and evil. The artist's own explanation of the mural is as follows:

The subject of this mural treats the continual struggle waged by man to free himself from the forces and conditions which restrict his material, physical and moral well-being. These forces are symbolized by the two figures in the foreground representing sinister parties that usurp the wealth and power of the state to the detriment of the majority of the people in the commonwealth. The figure on the left, in the act of throwing the dice, may well represent the waste and misuse of resources by those who accumulate wealth without any beneficial contribution whatsoever to the community. The figure on the right represents the corrupt official. Their surrounding is one of chaos and non-productivity. The central figure represents the contributing groups of society, smiting to overcome the maleficent power that retards progress. The monumental figure in the center of the background represents man having achieved by his struggle the desired freedom. He is depicted in the act of sowing and symbolizes productiveness. The surrounding area is one of unlimited horizon and possibility of development.[9]

The mural's theme undoubtedly foreshadowed the years of political reform in Louisiana from 1940 to 1948. The "Louisiana Scandals" of the late 1930s exposed the widespread corruption of business and state officials to the rest of the nation. For eight years Governor Sam H. Jones and his successor, James "Jimmie" Davis, sought to restore integrity and honor to Louisiana politics. Albrizio captured the sentiments of many Louisianians by illustrating the attempt of the average citizen to overturn the power of corrupt political leaders. Albrizio always saw his murals not only as art, but also as an important means of teaching: "The conditions which beset people must be overcome. Art should awaken people and put them to work. The artist should choose his subject matter from things pertinent to existing conditions not vagaries of the inconsequential kind."[10]

The triangular mass of interweaving angles creates an intense and forceful statement exemplifying the "continual struggle waged by man" as Albrizio defined it. The angularity and harsh brushstrokes recall the works of Mexican muralist José Orozco in his *Epic of American Civilization*, painted in 1934 at Dartmouth College's library. In particular, the panel *The Departure of Quetzalcoatl* (plate 39) was a likely influence, as it has the same massing of figures and a similar arm placement of the figure at the apex of the pyramidal mass.

THE MOVEMENT TOWARD ABSTRACT EXPRESSIONISM

By the 1940s, American artists were showing a greater interest in imaginative interpretations, personal viewpoints, and expressions of emotion as opposed to the presentation of fact. The government programs of the 1930s had reinforced the popularity of realistic painting to accommodate an American public that was primarily rural and small-town. After World War II, the artist was no longer visually speaking to a provincial America. Many Americans had traveled overseas, and many Europeans had relocated in America. Albrizio also transitioned from the American Scene realism of the 1930s to more imaginative and introspective works in the 1940s—particularly in his easel paintings.

In April 1943, the LSU Gallery of Art exhibited Albrizio's abstract expressionist works. "The things I'm showing are the result of my work in attempting to solve the problems confronting an artist. An artist tries to communicate ideas and experiences, and the nature of these ideas and experiences constitute the subject matter of his work. I suppose

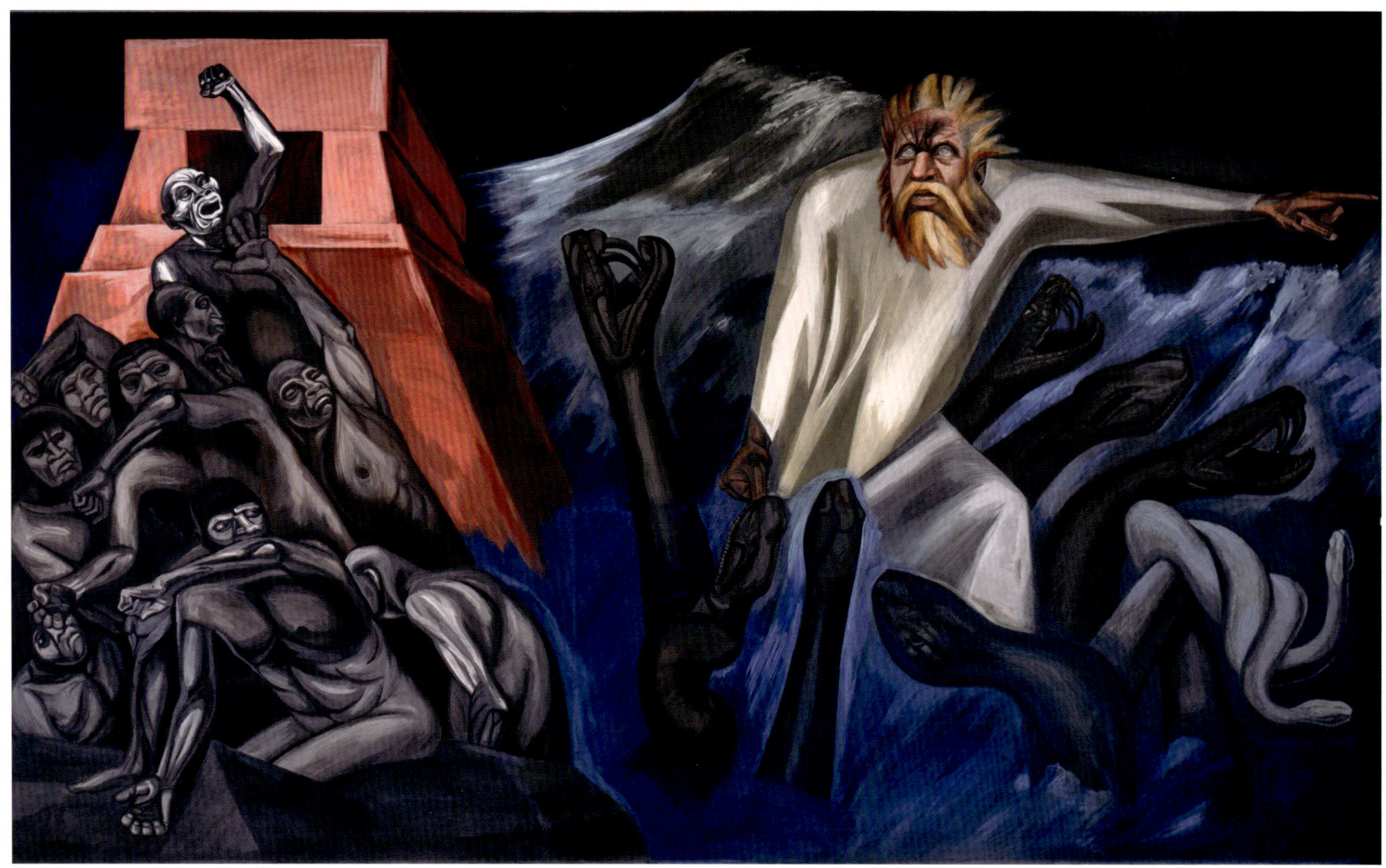

Plate 39.

José Clemente Orozco, Mexican, 1883–1949, *The Epic of American Civilization: The Departure of Quetzalcoatl* (Panel 7), 1932–34, fresco. Hood Museum of Art, Dartmouth: Commissioned by the Trustees of Dartmouth College; P.934.13.7.

one concludes that after seeing this work, people will get an idea of my viewpoint of life, my ideas and environment."[11] In *Four Horses,* for example, painted in 1945, he works in a frenzy of color and movement. The exuberant, violent brushstrokes of the four horses of the Apocalypse reveal the spirit of abstract expressionism.

Albrizio took a sabbatical from the university in 1943 and again in 1945 when he was granted the Julius Rosenwald Fund fellowship. Both times, he traveled to New York City in the hope of securing a large exhibit. His painting *Duality,* c. 1945, received honors at the 1945 Armory Show. In 1946 he was finally offered an exhibition at the well-known Passedoit Gallery. Albrizio was elated to display what he considered to be the "beginning of his creative painting." He felt that he had finally found the "form for what goes on in the artist's mind."[12] His one-man show was well received. It featured his work from 1940 through 1946 and allowed the viewer "to face the fearfulness of the late war, and to find a way out of chaos in the lovely passages of the planetary themes."[13]

As though exhausted from the tumultuous, throbbing energy of recent years, Albrizio now shows in his paintings a harnessing of previous exuberance into controlled orbs and ovals reflecting not the atrocities of life, but the sublime powers that govern living things. "With the feeling of the passionate reformer, there is also in his work a regard for subtler universal concepts," wrote the art critic of the *New York Herald Tribune.* "Albrizio's potent insight into large problems presents a good deal for serious consideration on a philosophical basis."[14]

Because of his achievements, Albrizio's Rosenwald fellowship was extended through 1947. He returned to Baton Rouge late in 1947 to continue his work at LSU. In 1948 he held a solo show at the Delgado Museum of Art in New Orleans, which included many of the same works shown at the Passedoit in New York. The influence of these paintings on Albrizio's future murals was considerable. Not only do details appear in later frescoes, but also the motivation behind this work helped to change Albrizio's approach to mural painting. Murals of the 1940s and '50s in the United States also became more symbolic and philosophical. The narration of American Scene painting had given way to serious and more speculative thought.

7.

The Murals of the Waterman Steamship Corporation, Mobile, Alabama

IN 1949 ALBRIZIO AGAIN TOOK LEAVE FROM his teaching duties at LSU to undertake a monumental endeavor, the painting of the frescoes in the new Waterman Building in Mobile, Alabama. It had been nine years since he completed his last government-sponsored fresco in the Iberia Parish Courthouse, and enthusiasm for regional-themed mural art had long since peaked in America. The break from wall painting proved to be a beneficial respite for the artist. He brought renewed energy to the Mobile assignment along with exciting ideas he had recently explored in his easel painting. He felt a restored artistic freedom without the tedious demands of the federal art agencies, and a robust and creative vision spurred him forward as he began this two-year enterprise.

THE WATERMAN BUILDING

The 18-story Waterman Building was constructed in 1948 to house the offices of the Waterman Steamship Corporation. At the time, the Waterman Corporation owned and operated forty-five vessels that carried goods to major world markets. The small company began in 1919 with a single steamer known as the *Eastern Sun* traveling from Mobile to Liverpool, England. After World War II, the company was rolling in profits and decided to build a suitable structure for its home office. The $3 million edifice was an imposing addition to downtown Mobile. The murals decorated its 2-story lobby.[1] In the center of the lobby was a 12-foot revolving globe, above which was a frescoed dome of the heavens. Around the walls were seven panels depicting various aspects of maritime commerce (plate 40).

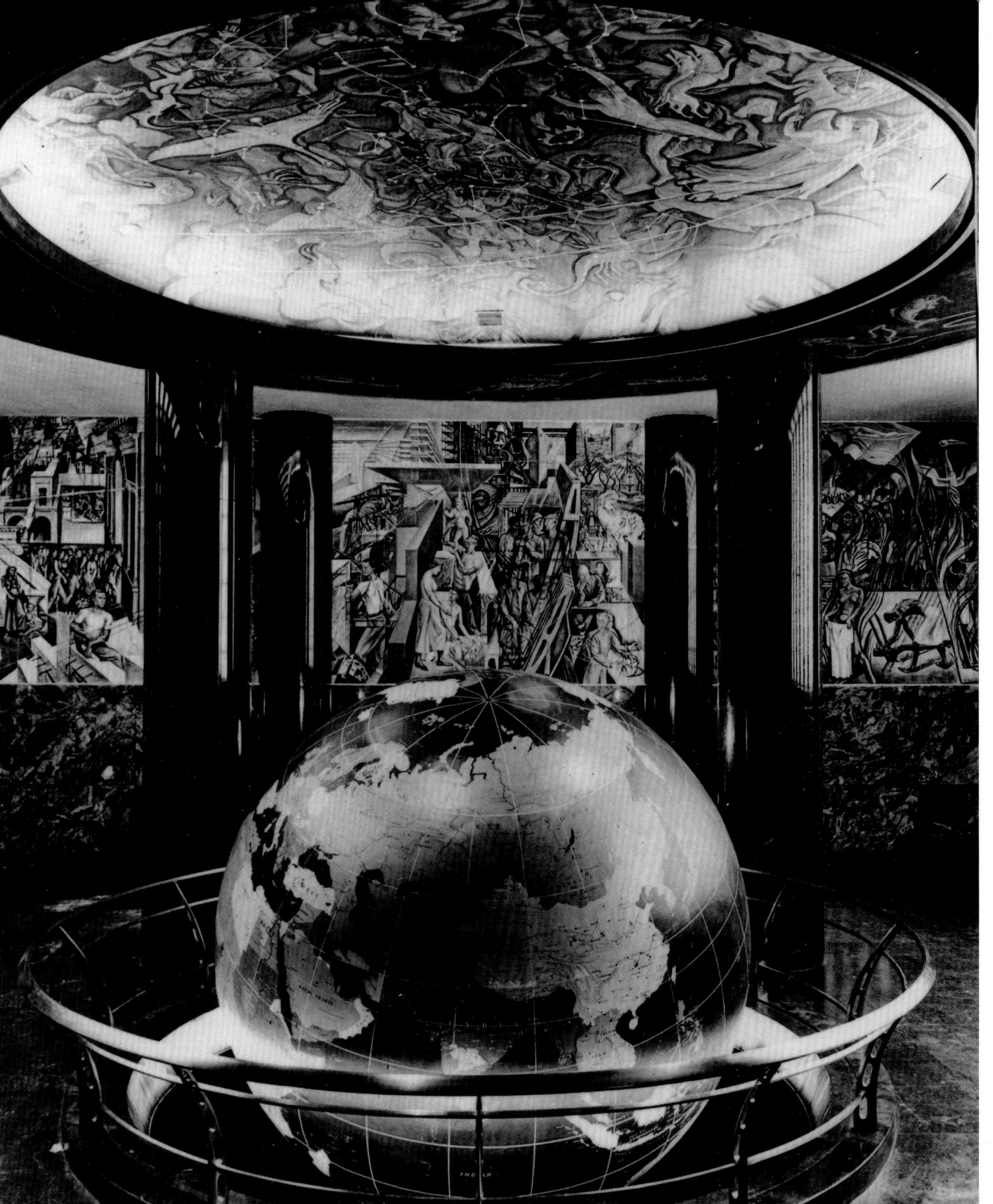

Plate 40.
Lobby of the Wachovia Building (formerly the Waterman Steamship Building), Mobile, AL. Photo courtesy of C. T. Mayer, The Doy Leale McCall Rare Book and Manuscript Library, University of South Alabama.

Albrizio and his student assistant, Jack Hastings, worked in a small studio in the nearby Salvation Army building, where they prepared life-size drawings for the seven panels and dome. After almost a year of preparatory work, the drawings were complete. Albrizio and Hastings then spent an additional thirteen months in the actual painting of the building interior.[2]

For twenty-five years, the Waterman Building's lobby was a frequent stop for locals and schoolchildren. The rotating globe was finely painted with a scale replica of the countries of the world as they appeared in 1948. Partially recessed into the marble floor, it was tilted at precisely 23½ degrees on its axis and moved at the same speed as Earth's rotation. A brass rail surrounded it.

In 1955, McLean Industries purchased the building and renamed it the Roberts Building, after longtime Waterman executive E. A. Roberts. In 1973 Commercial Guaranty Bank bought it, and the lobby became an active banking area. The revolving globe was removed and relegated to storage. In 1978, the University of Alabama acquired the globe and in 1998 installed it in the university's basketball complex, the Mitchell Center. A bank currently occupies the ground floor of what is now known as the Wachovia Building. Fortunately, the frescoes remain intact, and the masterful dome still creates a heavenly sphere overhead. The elegance of the once-grand lobby is gone, but the beautiful works of art remain due to the enduring permanence of fresco.

THE MURALS

As one of the largest fresco cycles in the United States since the work of the Mexican muralists in the early 1930s, the Waterman series was sure to gain national acclaim. Long after the idea of public art had faded from the American focus, Albrizio continued to believe in and promote the need for all-inclusive, accessible art throughout his career. His enthusiasm drove him to acquire mural commissions into the 1940s, '50s, and '60s. His foremost concern with the Waterman murals was their acceptance by the citizens of Mobile. "I hope the people of Mobile like it," he said. "[I want to take] art out of the gallery and into a place where it can be seen in everyday life."[3]

The frescoes of the Waterman cycle depict alluring themes of foreign lands and travel. A cluster of tropical trees here, bits of ancient architecture there, indigenous carvings from distant lands—each visual fragment suggests thoughts of one exotic port or another. The murals, however, are intricate and complex and hold many in-depth messages beyond what an initial glance might suggest. Albrizio chose to incorporate the themes of commerce and navigation, which he felt best represented the goals of the Waterman Company and the shipping industry. Three of the seven wall panels depict commerce and trade, four explore the classical elements, and the great dome illustrates the constellations, a guide for seafarers for centuries.

Plate 41.

Commerce and Migration, 1940, fresco, Wachovia Building, Mobile. Photo by Chad Riley.

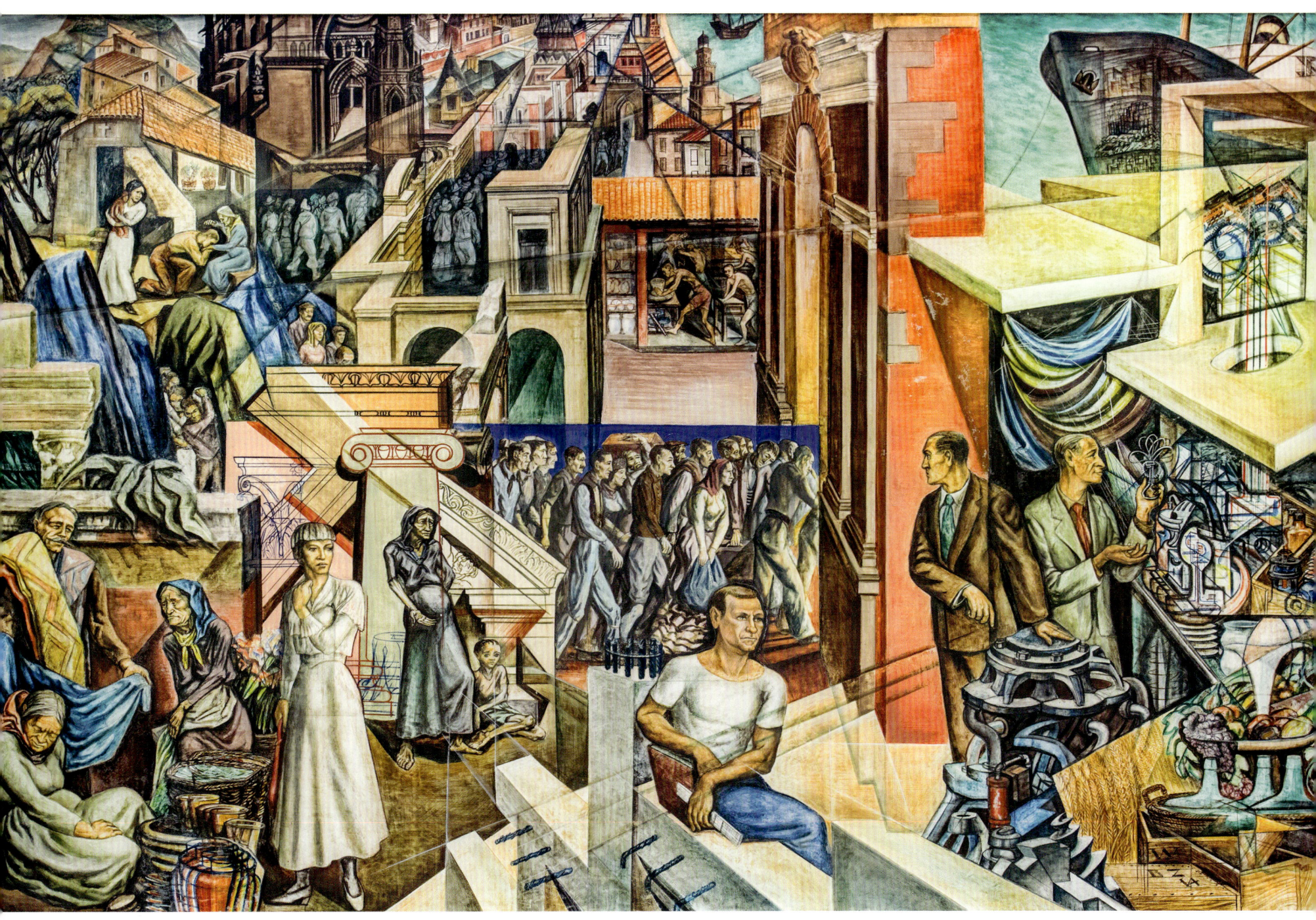

COMMERCE AND MIGRATION

Albrizio based his visual narrative on the belief that trade brings the exchange of ideas as well as goods. The panel *Commerce and Migration* shows developing cultures as they glean information from other civilizations (plate 41). A mass exodus from the Old World to a land of opportunity is symbolically portrayed by emigrants marching through an arched gateway toward a new life. For this son of Italian immigrants, migration to a land of opportunity was a close experience. The ghostly outlines of explorers in the upper left corner is a reminder that cultural exchange is not new; it began thousands of years ago.

Albrizio gives a nod to the Old World artisans who stayed behind and chose not to advance to new lands. The handmade wares honor vintage traditions. Standing before the ruins of classical architecture, these figures mark the division between past and present. A lush still life of fruit, grapes, and wheat touches upon the prosperity awaiting those who might seek it.

At bottom center, shown seated upon the foundation of a modern structure, is a self-portrait of Albrizio.[4] His position suggests not only his past training as an architectural draftsman, but also his place in both the Old and New Worlds. To the right, the man in the brown suit is believed to be one of the board members of the Waterman Corporation, and next to him, the man in the green jacket is possibly one of Albrizio's painting assistants on the project.[5]

Particularly notable are the subtle overlays of color that accentuate the converging planes and lines found throughout the panels. For example, the diagonal lines originating in the center of the first panel ultimately meet in the adjacent panel.[6] These lines and planes sweep across the compositions, creating strategic focal points. According to the artist, they symbolize infinity and continuity.

The extreme sense of geometry in the Waterman cycle is probably a result of the qualities that Albrizio had recently explored in his easel works and, of course, the advance of abstract painting as a current trend in American art. Albrizio was careful, however, not to permit his use of abstraction to overwhelm his audience. "The function of mural painting is preeminently social," he explained. "It allows less whimsical treatment of an idea because the artist must hold himself in check during the course of his work. His first objective must always be to give his painting a meaning for all classes of people."[7] The broken and angular divisions within the Waterman cycle seem to allow the artist an interest in abstraction within the restricted confines of "readable" mural art. The compositional layout is certainly evocative of Thomas Hart Benton's "disjointed perspective." Benton used this notion of

Plate 42.

Effects of Commerce on Primitive People, 1940, fresco, Wachovia Building, Mobile. Photo by Chad Riley.

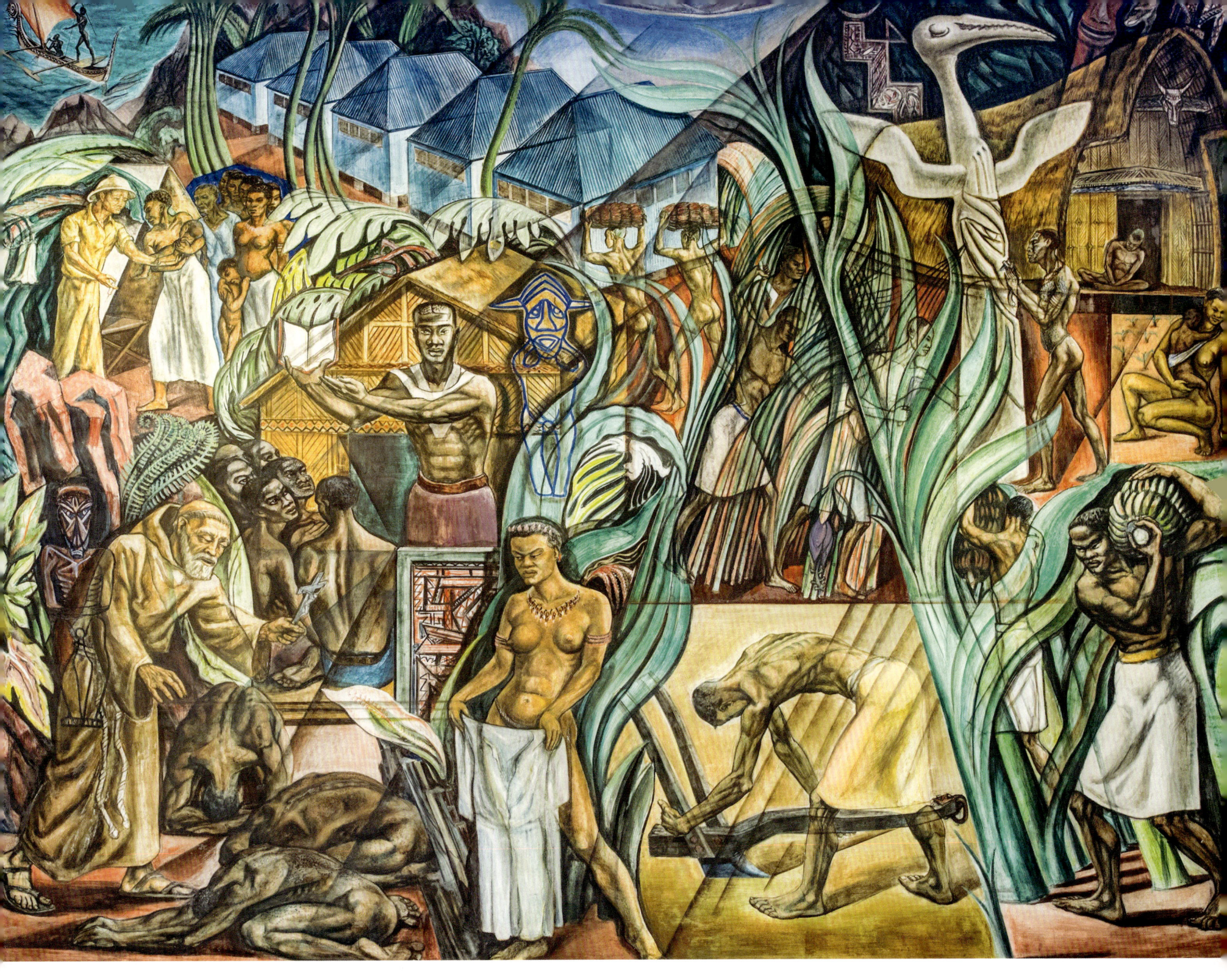

piecing together different scenes within a single frame to create turbulent rhythms that suggest rapid growth and energy.[8] Albrizio experimented with this technique as early as 1938 in his paintings at the Capitol Annex and the Shreveport frescoes, but he brings it to a more sophisticated level by the end of the 1940s in Mobile.

EFFECTS OF COMMERCE ON PRIMITIVE PEOPLE

Effects of Commerce on Primitive People serves as a companion piece to *Commerce and Migration* (plate 42). With commerce came missionaries, doctors, and educators, who introduced new ideas and brought tools and practices intended to improve basic standards of living. To show that all new ideas were not readily accepted, Albrizio includes the figure of a native woman apprehensively examining a modern dress. To the right, a man inspects a newfangled farm implement—a plow.

Especially noticeable is the dynamic angle of huts cutting into the frame. The downward thrust of the plant shaft balances this diagonal that pushes into the composition. An airplane passes through the darkness of the past into the light of the future.[9] Albrizio again uses the disjointed perspective to group areas within the collage-like composition. The jungle growth strewn throughout the painting serves to composi-

tionally tie areas together while adding a sensuous contrast to the angularity of the extended lines and planes that the artist defined as "infinity."

CIVIC WELL-BEING

Albrizio centers the third panel in the commerce triad between the other two to tether the threesome. *Civic Well-Being* shows in the lower right corner those who manage and guide the future through their executive positions (plate 43). As in most Albrizio murals, these are portraits of significant individuals who were part of the project. The man in the brown suit with his head resting upon his hand is E. A. Roberts, an executive of the Waterman Corporation.[10] Behind him is Waterman himself,[11] and below the two is John Platt Roberts, the brother of E. A. Roberts and a building architect.[12] At upper right, several notable buildings stand above the city's Bienville Square. A Mardi Gras parade passes alongside the square in Mobile as a historical reference to the city where the earliest celebration of Mardi Gras in the United States occurred, in 1703. The surrounding scenes in the panel show the many ways life is improved by modern innovations. Figures fade in and out of their environment, uniting man, his work, and the world that he ultimately creates for himself.

Plate 43.
Civic Well-Being, 1940, fresco, Wachovia Building, Mobile. Photo by Chad Riley.

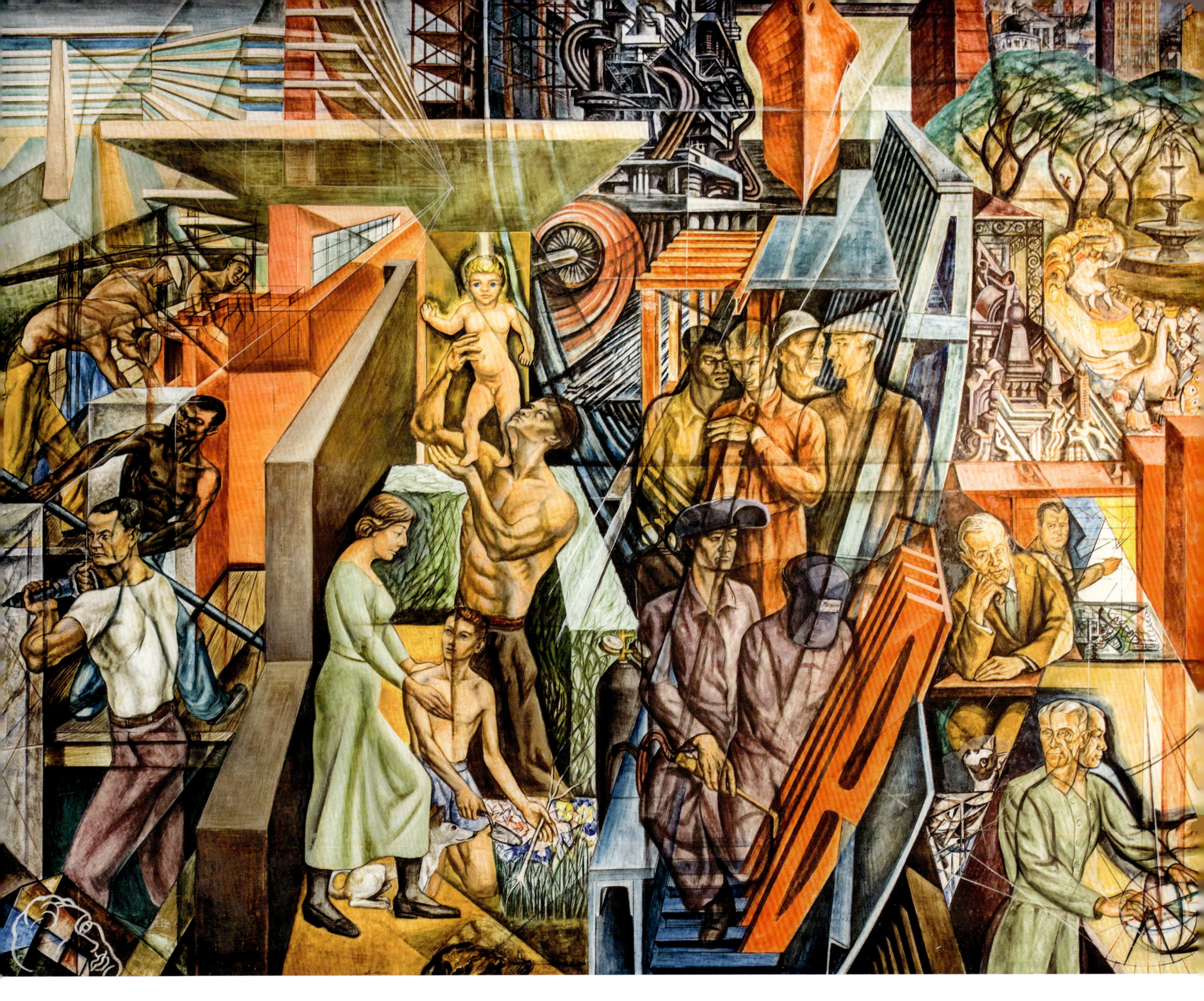

The panel's center focuses on the family as part of a well-ordered society. To Albrizio, the care and welfare of man began at home. The family circle is supported by the father, who holds his young son upon his shoulder. Before him is the mother—a portrait of Albrizio's wife, Jean—and an older son.[13] The older son holds a sapling to symbolize future generations. At the woman's feet is a dog, sign of fidelity, and in the foreground a rock alluding to the foundation that the family provides.

Herndon Inge Jr., a cousin of Jean Albrizio, remembered walking to work every morning in downtown Mobile and passing the Waterman construction site along his way. He would see Jean sitting on a stool reading and watching Albrizio at work.[14] Very little is recorded about Albrizio's wife. It's worth noting, however, that family themes are often used in Albrizio's works, and portraits of his wife figure prominently in his murals. He also painted several oil portraits of her that are in private and museum collections. Their marriage ended in separation, but no divorce papers were ever found. They had no children.

Conrad and Jean did not seem to be living together in the 1950s, although there is at least one very poignant letter written from Conrad to his wife in 1958 while she was living in Alabama and he was en route to Venice to research the construction of a mosaic mural. He was on board a small ship, the SS *Mongioia,* which was carrying only about ten passengers and crew members. His mood was somber and lonely as evidenced by a 16-page letter in which he journaled about his voyage and his feelings. He comments on the other passengers, the food on the ship, the blue of the ocean, his anticipated project, and his restlessness and emptiness. "But I am much alone and I find myself most of the time in 'thoughts' which are not really thoughts but a continual review of what at one time must have been thoughts. It is as though I cannot get away from being forced to see an old movie every inch of scene known and anticipated, relentless and overbearing."[15] He may be attempting a reconciliation with his wife, although he never says that directly. Albrizio continues with these heartfelt passages throughout the letter. He tells Jean that perhaps what is causing his restlessness is her absence. He also wonders if she will answer his letter.

Jean died in October of 1958. Whatever transpired between them during their married life was seemingly left unfinished. Albrizio continued to use the family as a theme in his work, creating one of his most well-known murals, the mosaic *Family Life,* in 1964 for the Algiers Mental Health Center in Algiers, Louisiana (see plate 86).

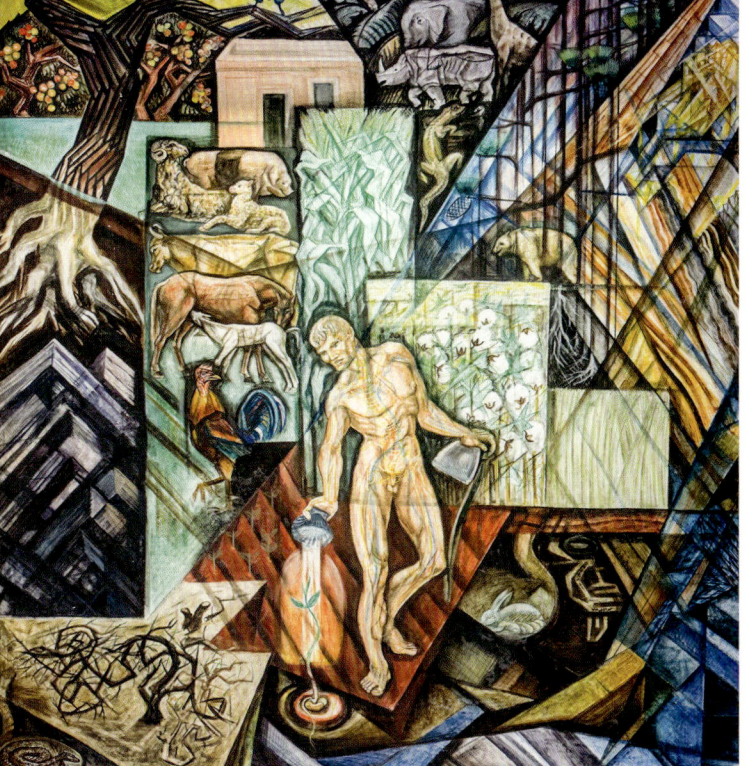

Plate 44.

Land, 1940, fresco, Wachovia Building, Mobile. Photo by Chad Riley.

Plate 45.

Water, 1940, fresco, Wachovia Building, Mobile. Photo by Chad Riley.

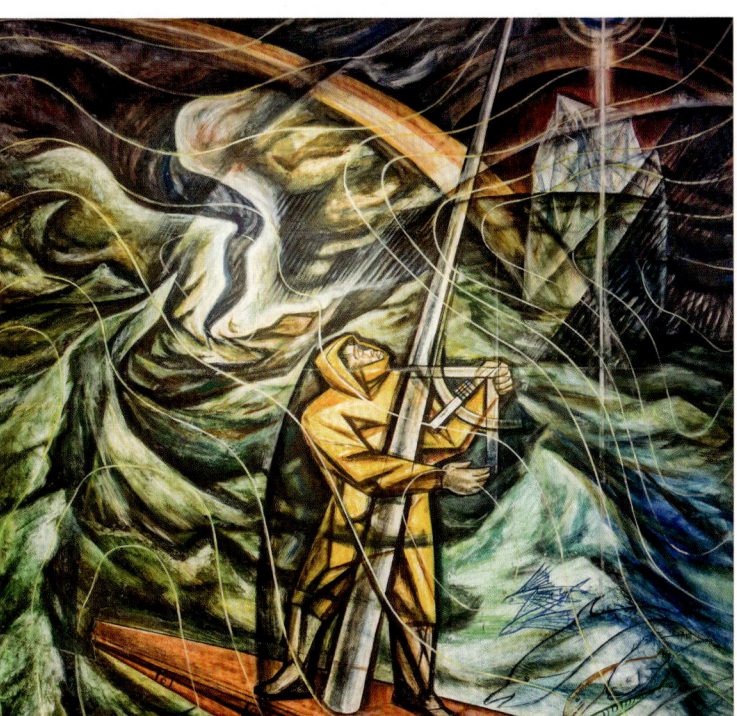

LAND

The remaining four panels of the Waterman cycle depict the four classical elements of earth, water, fire, and air. Albrizio's symbolic and mythological interpretation of these elements begins with *Land,* the source of raw materials that in turn yield products for trade (plate 44). At the center of the panel are farmed fields of corn, cotton, and wheat amidst rich and fertile soil. The rectangular strip features a column of domesticated animals before a man-made shelter. The periphery is comprised of beautiful details of nature's wilderness. Emerging through the maze of grids and diagonals are renderings of fruit trees, wild jungle animals, plants, and forest creatures. Underground are the habitats of rabbits, snakes, ants, and rodents. The black diagonals, like leading on a stained-glass window, accentuate the figures against the muted hues of earth and sky. This tightly interwoven mesh represents the inextricable union of man and nature. Even the figure of the man seems to be grounded in the earth as the veins and arteries of his body become the roots and stems of the plants around him.[16]

WATER

In *Water,* the swirling, untamable violence of the sea threatens a lone sailor on the remains of his vessel (plate 45). The radiating and converging lines of the previous panels are now undulating contours sweeping across the surface like torrential wind and rain. The threatening forms of a tornado and glacier are offset by an unexpected rainbow leaping across the sky. The sailor holds a sextant for aid in navigation as he stands helpless and unprotected, looking toward the North Star for hope and direction. The North Star shines forth in the shape of a cross, reiterating its function as a mark of salvation.

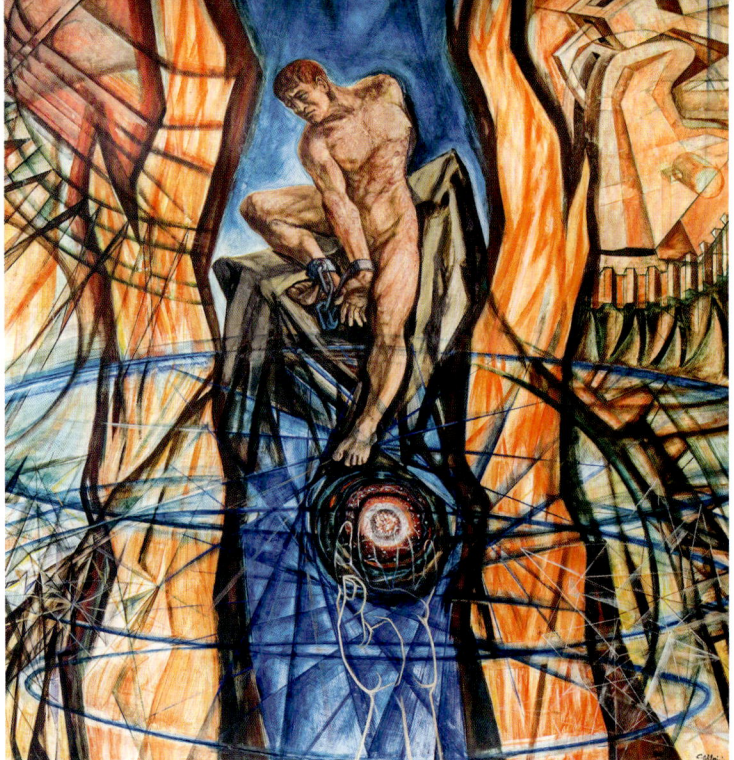

Plate 46.

Fire, 1940, fresco, Wachovia Building, Mobile. Photo by Chad Riley.

Plate 47.

Air, 1940, fresco, Wachovia Building, Mobile. Photo by Chad Riley.

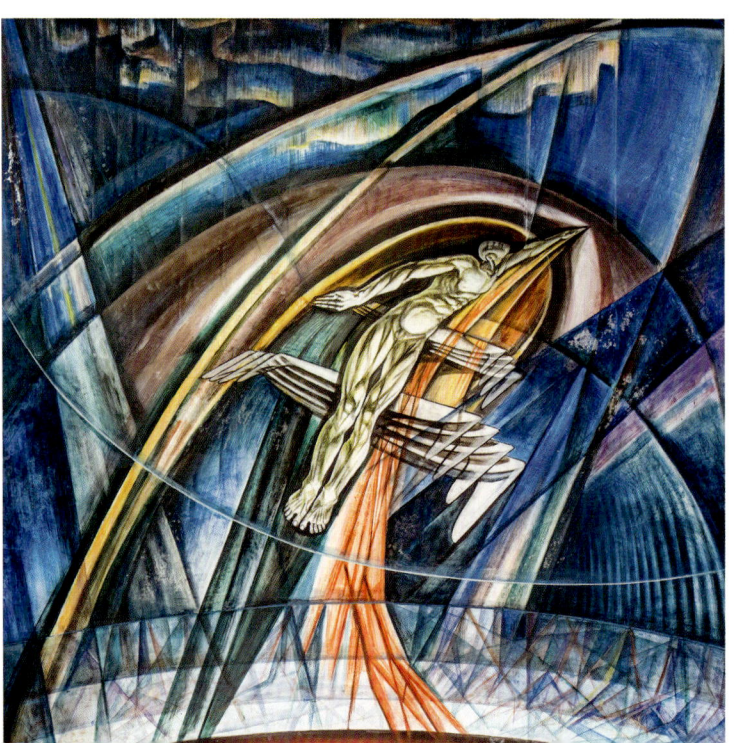

In the same 1958 letter written to Jean from the SS *Mongioia,* Albrizio notes: "This afternoon I was shown how to use the sextant. It is something I have always wanted to do . . . ever since I used the sextant symbolically in the sea panel of the Waterman murals." He continues a lengthy and detailed explanation of how a colored glass drops in front of a lens allowing a view of the sun in relation to the horizon, creating an angle from which latitude and longitude can be calculated. "I was quite thrilled by the whole procedure."[17]

FIRE

Fire takes its subject from the mythical tale of Prometheus, a Titan who stole fire from the gods to give to mankind (plate 46). For this deed, he was chained to a mountain and left to the mercy of vultures. Albrizio portrays Prometheus bound in chains, reaching down to take the gift of fire, which is ominously portrayed as the nucleus of an atom. The dynamic orbital movements aptly illustrate the force of atomic power. Repeating vertical columns of orange, red, and yellow hues flank the intense cobalt blue area that anchors the central figure of Prometheus. Albrizio depicts fire as the source of heat and energy, which in turn enable the manufacture of goods for trade.

AIR

As the companion panel to *Fire, Air* also takes its subject matter from ancient myth (plate 47). Man soars through space upon the wings of his own invention—just as Icarus flew through the air on man-made wings of feathers and wax. Elliptical, stair-stepped platforms behind the figure abstractly represent the "wings of man," which propel him into the unknown. Soaring into the darkness, man is pierced by the rays of the sun.[18]

THE DOME

The final realm of the Waterman cycle is the two-story dome, which hovers over the center of the lobby (plates 48 and 49). Its design consists of a chart of the heavens surrounded by an encircling band of red that contains the twelve signs of the zodiac in grisaille. Around the outer rim of the band are the four points of the compass precisely positioned to indicate true north. Around the inner rim are hour circles of the celestial sphere.

The dome itself depicts constellations of the summer and winter skies superimposed one upon the other. The figures of the summer sky, as seen on July 15, are painted in brilliant colors. The locations of the stars are designated by the placement of metal discs of varying sizes, which have been sunk into the plaster. Across the southern part of the dome is a silver arc that represents the celestial equator, the imaginary line that laterally divides the celestial sphere just as the equator divides the earth. The gold arc represents the ecliptic equator, the imaginary path of the sun's journey as it travels through the heavens.[19]

The constellations of the summer sky are easily discernible. In the center is Hercules, sometimes known as the Kneeler. He is clad in the skin of the Nemean lion, which he had killed, and he holds the three-headed dog Cerberus, watchdog of Hades. Cygnus, the swan, is to the right and located within the Milky Way, painted as a transparent overlay across the dome. Ursa Major, or the Great Bear, is to the lower left of Hercules, and the graceful Virgo circles upward (plate 50). Due to Albrizio's precise positioning of these figures, they seem to float through the heavens with no sense of tension or crowding. The careful balance of color and the assuredness of drawing give a harmony and stability to what otherwise might be a hodgepodge of overlapping shape and color.

Painted underneath this magnificent vision of the summer sky are the major constellations of the winter sky as seen on January 15. To avoid confusion, the winter constellations are painted in grisaille, as are the signs of the zodiac in the encircling red band (plates 51 and 52). By comparing the summer constellations to their positions in the winter sky, it is easy to see the change in location of the constellations over a six-month period.

The dome is a remarkable design feat and a technical tour de force as well. Albrizio found that the dome was already finished with a dry gypsum plaster when he came to the Waterman Building. As gypsum does not take fresco, an alternate medium had to be employed. During the 1940s, the advent of ethyl silicate paints gave artists a new option for outdoor works. The paint's primary advantage was resistance to deterioration. This made it ideal for modern outdoor murals threatened by industrial pollution. Moreover, the medium could be used on a dry surface; it could be applied with a brush, producing brilliant hues similar to fresco painting.[20] With the assistance of E. B. Newton of the Carbide and Carbon Chemicals Corporation, Albrizio obtained a workable formula. It consisted of:

- 8 g Vinylite XYHL solution (gives viscosity; good suspension of pigment within the medium)
- 12.5 cc 91 percent isopropanol
- 2.5 cc 1 percent hydrochloric acid
- 26.5 cc condensed ethyl silicate[21]

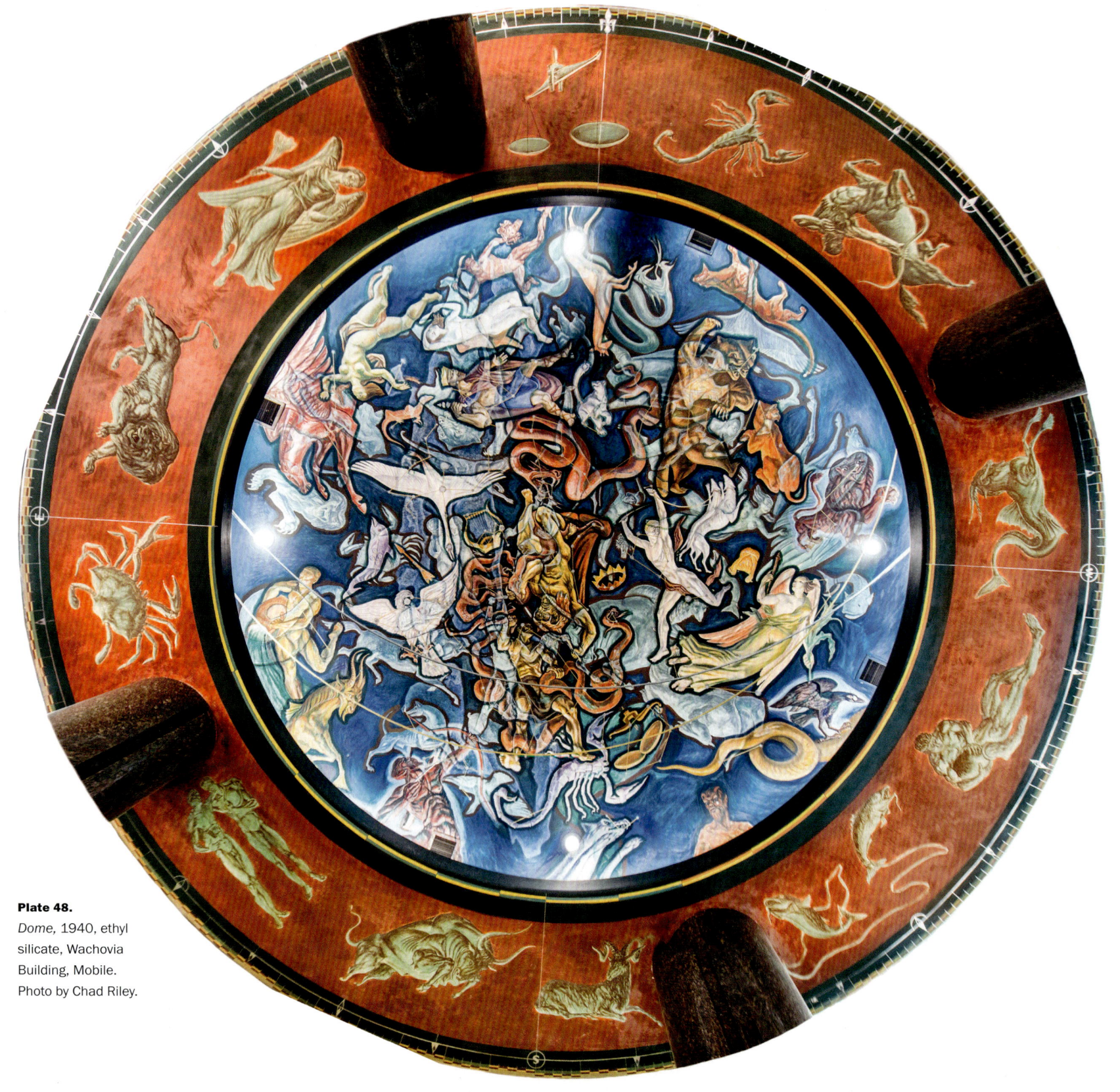

Plate 48.
Dome, 1940, ethyl
silicate, Wachovia
Building, Mobile.
Photo by Chad Riley.

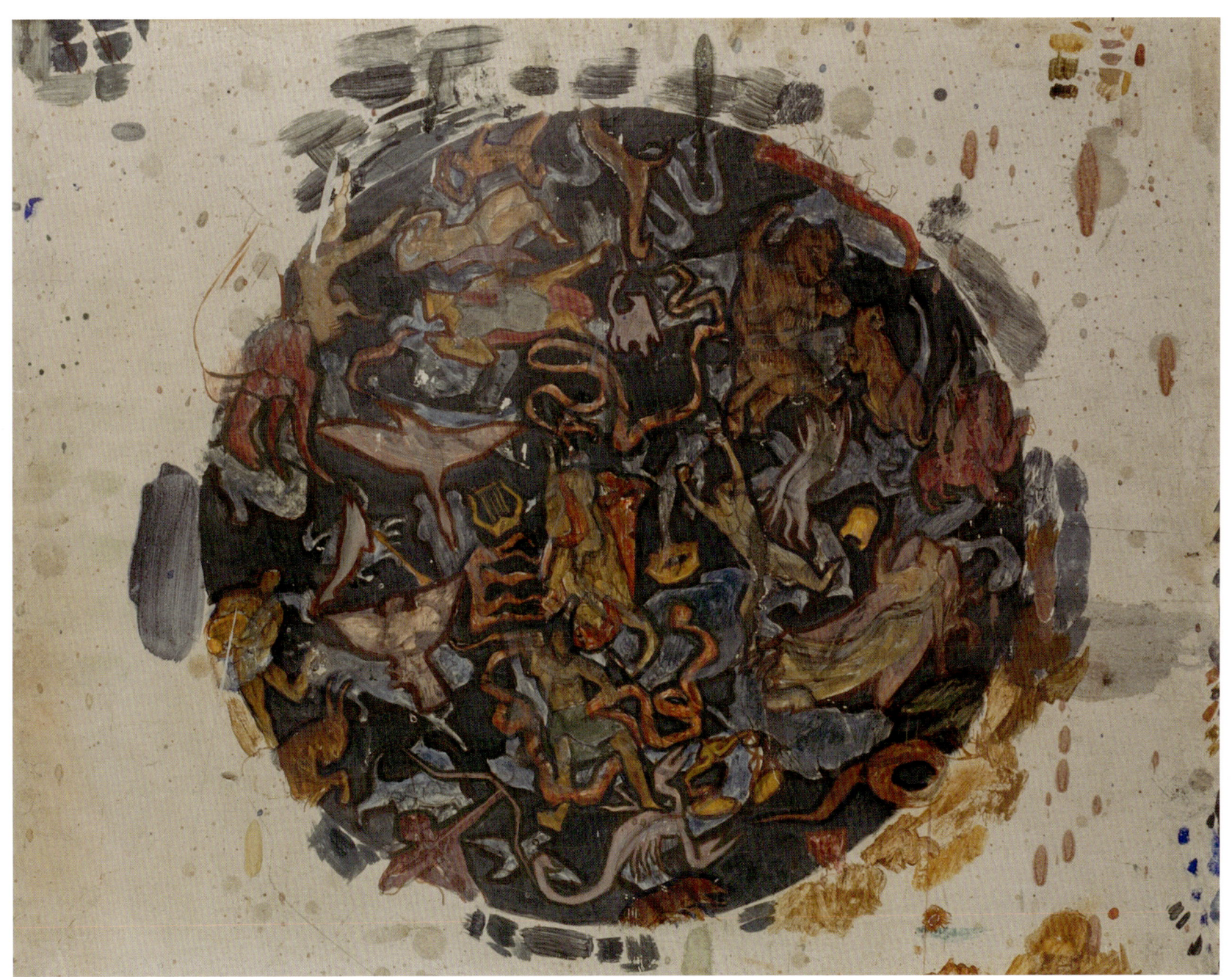

Plate 49.

Study for Ceiling Mural, Mobile, Alabama, 1940, oil on board. The New Orleans Museum of Art: Gift of an Anonymous Donor, 85.104.

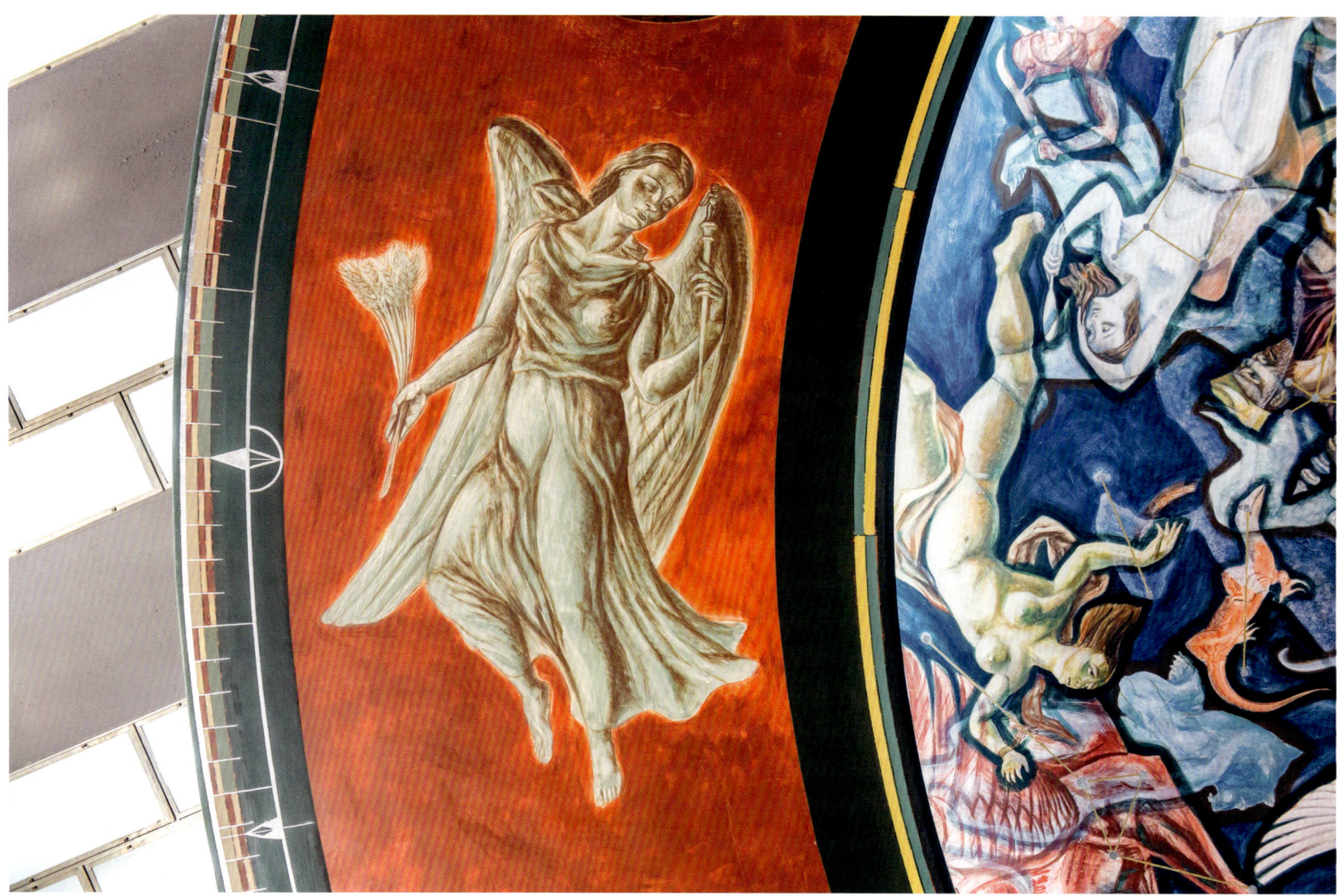

Plate 50.
Dome (detail), Virgo. Photo by Chad Riley.

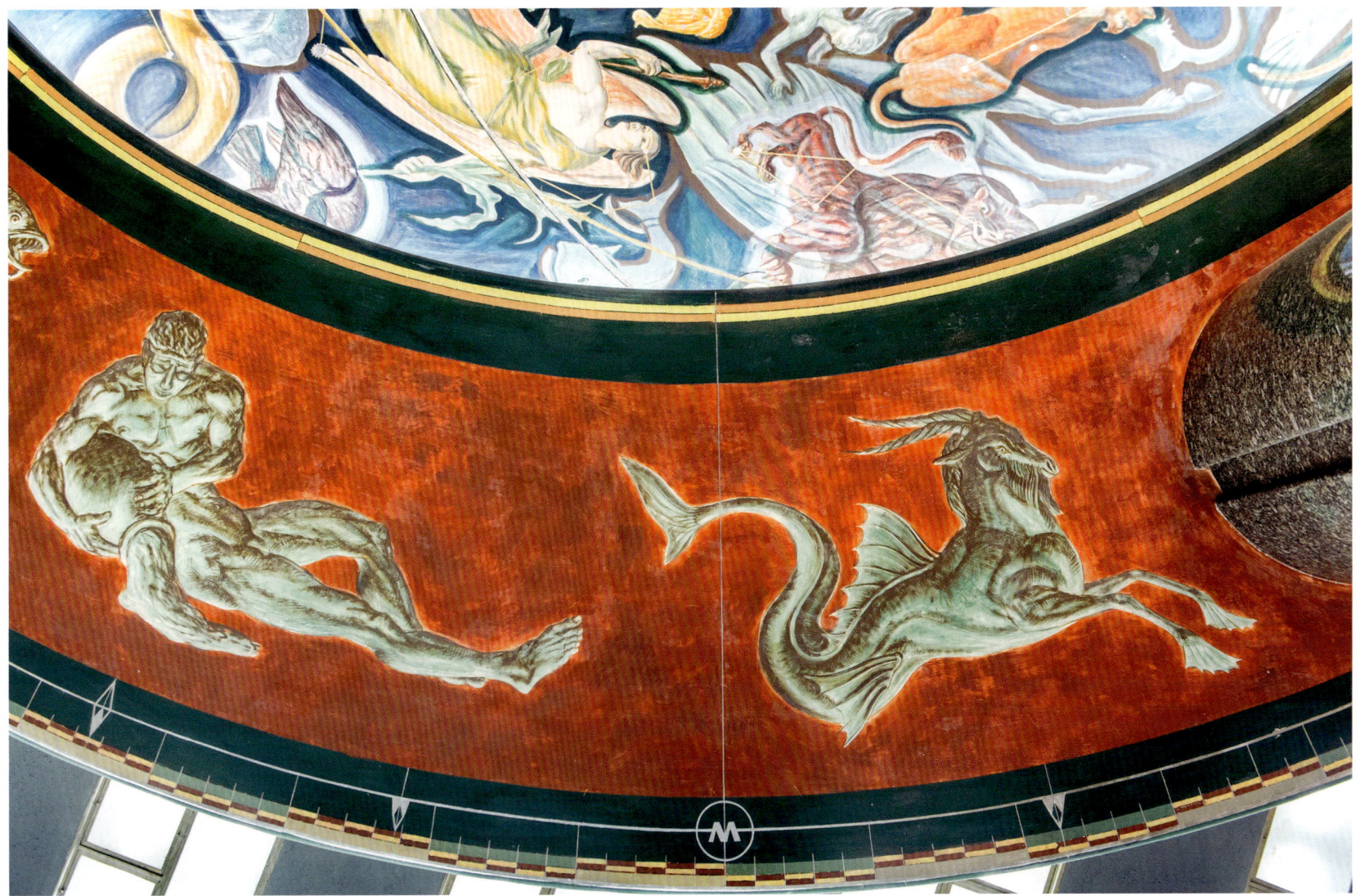

Plate 51.

Dome (detail), Aquarius and Capricorn. The exact notation for west is noted on the circumference of the dome. Photo by Chad Riley.

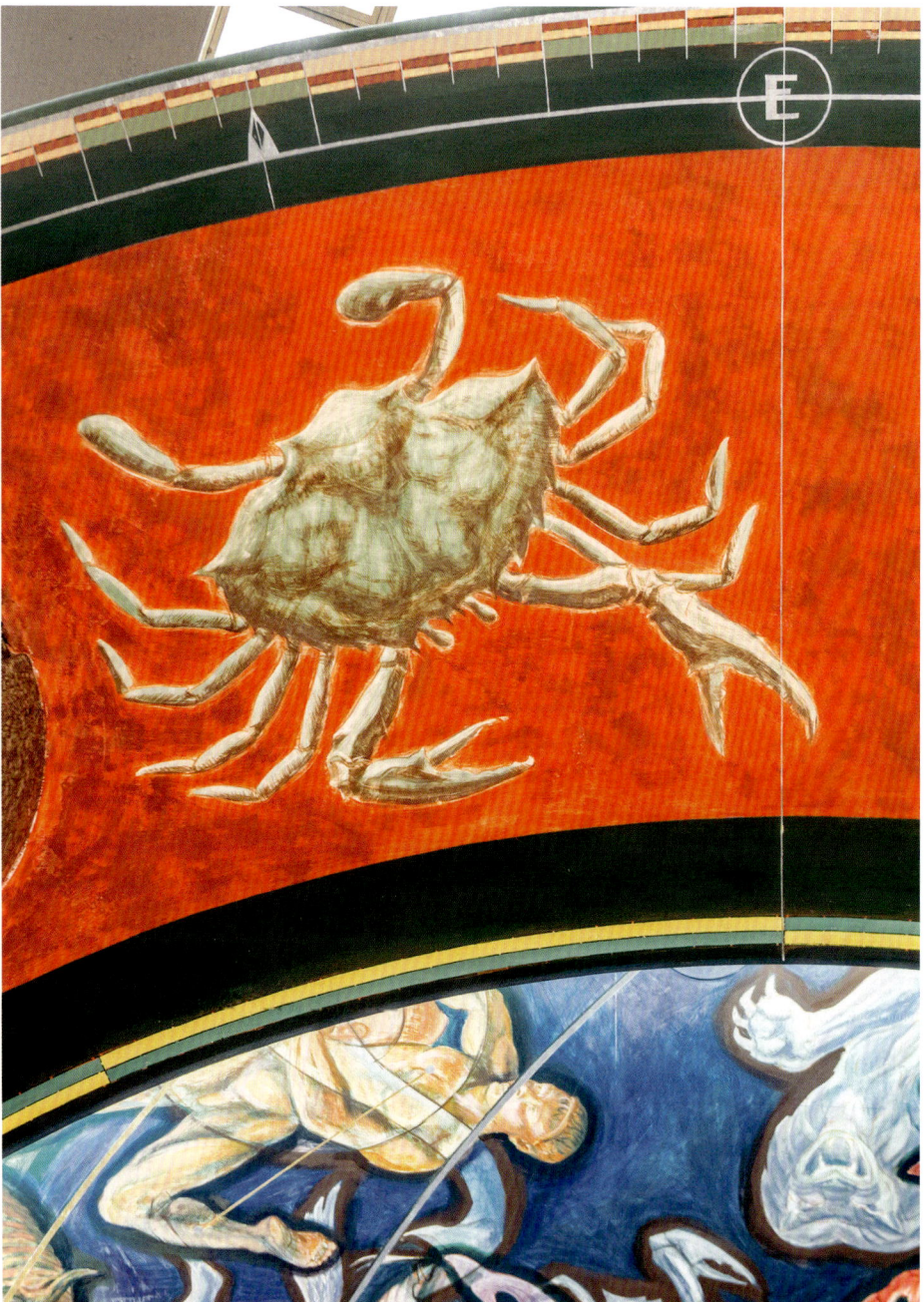

Because the painted dome looked like fresco, it formed a homogenous unit with the seven fresco panels. "The paint literally turns to colored stone," explained Albrizio of this new technique. "A rag comes away unstained when wiped across the painted surface and the colors are even fire retardant."[22] Despite ethyl silicate's ease of application and similar appearance to fresco, Albrizio continued to work in true fresco for later works. He believed that the effect of ethyl silicate paint does not equal fresco's subtle beauty. For Albrizio, convenience could not outweigh aesthetic value.

Plate 52.

Dome (detail), Cancer. The exact notation for east is noted here. Photo by Chad Riley.

8.

The Murals of the New Orleans Union Passenger Terminal

AFTER COMPLETING THE WATERMAN project, Albrizio returned to teaching at Louisiana State University. Although he worked in Baton Rouge, he now maintained an apartment and studio in the French Quarter. "New Orleans is where I want to live and I will just have to be a commuter to Baton Rouge!" he exclaimed.[1] His connections with the Arts and Crafts Club and the lingering members of the community from the 1920s were enough to keep him coming back to the "old neighborhood."

In 1951, Albrizio painted a small fresco for the Pan-Am Southern Corporation's building on Lee Circle in New Orleans (plate 53). The mural was a single panel representing oil production and refining. In the upper left corner, workers are interwoven with a drilling rig as they have become one with their labor. Below is the stark, white contour of a "Christmas tree," a series of valves used to regulate oil flow. As production progresses, oil moves to large furnaces for vaporizing. The seemingly endless entanglement of pipes on the right side of the composition represents oil vapors as they are taken to fractioning towers where they are made into benzene, naphtha, gasoline, and so on. The lighter palette represents the lighter oils and vapors.[2] The building still stands, now as a housing facility. The interior fresco has been covered by several layers of white paint but could still be resurrected if a future owner desired.

Later that year, Albrizio received a commission to execute decoration in fresco for the new Union Passenger Terminal in New Orleans. The members of the passenger terminal committee were not identified in related correspondence, but it is likely the building architects and city officials comprised the group. The committee based its decision on Albrizio's recent Waterman cycle as well as his frescoes throughout Louisiana.[3] The terminal would be the artist's most illustrious project to date.

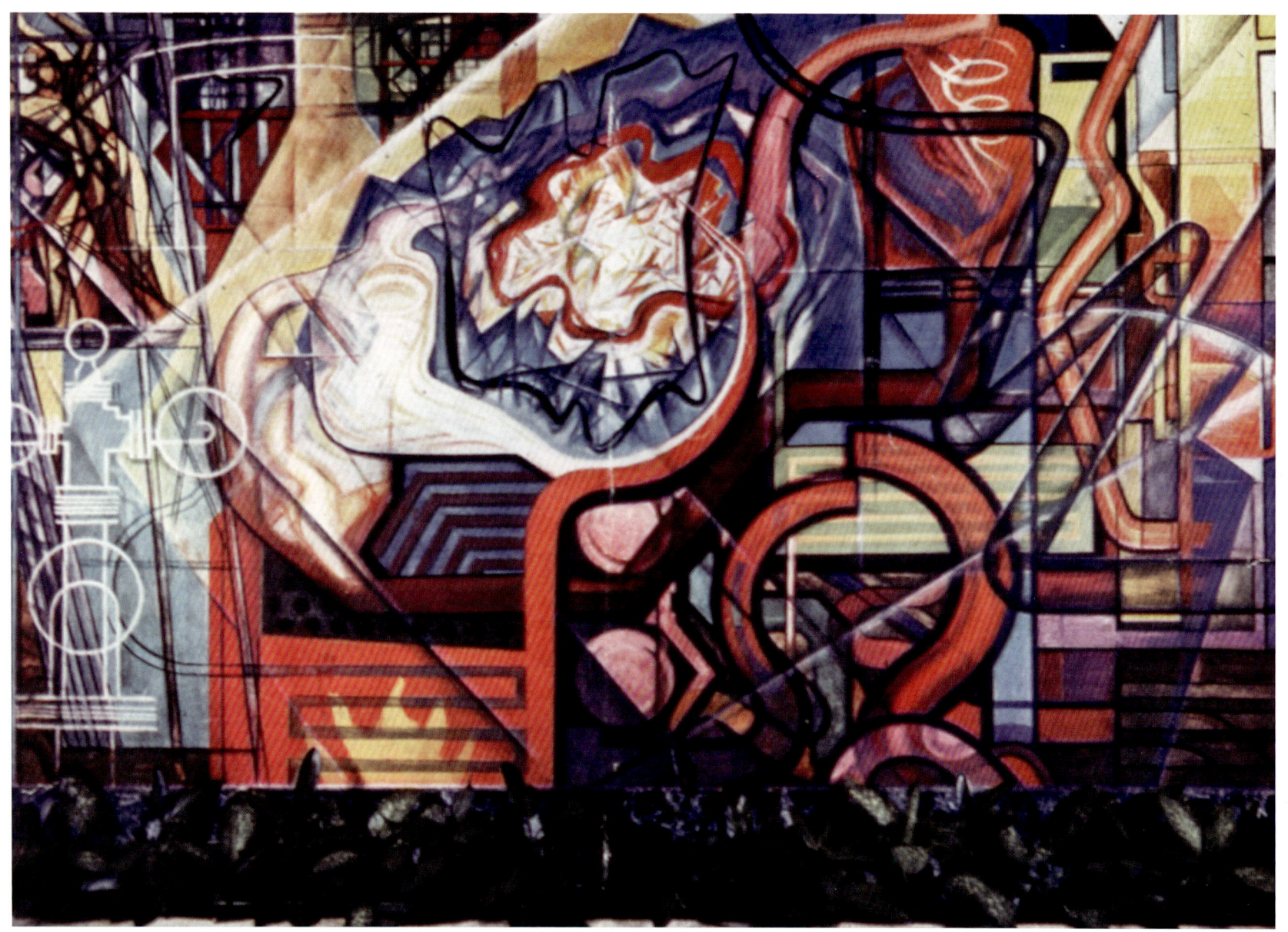

Plate 53.
Pan-Am Building fresco, 1951, Lee Circle, New Orleans (now Tivoli Place, fresco covered). Author's collection.

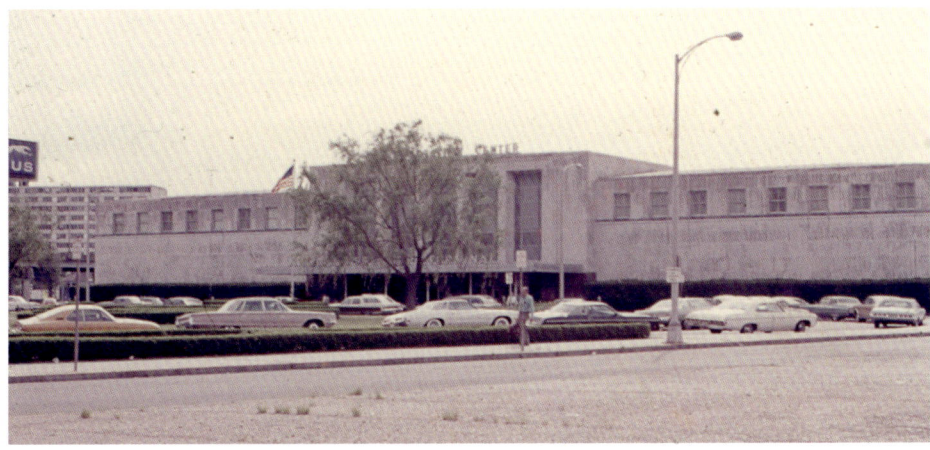

Plate 54.
New Orleans Union Passenger Terminal (NOUPT) exterior. Author's collection.

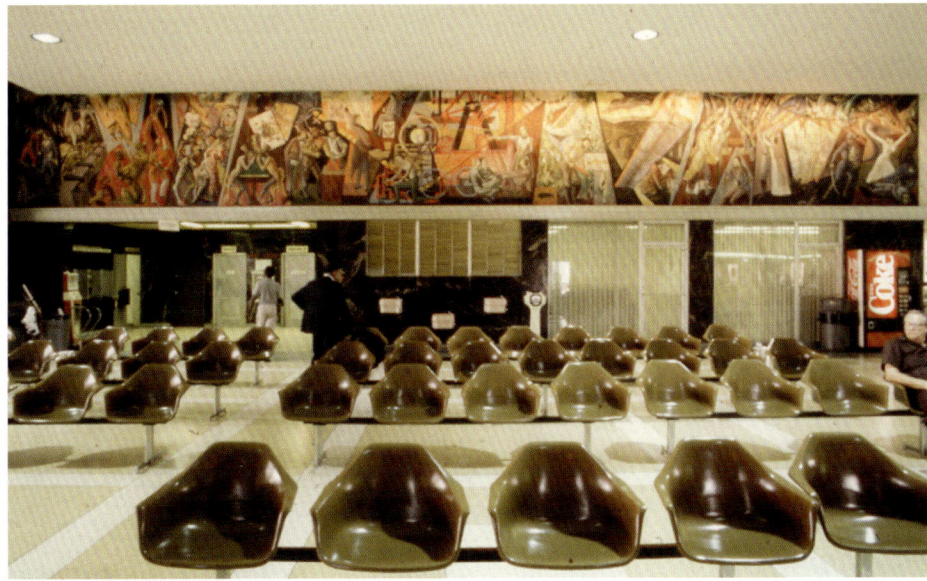

Plate 55.
NOUPT interior. Photo by Jackson Hill.

One year earlier, the citizens of New Orleans had reelected deLesseps Story "Chep" Morrison to his second term as mayor. Morrison represented a new era of modernism for the city. The Independent Citizens Committee, a group of political reformers, had sought a candidate who would challenge the old political ways in New Orleans. They touted Morrison as a revisionist and enthusiastically watched as New Orleans's architecture and skyline began to change under his new regime. A modern, more sophisticated look prevailed as the city embraced an innovative post–World War II image. Morrison welcomed the establishment of numerous oil industries and white-collar corporate offices in downtown New Orleans. Construction of the Union Passenger Terminal was one of the major projects he sanctioned. Built at a cost of $18 million, it was dedicated on May 1, 1954 (plate 54).[4]

The terminal had an immense concourse designed to display 2,166 square feet of fresco painting depicting the important events in Louisiana history. Six months of concentrated reading on the state's history enabled Albrizio to select events that he felt would best exemplify the "making" of Louisiana.[5] The action-packed and often flamboyant past presented him with a considerable challenge. "It wasn't a question of what to include," says Albrizio; "it was what had to be culled from the wealth of material at hand."[6] After careful consideration, he chose numerous key events that encapsulated some 435 years.

The terminal's concourse is one giant rectangle. The two long walls contain frescoes, two panels on each wall (plate 55). The two short walls contain glass doors that allow access to the terminal space. Located just below the 18-foot ceiling,

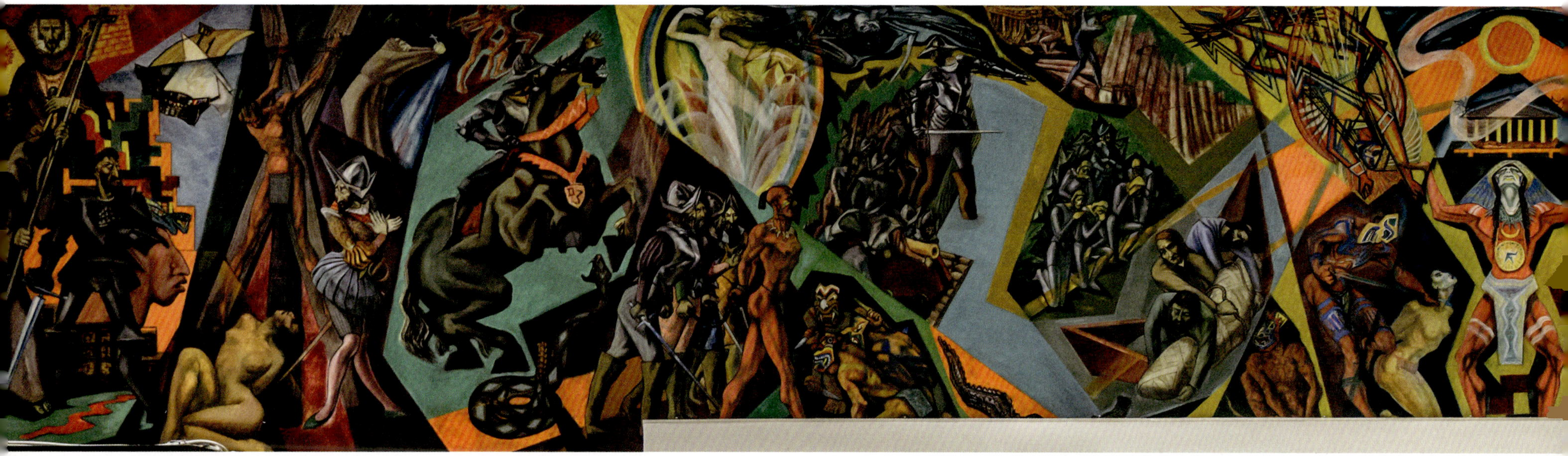

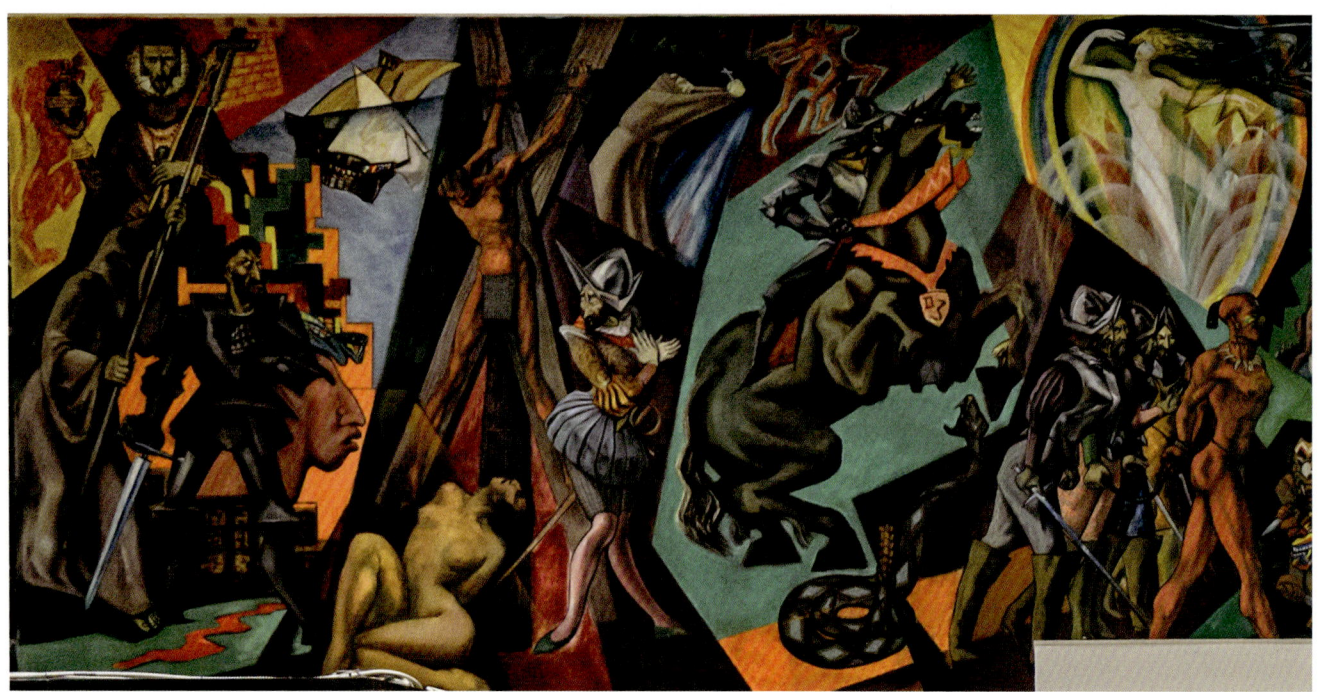

Plate 56.

Overview, *Age of Exploration,* 1954, fresco, NOUPT, New Orleans. Photo by Jackson Hill.

Plate 57.

Age of Exploration (Section 1), 1954, fresco, NOUPT, New Orleans. Photo by Jackson Hill.

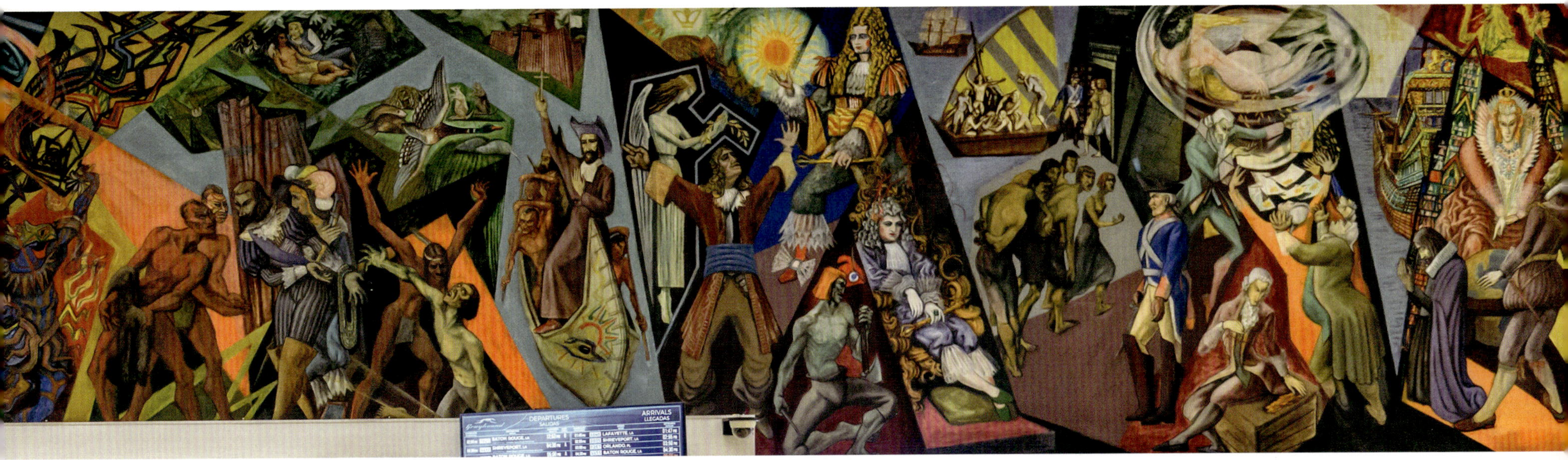

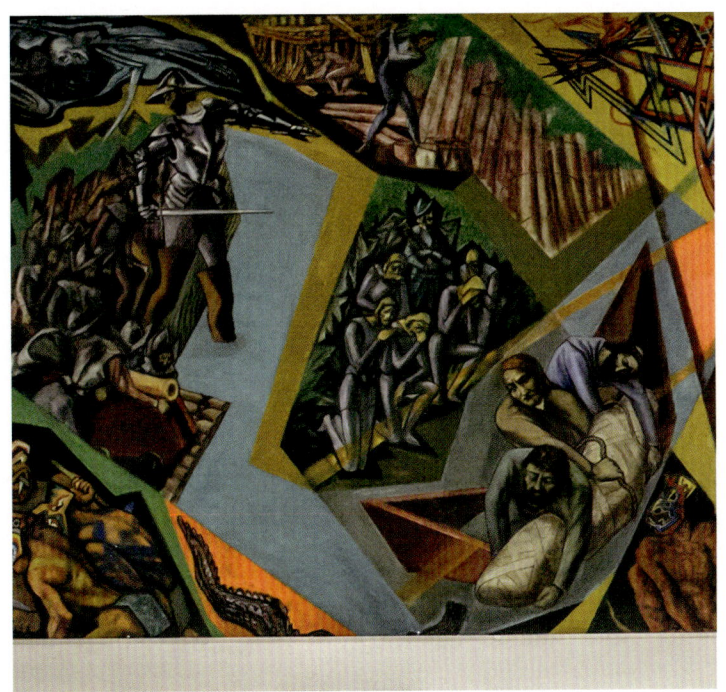

Plate 58.
Age of Exploration
(Section 2), 1954,
fresco, NOUPT, New
Orleans. Photo by
Jackson Hill.

each of the four panels measures 61 feet, 4 inches by 8 feet, 10 inches. Albrizio spent two years preparing the preliminary sketches, which resulted in four major historical divisions to coincide with the four panels. Panel 1 (*Age of Exploration*) and Panel 2 (*Age of Colonization*) are on one wall, directly across from Panel 3 (*Age of Struggle*) and Panel 4 (*Modern Age*). Panel 1 faces Panel 4, and Panel 2 faces Panel 3. They were placed so that the viewer could walk around the terminal and "read" the story of Louisiana history in sequence. The design relationship between Panels 1 and 4, and Panels 2 and 3, is important because the panels are visually linked across the terminal from one another.

Albrizio wanted to present not merely historical events but the humanistic interactions within those events—the spirit of the subject rather than the details. He maintained, however, that subject can never overrule matters of form and color. Chronological events and symbolism are often even anachronistic where the change yields a better design.[7]

After the opening of the terminal, New Orleans police had a difficult time identifying vagrants and loafers, according to a *Morning Advocate* article in December of 1954. Many "vagrants" turned out to be art lovers admiring the murals. The manager of the station, C. J. Wallace, said he couldn't even venture a guess at the number of visitors who came just to look at the artwork.[8]

AGE OF EXPLORATION

(Plate 56)

Albrizio begins the visual history of Louisiana with Spain's arrival in the Americas (plate 57). The king of Spain, flanked by royal arms and Spanish ships of conquest, sends missionaries and conquistadors to the Americas. Spanish domination is shown in the cruel treatment of the indigenous peoples: a conquistador arrogantly stares at the distorted and tormented figure of a native woman, while a proud warrior is led away at sword point. The promise of Ponce de Leon's Fountain of Youth and the chance of discovering gold motivated many early explorers, as depicted in the right-hand portion of this first section.

The second section of *Age of Exploration* highlights Hernando de Soto's 1541 discovery of the Mississippi River. After his death in 1542, de Soto was buried in the river (plate 58). Albrizio uses the Mississippi as a thread to visually connect the many sections of the expanded composition.[9]

The dramatic rendering of figures creates an exquisite theatrical interplay of characters throughout the terminal's panels. Geometric forms often function like spotlights to accentuate the scenes. The "disjointed perspective" Albrizio shared with Thomas Hart Benton in the 1930s has now evolved into a more stylized form through the influence of abstraction. Each panel required many studies to find the perfect juxtaposition of shape and color (plates 59 and 60). Their careful placement creates a beautiful visual rhythm along the extended wall space.

After drawing and design considerations were satisfied and color problems were solved, the artist prepared the final grid drawings to transfer the work to the wall surface. Life-size drawings were attached to the wall and the lines pricked with a nail through which powdered charcoal was

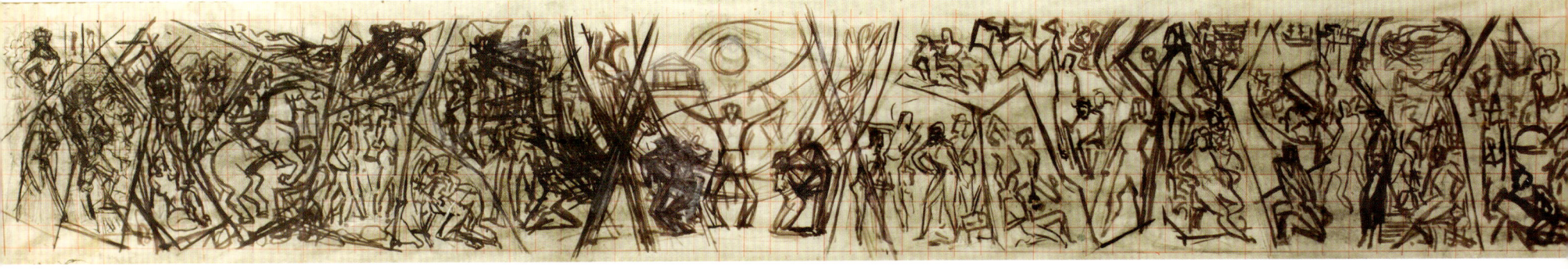

Plate 59.

"Age of Exploration" New Orleans Union Passenger Terminal Mural Study, 1954, ink and graphite on graph paper, 8 × 47 inches, LSU Museum of Art, 2005.2.4. Purchased with funds from the Paula Garvey Manship Endowment, Lucy D. Robinson, and Michael D. Robinson. Photography: Malarie Zaunbrecher.

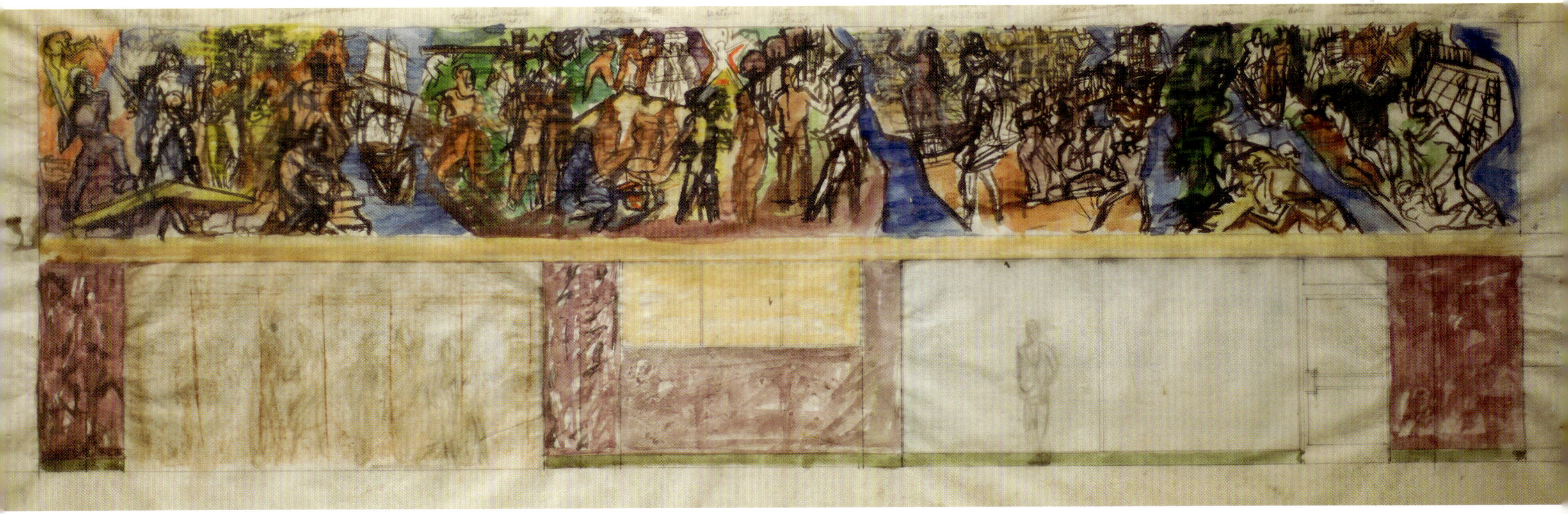

Plate 60.

"Age of Exploration" and "Age of Colonization" New Orleans Union Passenger Terminal Mural Study, 1954, graphite and watercolor on paper, 12 × 34 inches, LSU Museum of Art, 2005.2.3. Purchased with funds from the Paula Garvey Manship Endowment, Lucy D. Robinson, and Michael D. Robinson. Photography: Malarie Zaunbrecher.

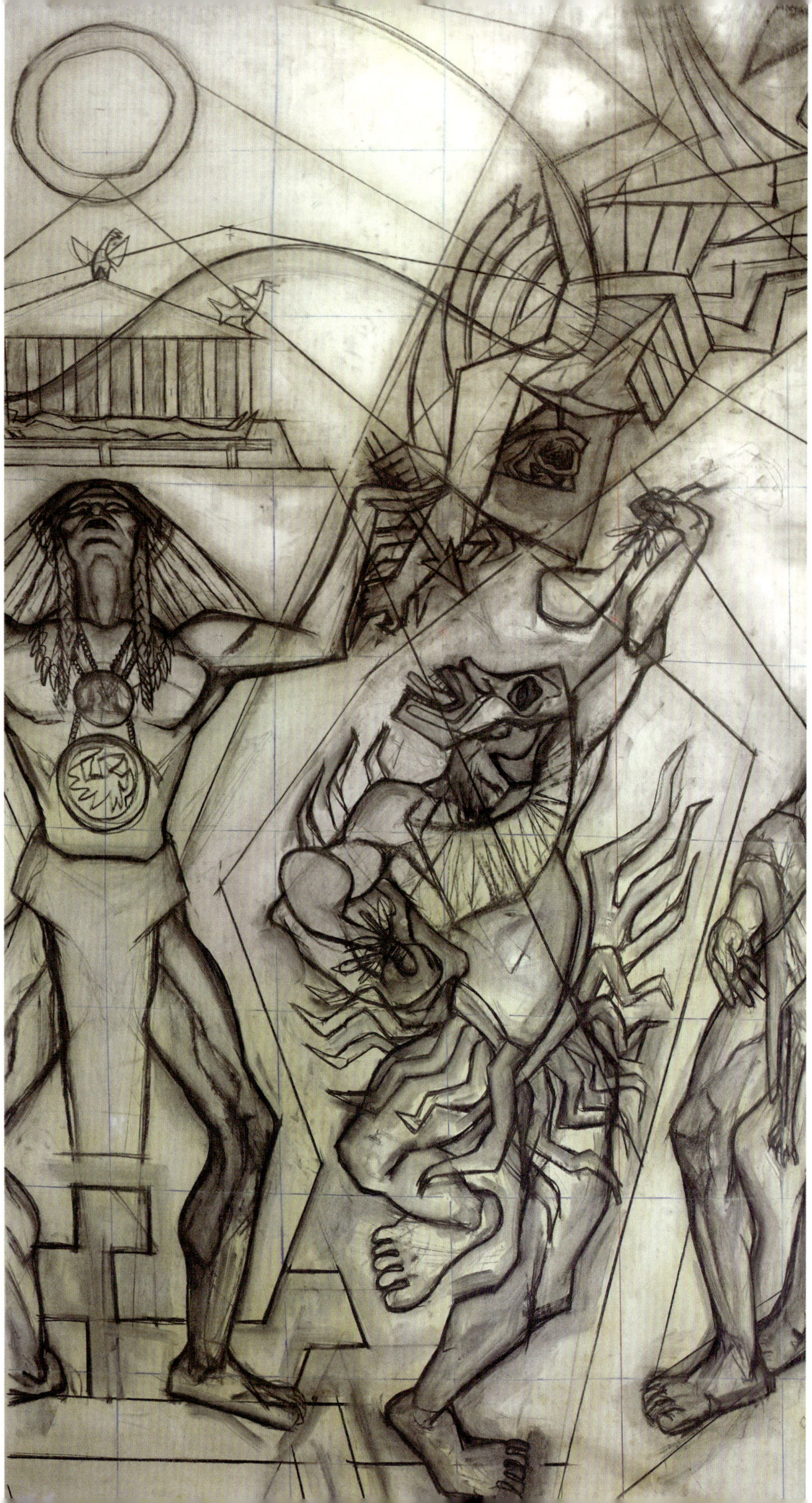

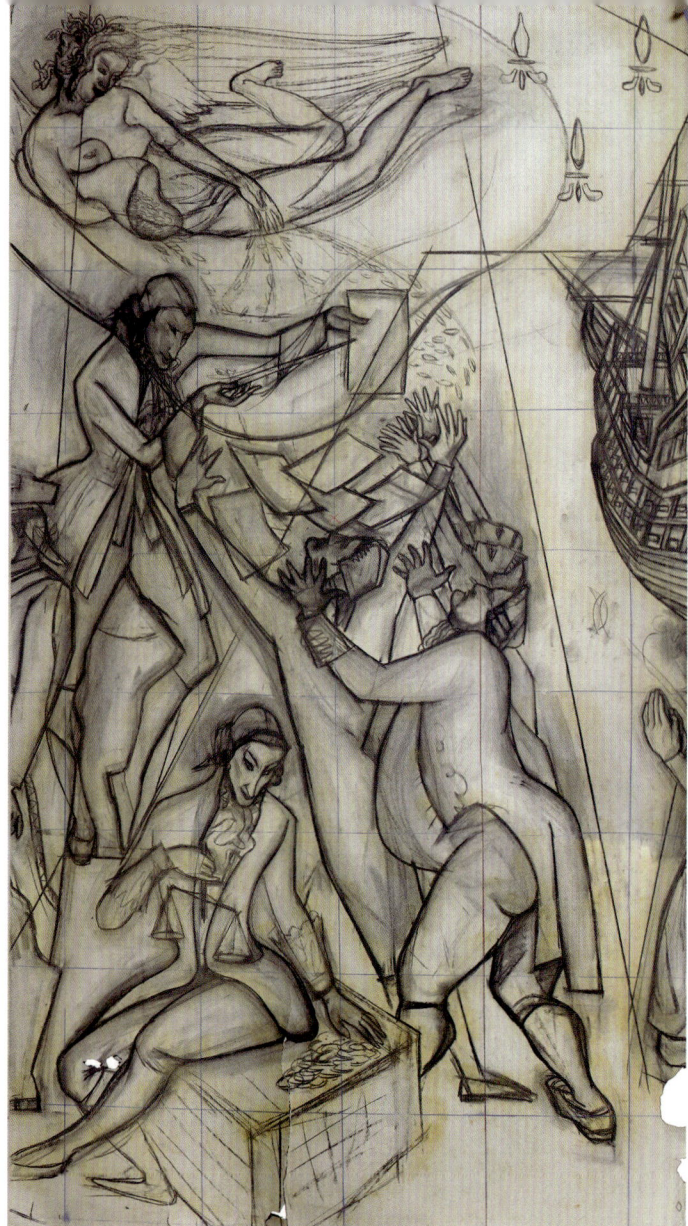

Plate 61.
Grid drawing for *Age of Exploration,* 1954, charcoal on newsprint. Courtesy of the Louisiana State Museum. Photo by Patrick Barnes.

Plate 62.
Grid drawing for *Age of Exploration,* 1954, charcoal on newsprint. Courtesy of the Louisiana State Museum. Photo by Patrick Barnes.

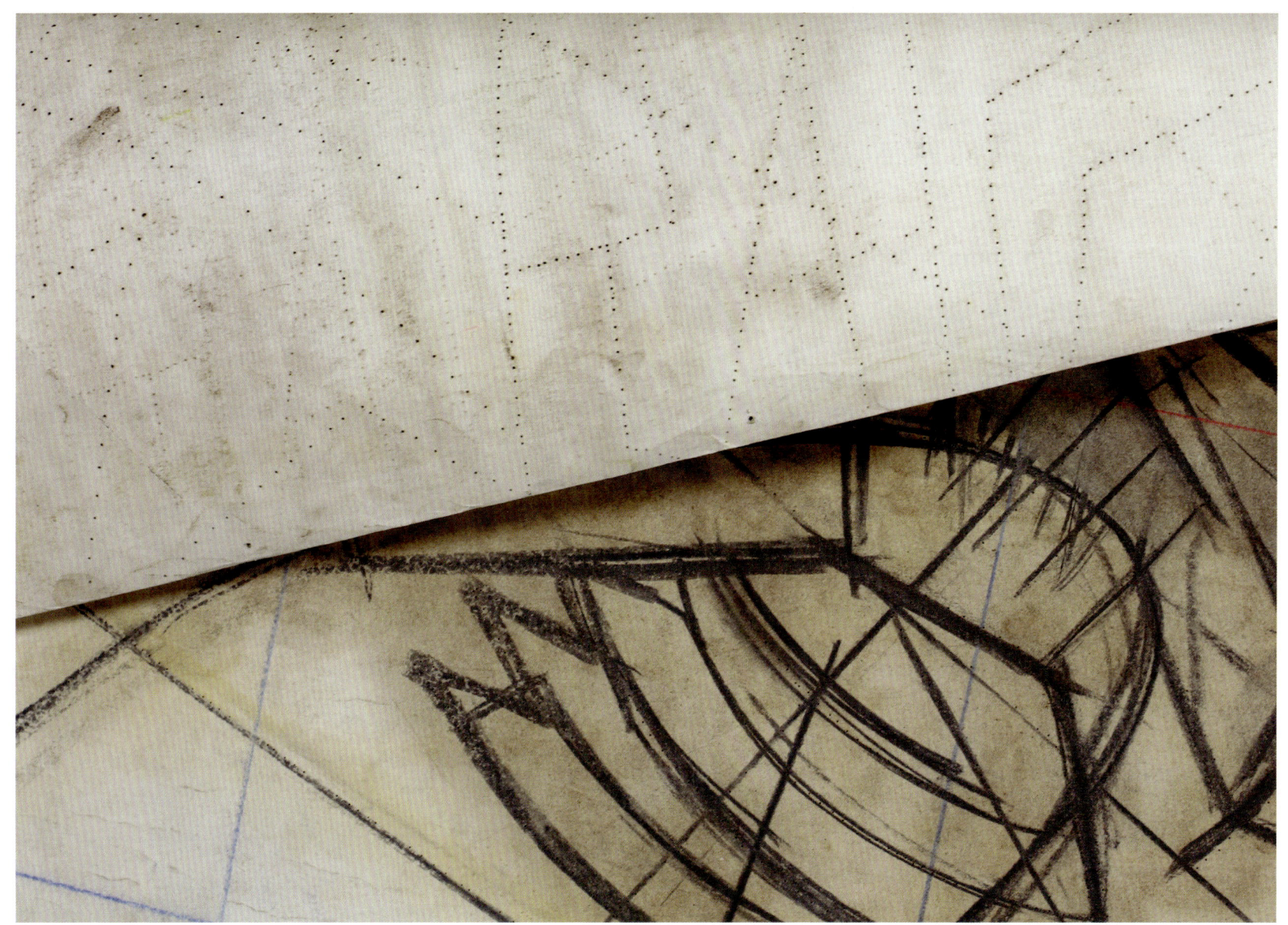

Plate 63.
Grid drawing showing pricks for transfer, 1954, charcoal on newsprint. Courtesy of the Louisiana State Museum. Photo by Patrick Barnes.

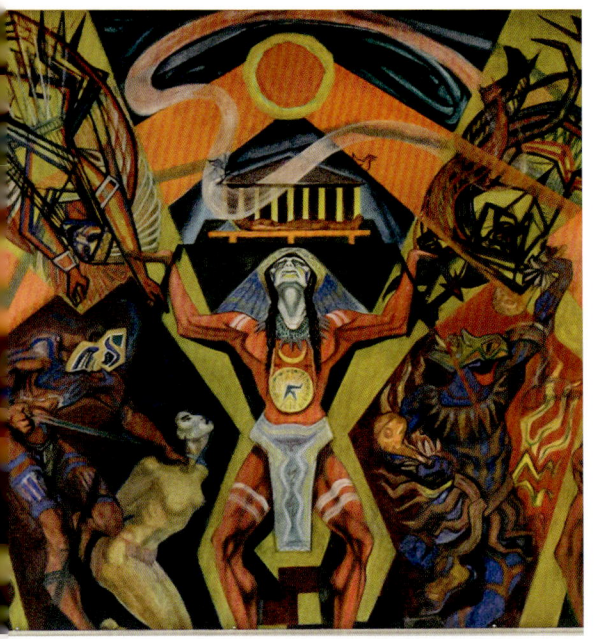

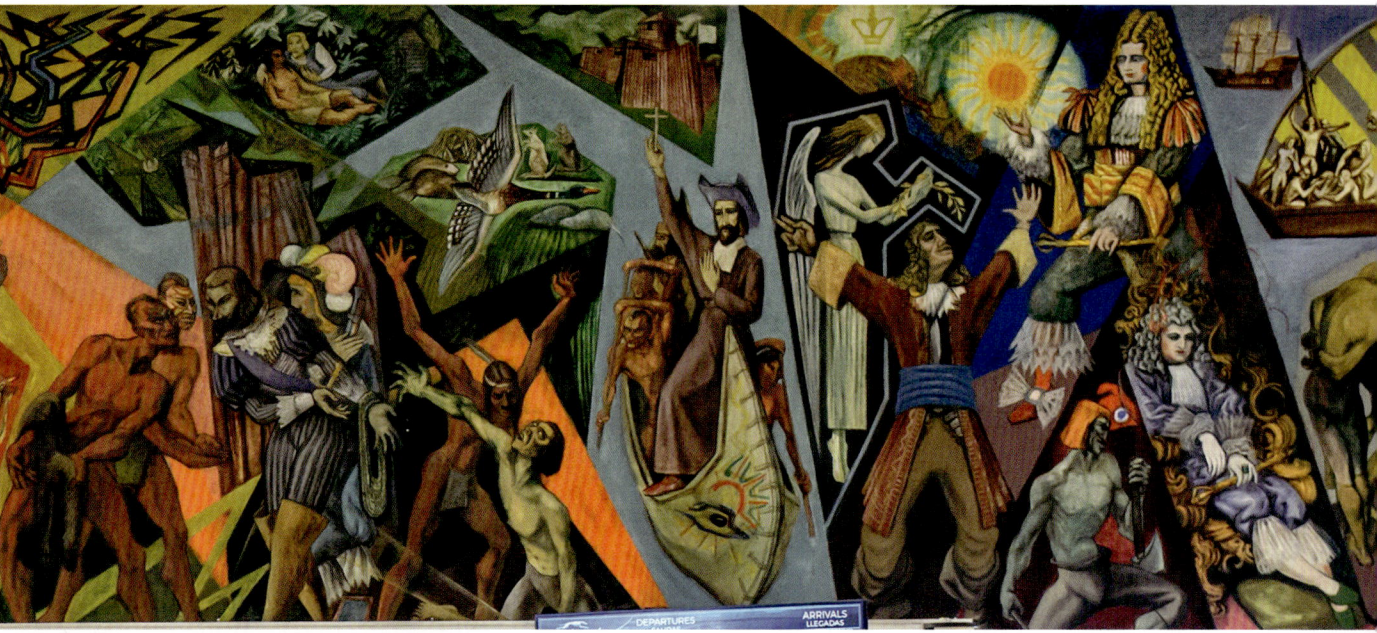

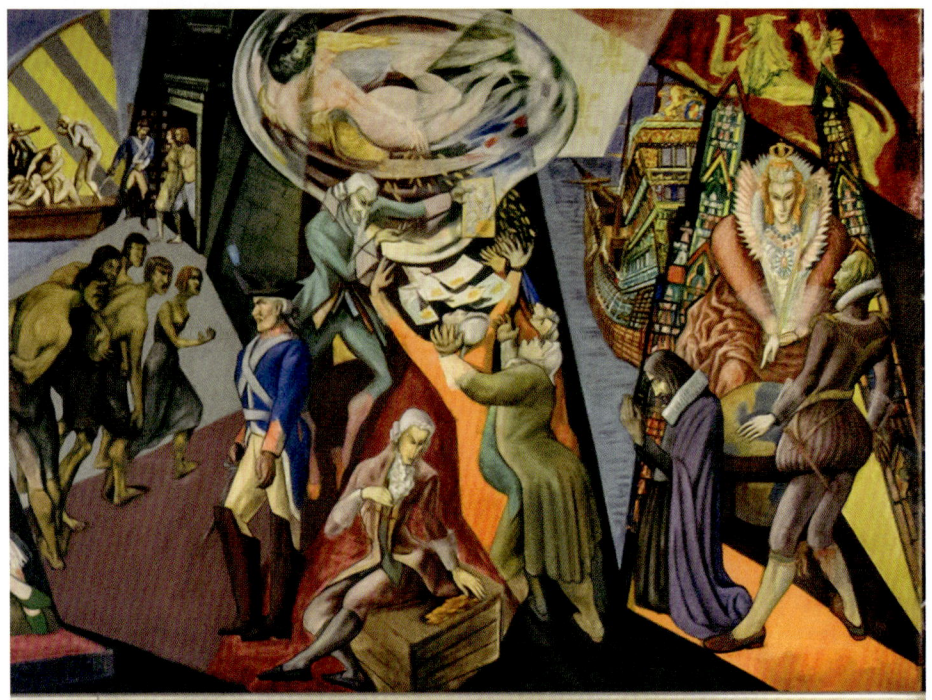

Plate 64.

Age of Exploration (Section 3), 1954, fresco, NOUPT, New Orleans. Photo by Jackson Hill.

Plate 65.

Age of Exploration (Section 4), 1954, fresco, NOUPT, New Orleans. Photo by Jackson Hill.

Plate 66.

Age of Exploration (Section 5), 1954, fresco, NOUPT, New Orleans. Photo by Jackson Hill.

pounced. This allowed the lines to be transferred to the wall surface. Two grid drawings are shown here, as well as a grid drawing showing pricks for transfer (plates 61–63).

The third section, which supports the center of the *Age of Exploration* panel, depicts a native sun worshiper (plate 64). The figure stands beneath a temple. Overhead the sun emits two powerful rays that envelop the bygone civilization. Symbols of good and evil fly from the figure's hands in the energy of opposing forces, a recurring theme in the mural.[10] The colors are intense and acrid and the contour is severe. "All figures are used symbolically," wrote Albrizio, "as are the colors and elements of design."[11]

In Section 4, France is introduced as the second rival for Louisiana soil (plate 65). Unlike the Spanish, the French are portrayed as establishing friendly relations with the indigenous people. They amicably barter beads for furs and share the mystery of the magnifying glass with their American Indian friends. French and Native Americans marry, and French settlers usher missionaries down the Mississippi River to Louisiana. Louis XIV, the Sun King, and his court listen to French explorers enthrall audiences with the tales of riches and wealth found in the New World.

In Section 5, excited investors await great fortune, but "John Law's Bubble" or "The Mississippi Bubble" turns out to be nothing more than a dream (plate 66).[12] Albrizio depicts the event in the same manner as the Fountain of Youth, as a fantastic notion that enticed anxious outsiders. The Queen of England sits majestically before her explorers. Supported by symbols of wealth and the Crown, the third contender for Louisiana has now arrived.[13]

AGE OF COLONIZATION
(Plate 67)

The mural's second panel, *Age of Colonization,* begins with the settlement of Louisiana by pioneers from the east (plate 68). Early settlers needed the aid of Native Americans and learned to pit one tribe against another. Through this conspiracy, early colonists learned the war tactics of the Indians and ultimately gained their lands by force.[14] This section illustrates slavery of both Africans and Native Americans, which was practiced as early as the beginning of the 1700s.[15]

In a conversation in the 1980s, Albrizio's niece Anne Orvin explained her uncle's concern with acknowledging the contributions of under-recognized people in shaping the history of the state, in particular Native Americans and African Americans. "He wanted those people to be able to walk into the Passenger Terminal and see that their history was there," she said. "He even went so far as to count the number of figures of each race to make sure they were well represented."[16] It's interesting to note that in the mid-1950s discussions of segregation and equal opportunity were coming to the fore. The few African American artists working in New Orleans in the years of the Great Depression, World War II, and even the postwar era were rarely recognized as serious artists. Considered "self-taught," they only later were discovered by art scholars. A good example is Richmond Barthé from Bay St. Louis, Mississippi, who lived in New Orleans in the early 1920s. His extraordinary art skills were appreciated by many people, but he had no place to study or show his work. Funds collected by locals eventually enabled him to study at the Chicago Institute of Fine Arts at the age of 23.[17] Though

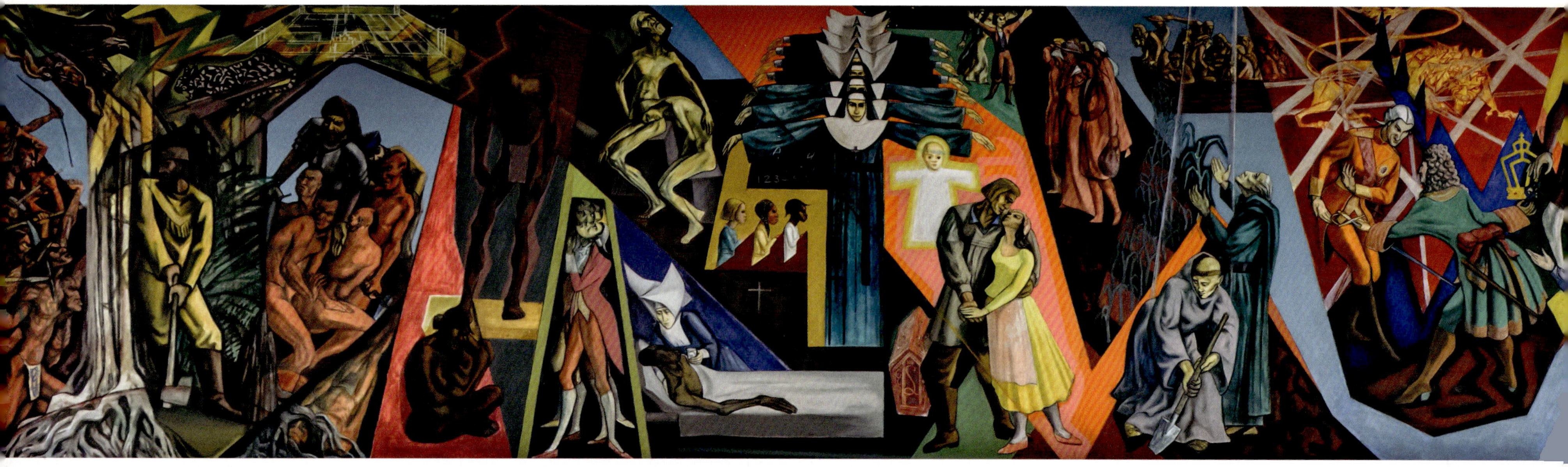

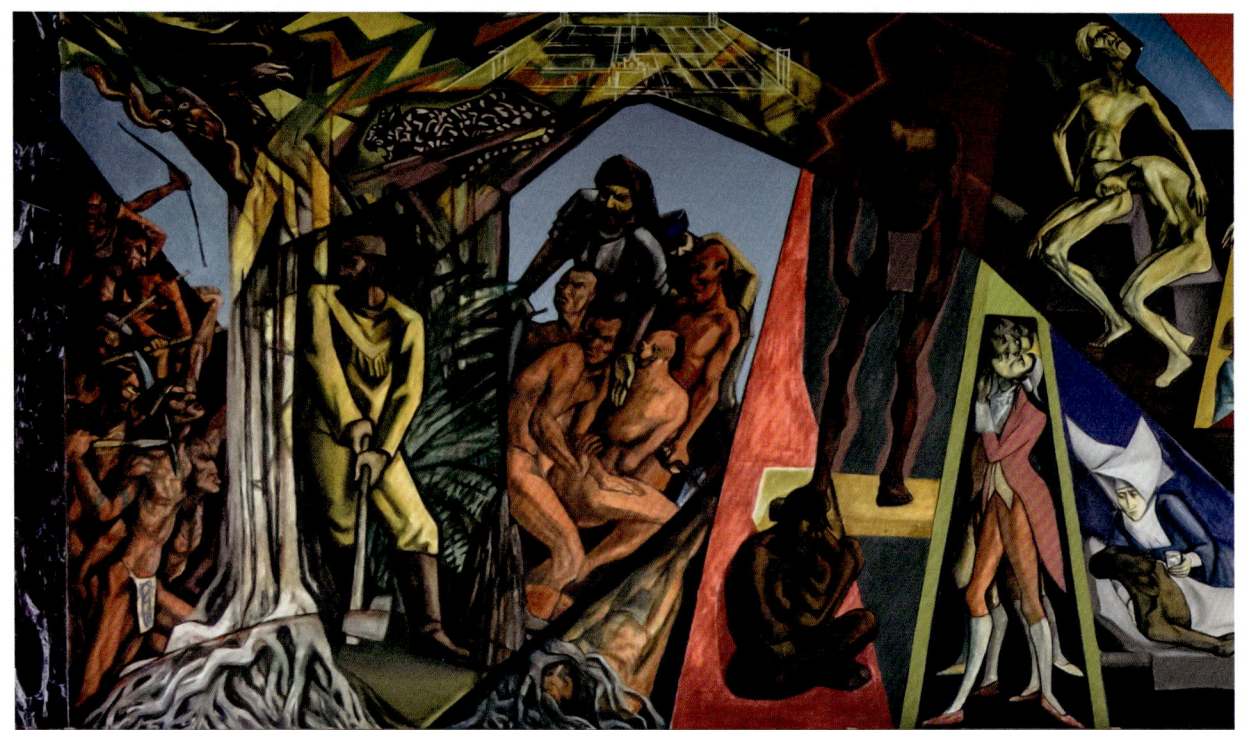

Plate 67.

Overview, *Age of Colonization,* 1954, fresco, NOUPT, New Orleans. Photo by Jackson Hill.

Plate 68.

Age of Colonization (Section 1), 1954, fresco, NOUPT, New Orleans. Photo by Jackson Hill.

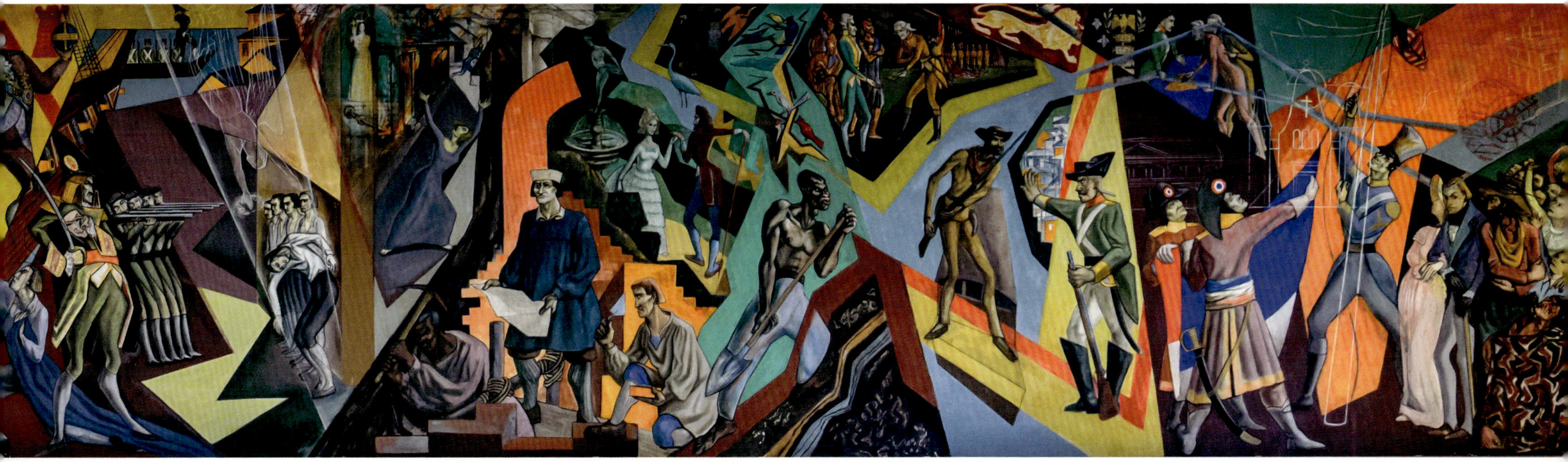

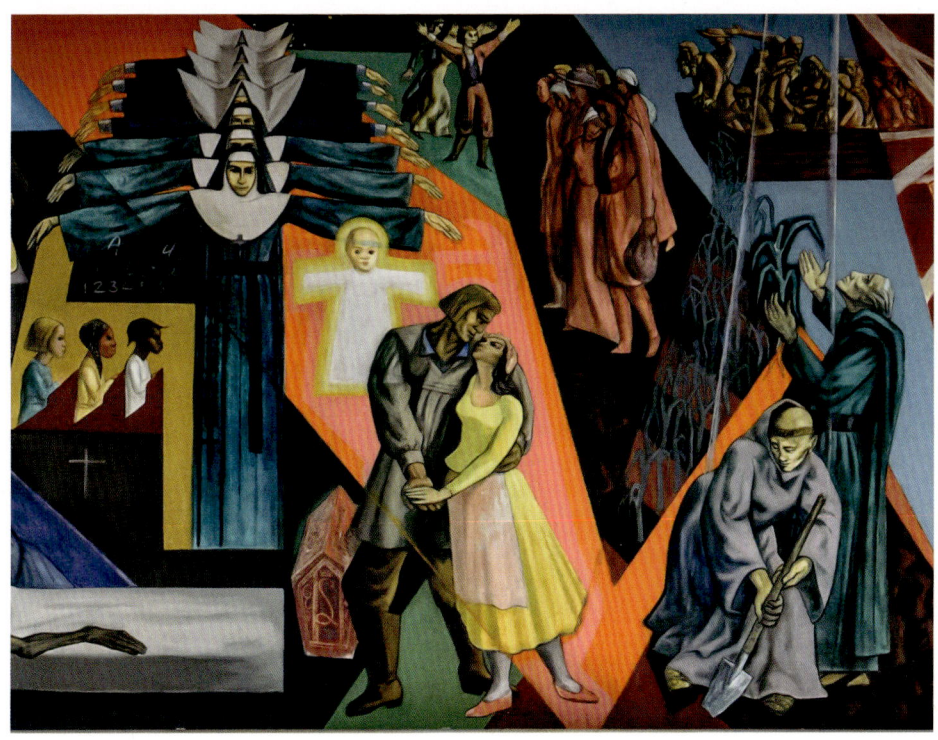

Plate 69.
Age of Colonization (Section 2), 1954, fresco, NOUPT, New Orleans. Photo by Jackson Hill.

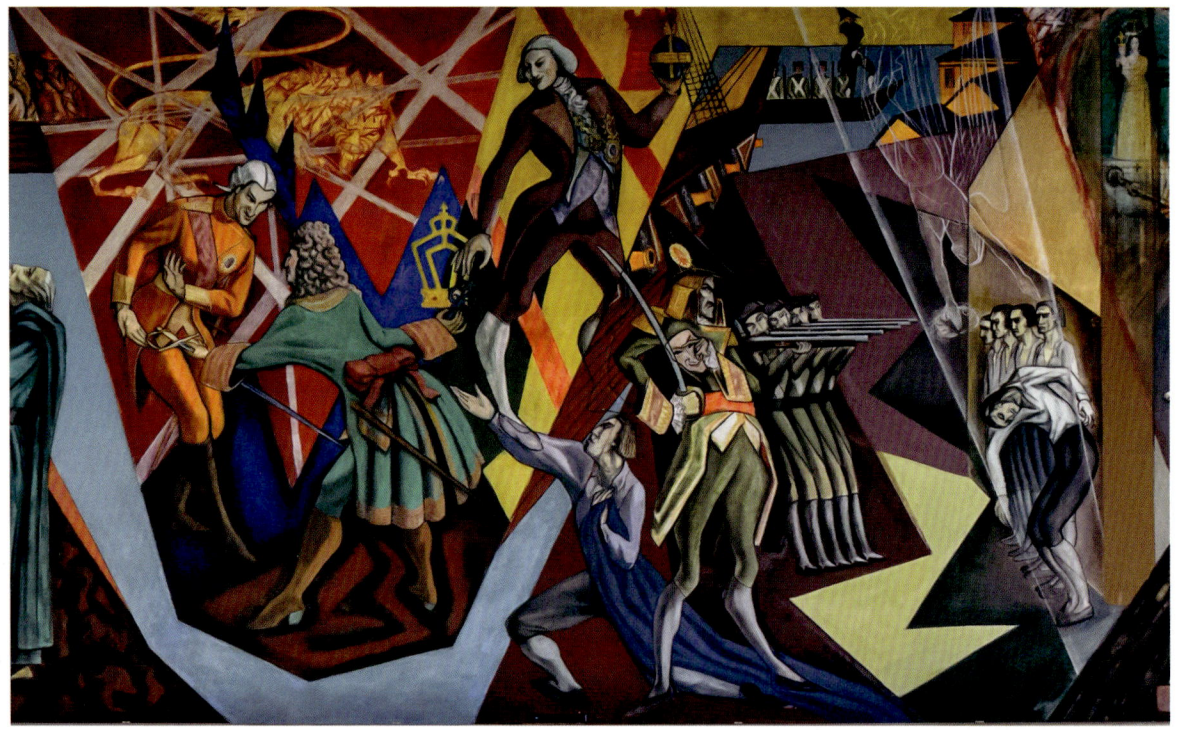

Plate 70.
Age of Colonization
(Section 3), 1954,
fresco, NOUPT, New
Orleans. Photo by
Jackson Hill.

unfortunately lost to New Orleans, he became part of the Harlem Renaissance.

The second section of Panel 2 depicts the charitable contributions of the Ursuline nuns and the Sisters of Charity (plate 69).[18] In 1727 the first Ursuline nuns arrived from France to provide education and medical services. Their devotion to educating young women and tending the sick without regard to race aided both French settlers and enslaved Africans.[19] Albrizio used the figures of the Ursuline nuns to create a striking repetitive pattern. Standing in

a line with their arms outspread in a cruciform position, the figures in their uniformity and stark simplicity create a strong decorative device. As symbols of strength and protection, the open arms of the nuns cloak the needy around them. Also under the aegis of the Ursuline nuns were the casquette girls, so called because of the small cases they carried containing their dowry from the king of France. These were young women brought from France to become the wives of French settlers and to establish families, symbolized by the figure of a small child standing beside the

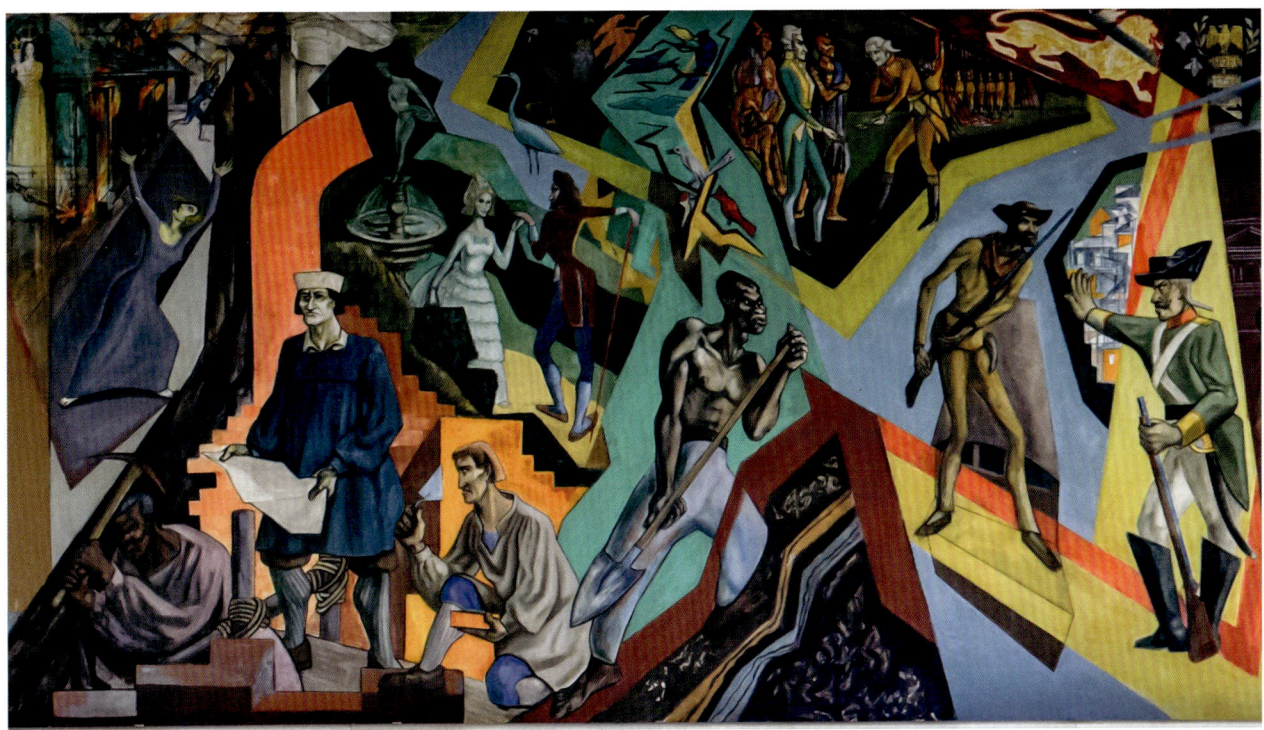

Plate 71.

Age of Colonization (Section 4), 1954, fresco, NOUPT, New Orleans. Photo by Jackson Hill.

nuns.[20] In this section Albrizio also acknowledges the considerable contribution that Jesuit priests made to the early French settlements through the cultivation of sugarcane, a practice they introduced to the lower Mississippi valley.[21] Rays from heaven stream down as if to aid the priest in his endeavors.

The central motif of the third section illustrates the surrender of the French colonies in Louisiana and Canada as a result of the French and Indian War (plate 70).[22] Dressed in blue with his back toward the viewer, a representative of

France cordially relinquishes Canada to the English, while secretly handing the key to the invaluable port of New Orleans to the Spanish. Below this triad, a French citizen of New Orleans pleads with France in protest of Spanish domination. To his right, the Spanish governor Alejandro O'Reilly, holding a mask of deceit, squelches resistance by capturing the insurgents through trickery and ultimately executing them before a firing squad.[23] An angel swoops down to protect the assassinated French protest leaders. Two radiating lines flanking the angel form a strong columnar

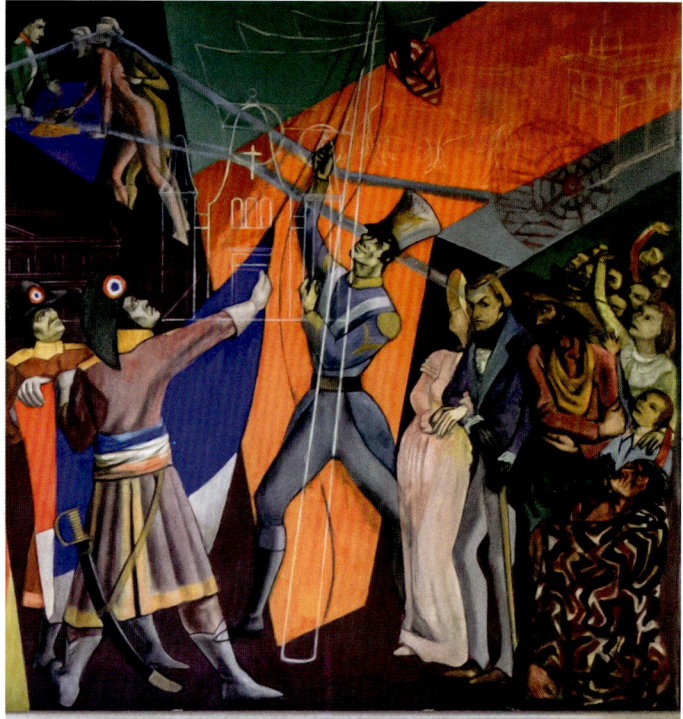

Plate 72.

Age of Colonization (Section 5), 1954, fresco, NOUPT, New Orleans. Photo by Jackson Hill.

support to the right of the central motif. This same support occurs to the left of center in the vertical rays that flank the Jesuit priest. The area between these two points is united by a broad, semicircular band of blue that gives prominence to the figures in the center. This band is the recurring symbol of the Mississippi River.[24] In this episode of Louisiana's history, it serves to bring the Acadians from Canada to Louisiana, where they no longer had to pledge allegiance to the unpopular English government and Anglican religion.[25]

Section 4 shows the devastating New Orleans fire of 1788 (plate 71). The flame of a votive candle placed on a home altar began a fire on Good Friday. Because the bells of the cathedral were not allowed to ring on Good Friday, the volunteer fire brigade could not be summoned and the fire burned uncontrollably, destroying most of the city.[26] The frantic figure of a woman gestures wildly as she conveys the desperation of the citizens over the resulting loss. The Spanish immediately began to rebuild the city, as shown by a small group of engineers and workers before partial structures of the new project. The Spanish continued to rule New Orleans and defeated the English in important battles in both Pascagoula and Baton Rouge. The broad, blue Mississippi appears once more. Here, it brings Kentucky traders on flatboats who demand entrance into the port of New Orleans.[27] Above this scene is a small segment that represents the secret negotiations that took place in 1800 resulting in the return of Louisiana from Spain to France.

The final section of the panel shows the Louisiana Purchase in 1803.[28] Representatives of France and the United States both thrust the American flag high into the air in commemoration of the event (plate 72). Ghostly contours of covered wagons, a missionary church, and a paddlewheel riverboat look to the future and the rapid settling of the West. Angry onlookers view the Louisiana Purchase as bewildering and unfair. America, with its language and its customs, was unfamiliar to the French of Louisiana. It was many years before the French readily accepted the American way of life.[29]

AGE OF STRUGGLE

(Plate 73)

The third panel begins with the Battle of New Orleans in 1815. The United States and Great Britain are symbolized by the American eagle and the British lion (plate 74). To the left, British agents attempt to enlist the aid of the notorious pirate Jean Lafitte, while Andrew Jackson leads American forces. To the right, the death of British general Edward Pakenham is shown.[30]

In contrast to the agonies of war, the next section shows the more festive side of New Orleans life with a throng of fantasy figures and revelers celebrating Carnival (plate 75). Gambling was also a favorite pastime, so much so that the Louisiana government enforced a tax on gambling and used the revenue to support the school system.[31] Albrizio has depicted three conniving gamblers scrapping around a card table. Above them hang two immense cards from which the pelican, seal of Louisiana, plucks sustenance. The hallowed halls of education are seen in contour in the distance.

The dramatic gesture of the teacher in the third section enthusiastically professes the discoveries taught in the many agricultural and mechanical colleges that were established in the mid-nineteenth century (plate 76).[32] Machines such as the cotton gin took the place of numerous enslaved workers and increased crop yields.

Section 4 shows the agricultural threats of the boll weevil and corn earworm. These were disastrous setbacks to southern farmers and required hastened advancements in methods of eradication (plate 77). Efficient means of shipping perishable goods became an important part of expanding marketing and sales in the agricultural business. The scourges of yellow fever, cholera, and malaria were common in the subtropical climate of Louisiana.[33] The artist shows Death enveloped in an acidic, yellow-green cloud of pestilence hanging over New Orleans. A writer during the 1853 yellow fever epidemic described the city: "The hum of trade was silent. The levee was a desert. The streets, wont to shine with fashion and beauty, were silent."[34] Albrizio captures this urban desolation fraught with disease and the dying. It was not until 1900 that medical research revealed the carrier of the dread yellow fever to be the mosquito.

The fifth and final section of *Age of Struggle* illustrates Louisiana faced with the challenge of secession (plate 78). A figure stands between shattered columns, representing the sentiments of Louisiana citizens divided over withdrawing from the Union.[35] The pinnacle of struggle in Louisiana—the Civil War—follows. Separation of loved ones, looting, death, and destruction are all represented along with the blockade of the Mississippi River. There is an abstract representation of immobilized ships crowded together in the port of New Orleans with St. Louis Cathedral standing nobly in the background. Most impressive is an arc that contains the Four Horsemen of the Apocalypse shown in a stricken frenzy across the sky.[36] The tumultuous interplay of the curves and shapes divorces this treatment from the general style seen throughout the rest of the mural. This detail strongly recalls the oil painting *Four Horses,* which Albrizio painted during the years of his Rosenwald fellowship.

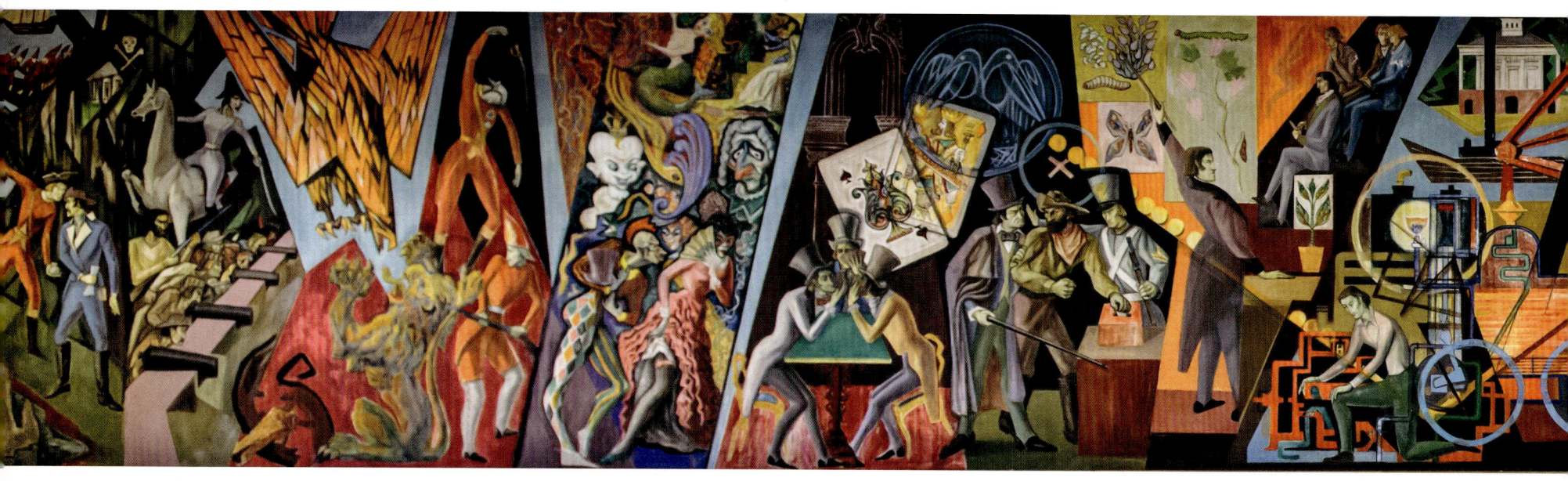

Plate 73.

Overview, *Age of Struggle,* 1954, fresco, NOUPT, New Orleans. Photo by Jackson Hill.

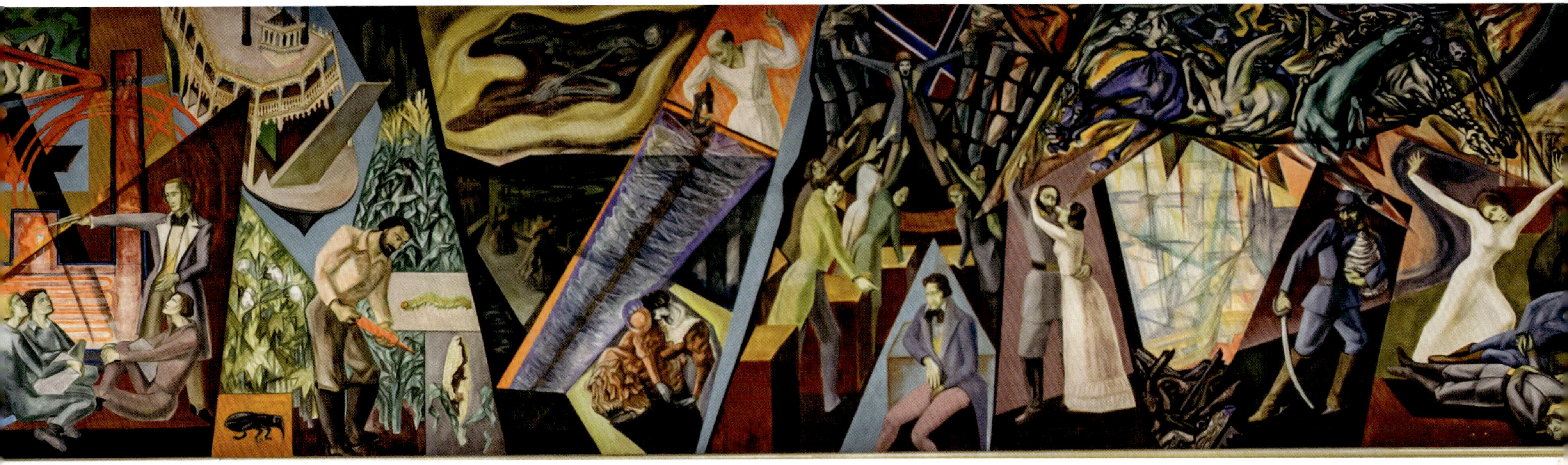

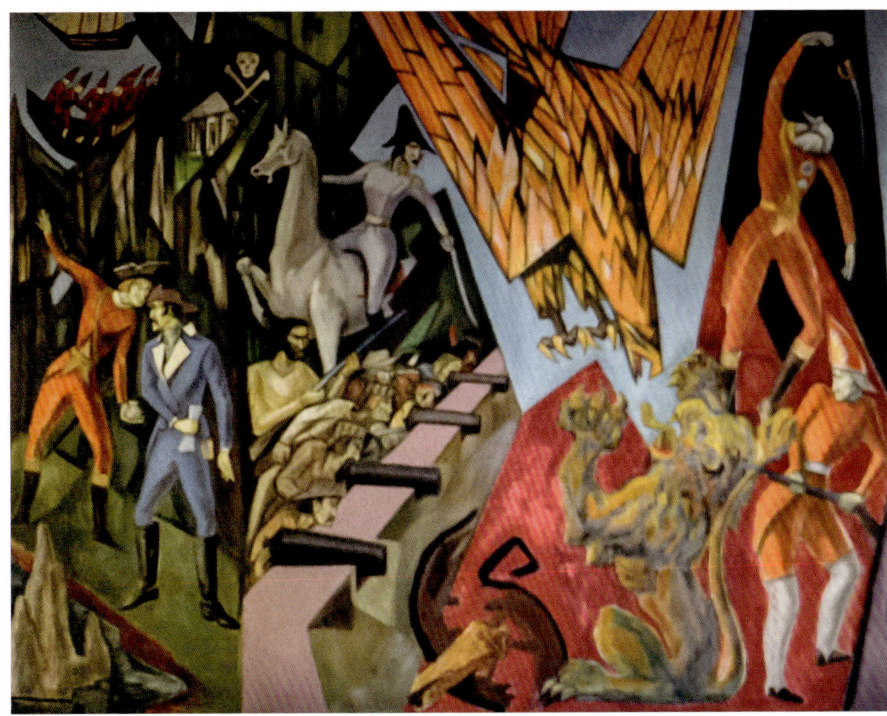

Plate 74.

Age of Struggle (Section 1), 1954, fresco, NOUPT, New Orleans. Photo by Jackson Hill.

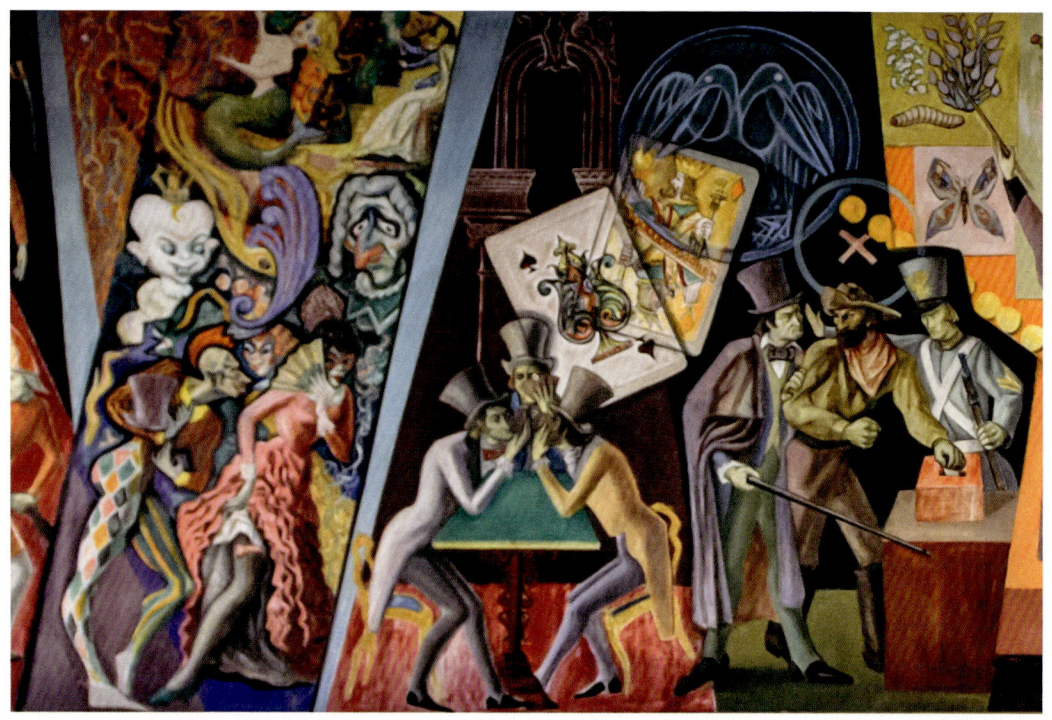

Plate 75.

Age of Struggle
(Section 2), 1954,
fresco, NOUPT, New
Orleans. Photo by
Jackson Hill.

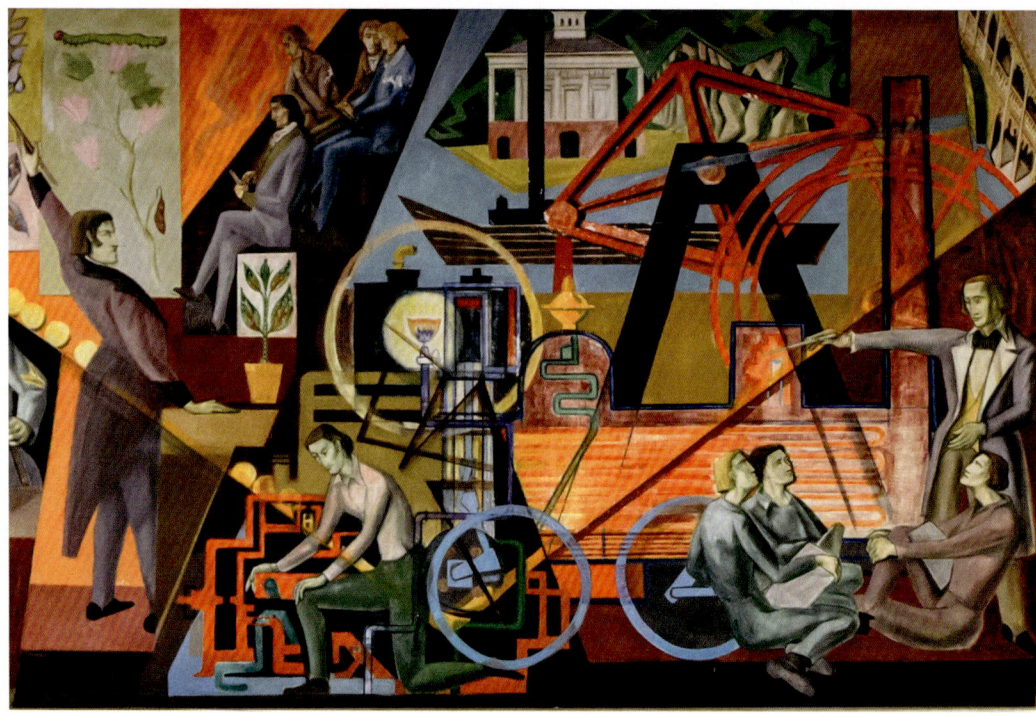

Plate 76.

Age of Struggle
(Section 3), 1954,
fresco, NOUPT, New
Orleans. Photo by
Jackson Hill.

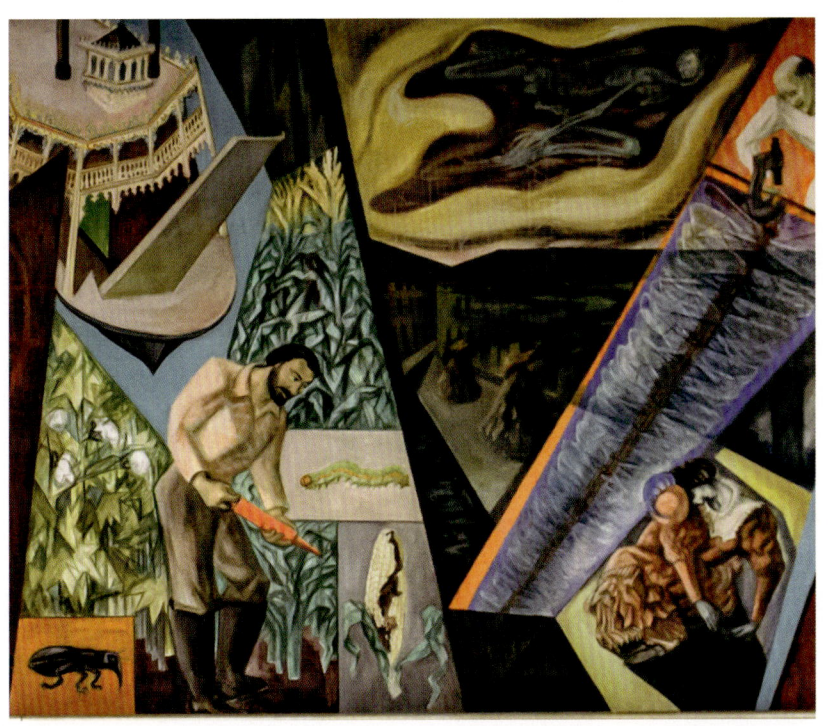

Plate 77.
Age of Struggle
(Section 4), 1954,
fresco, NOUPT, New
Orleans. Photo by
Jackson Hill.

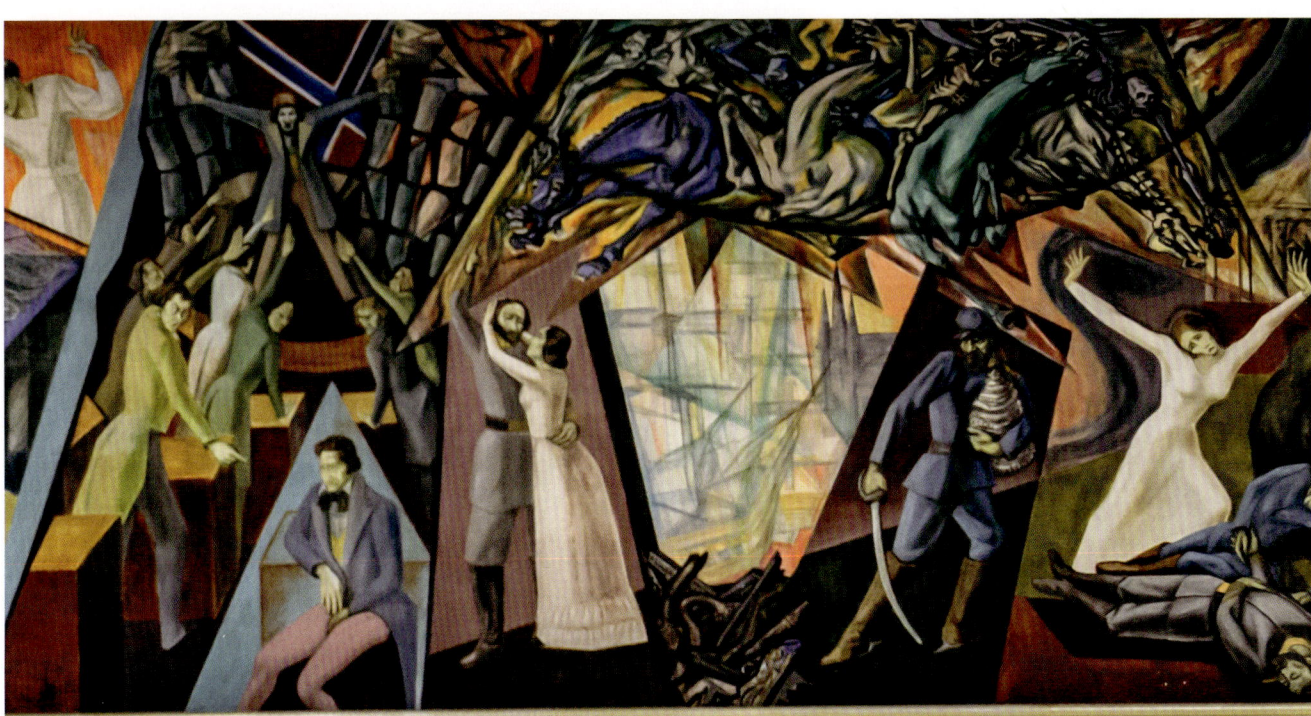

Plate 78.
Age of Struggle
(Section 5), 1954,
fresco, NOUPT, New
Orleans. Photo by
Jackson Hill.

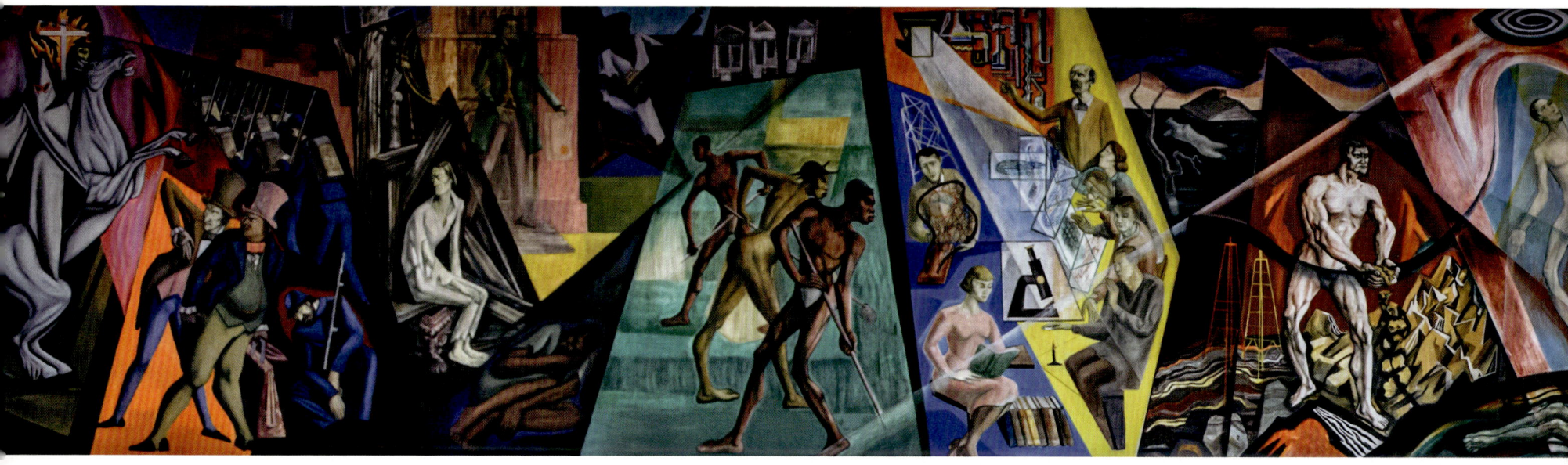

MODERN AGE

(Plate 79)

The fourth panel begins with the aftermath of the Civil War in Louisiana, a time of misery and chaos (plate 80). Albrizio depicts the fury and violence of the Ku Klux Klan through the raging white horse and rider who race across the alizarin crimson, cadmium scarlet, and turquoise blue landscape of a terrorized South. Carpetbaggers, as they were known, are portrayed as villainous characters shielding themselves from the terrorizing tactics of the Klan.[37] As the troops return home, the ravaged ruins of a once-glorious plantation and the impoverished and defeated owner remain behind. Below, an

enslaved African is shown sleeping, indicating that slavery in the South is laid to rest. A brighter background emerges as recuperative activities take place. Standing on the capitol steps, a government official holds the new State Constitution of 1879.[38] The state seal, "embossed" upon the scene, is a hopeful symbol of the perseverance of Louisiana's citizens.

Section 2 of *Modern Age* depicts the plight of the freedmen as foremost among unsolved problems (plate 81). Inexperienced in all but agricultural manual labor, many returned to the fields. Juxtaposed to that scene is the endowment by merchant Paul Tulane to the University of Louisiana for the promotion of education in New Orleans. His generous gift

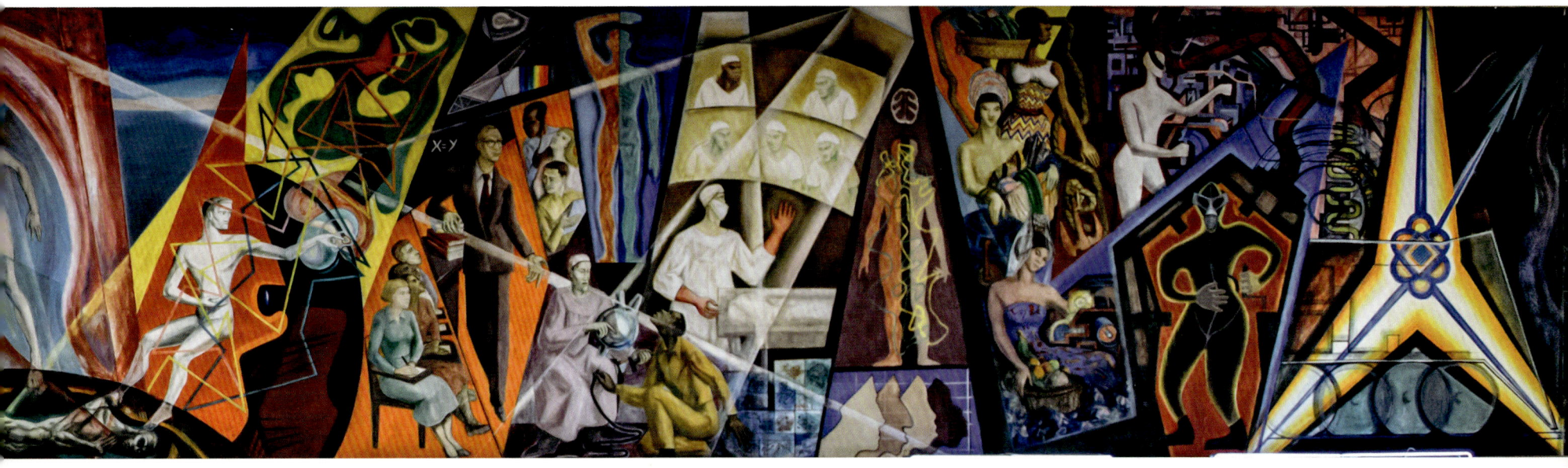

Plate 79.

Overview, *Modern Age,* 1954, fresco, NOUPT, New Orleans. Photo by Jackson Hill.

transformed the school into what is now Tulane University and set the stage for academic excellence and research in medicine, anthropology, and sociology.

Albrizio explained that he wished Panel 4 to mirror Panel 1 in design and spirit. In the third section of Panel 4, he represents humanity in its material, spiritual, and creative aspects with the ascending figure in the center paralleling the native figure in the panel directly across the terminal (plate 82). As the power of the sun's rays encompassed and nourished past Native American civilizations, the power of knowledge and the all-seeing "eye" of the divine encompass and give power to modern man. The first figure ties man with the material world. Seen amid the natural elements, man has the power to reap from the earth all its riches. He is also at the mercy of nature's power as represented by the flood and the ominous clouds in the background. The central figure represents the spiritual aspects of man, which allow him to transcend the material world and death. Albrizio's intention was to relate this transcending figure to the Christian idea of the Resurrection. Finally, creative man has his feet firmly rooted in the earth, using the fruits of his earthly environment to create a better existence.

The panel's fourth section depicts advancements in education (plate 83). A professor and his students are posi-

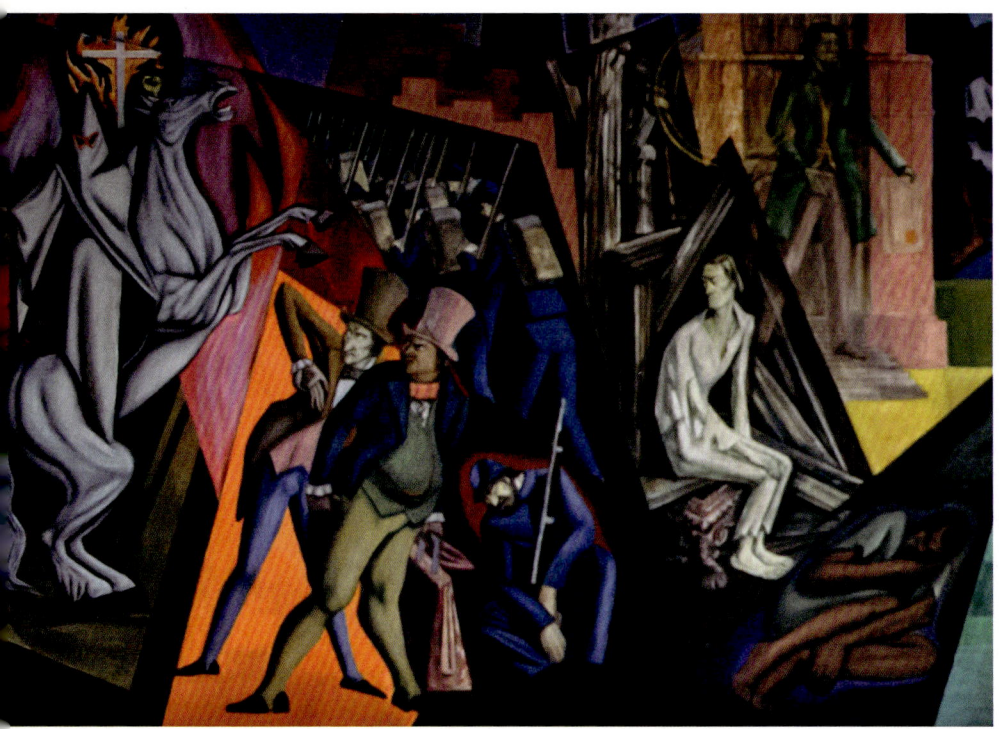

Plate 80.

Modern Age (Section 1), 1954, fresco, NOUPT, New Orleans. Photo by Jackson Hill.

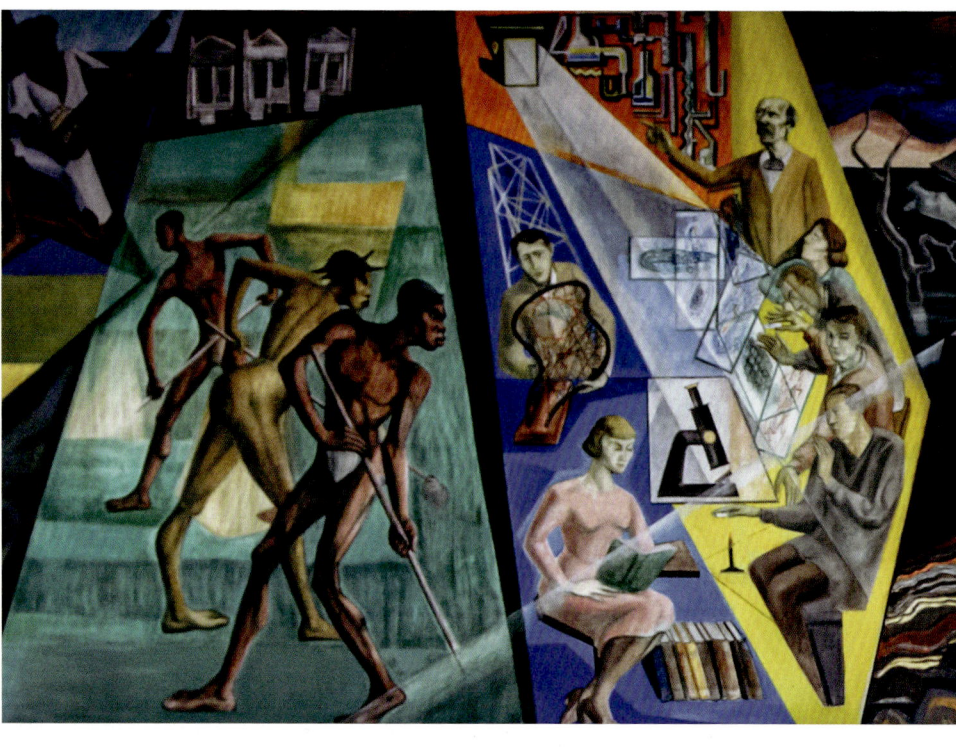

Plate 81.

Modern Age (Section 2), 1954, fresco, NOUPT, New Orleans. Photo by Jackson Hill.

tioned among radiating lines, which bind knowledge with the efforts of man and the advancements of the future. All races are shown as having equal opportunity in these educational endeavors.

Section 5 suggests the future conquests of space and atomic power (plate 84). The vertical strip of colorful figures on the left is almost an anomaly meshed between the representations and symbols of science. Elegantly and gracefully

posed, the figures provide a rich visual passage. Highlighting products of world trade, especially trade in the Caribbean and Central America, they signify the importance of New Orleans as a port and a transportation link with neighbors to the south. Representations of industry and technology form an undefinable assemblage of industrial workings. An alien being occupies a large portion of the foreground. The symbol of nuclear power in the conquest of space is represented

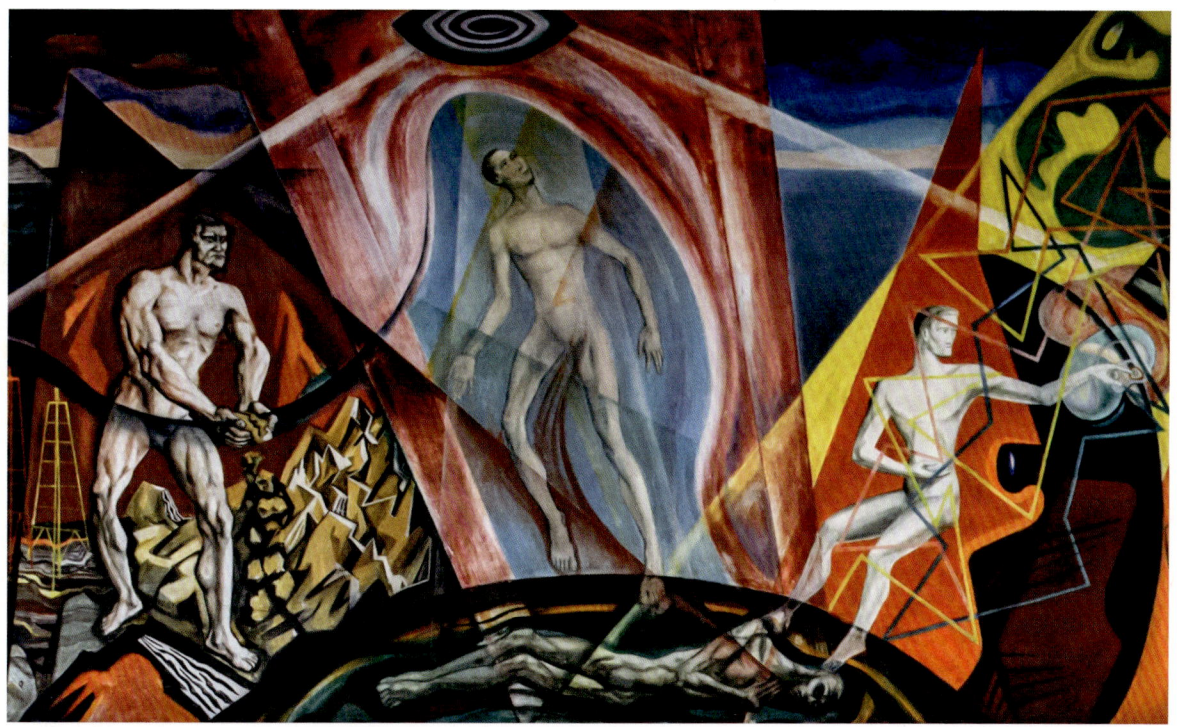

Plate 82.
Modern Age (Section 3), 1954, fresco, NOUPT, New Orleans. Photo by Jackson Hill.

within a tripointed structure reminiscent of a rocket.[39] The stability of this element creates a firm compositional anchor in the conclusion of the program.

TECHNIQUE AND STYLE

An interesting feature of the Union Passenger Terminal's cycle is that it employs not only fresco, but also the ancient technique of encaustic. Encaustic comes from the Greek word *enkaustikos,* which means "to burn in." Once the fresco has dried, heated beeswax and pigment are polished onto the surface to create a brilliant sheen. Albrizio used this technique at regular intervals to add a dull, satiny quality to the surface and give a contrast in texture.[40] He also added ground marble dust to his encaustic mixture, which he felt tied the murals to the marble used throughout the interior of the terminal.[41]

Compared to Albrizio's previous works, the terminal cycle displays yet another distinctive style for the artist. Abstract, decorative, and keenly design-oriented, the cycle has a feeling of intense theatricality. Many of the figures, with

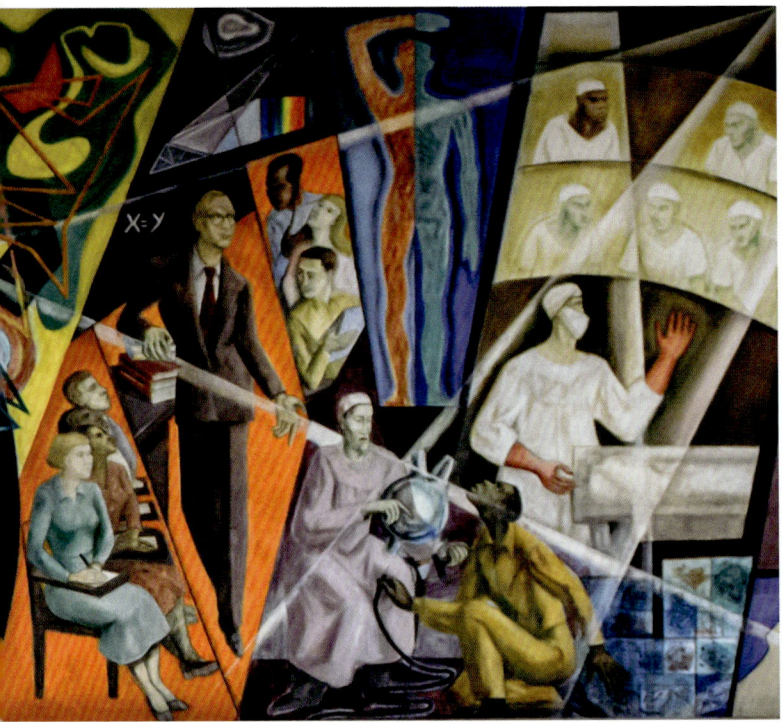

Plate 83.

Modern Age (Section 4), 1954, fresco, NOUPT, New Orleans.
Photo by Jackson Hill.

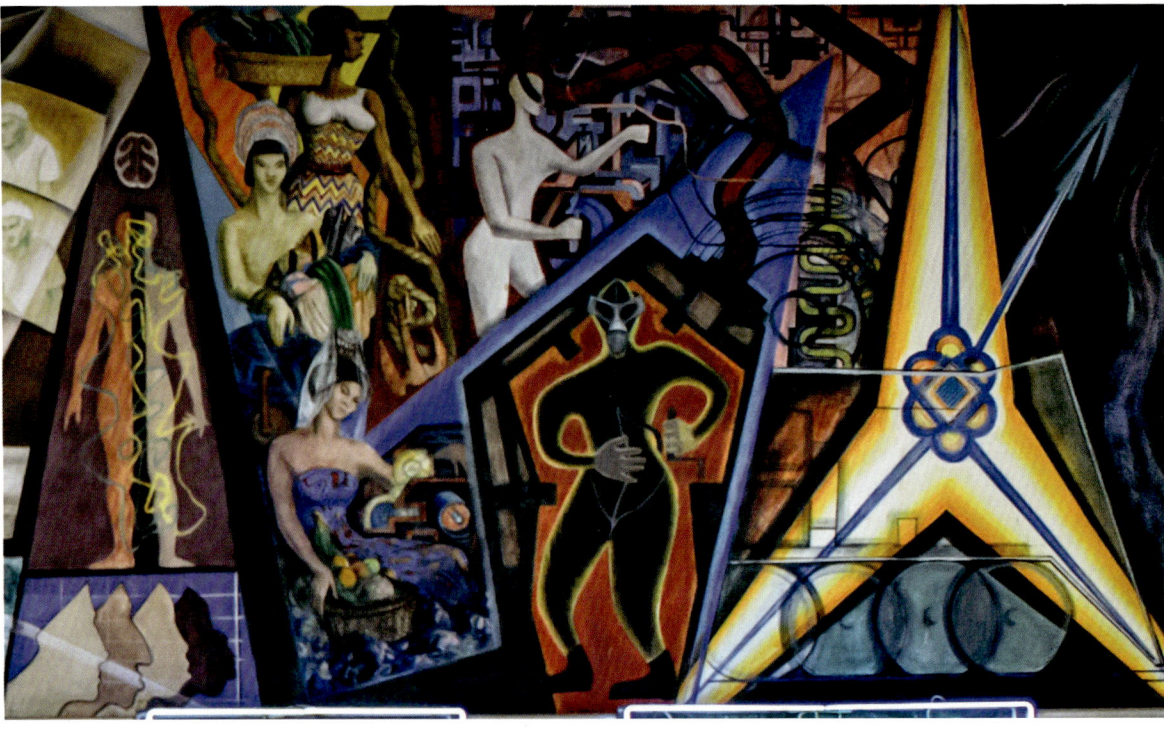

Plate 84.

Modern Age (Section 5), 1954, fresco, NOUPT, New Orleans.
Photo by Jackson Hill.

their exaggerated gestures and facial expressions, recall the figures in Albrizio's easel paintings of the 1930s, especially *Jordan* (plate 30). The geometric arrangement of the Waterman program, created by converging rays and planes, has here evolved into flat fields of color upon which the pageantry of events takes place. Certain episodes seem "spotlighted" by shapes of orange or yellow that set them apart from surrounding sequences. The intriguing shapes of these

background areas alternate between light and dark values to clearly separate the illustrated events. This value alternation also creates a visual momentum across the fresco that helps to move the eye from one sequence to another.

Compositionally, each of the four panels in this program is arranged around a central section. It is as if this central area tethers the otherwise unruly, outspread segments of the vast panel. Albrizio explicitly established this "compositional center" around a uniform theme. To the left and right of this focal point the remainder of the design forms a mirror image that helps to create a cohesive unit within each of the extended 61-foot panels. To unite the entire cycle, he relates one panel to another through either composition or subject.

The continuous narrative is tied together by interlocking compositional elements, such as the recurring band of blue symbolizing the Mississippi River. Albrizio also uses the opaque color shapes of the background as pieces of a puzzle that interlock and join the various scenes playing upon their surface.

This grand endeavor was the last fresco mural executed by Albrizio, and he saw it as the most important project of his career. It gave him the opportunity to immortalize in fresco a part of the country that he cherished. It also gave him the chance to offer the people of New Orleans and Louisiana something to be proud of, both as a work of art and as a reflection of their heritage. "I want this to be the best painting I have ever done," he said.[42]

9.

Beyond the Frescoes

BY THE TIME ALBRIZIO FINISHED THE murals in the Union Passenger Terminal, he had resigned from LSU and was living in New Orleans full-time. He and his wife were separated, Jean living in Alabama and Albrizio at a nineteenth-century townhouse in the French Quarter that had been divided into apartments. While living there, he painted a small fresco in the entryway of the building (plate 85). Measuring approximately 3 feet by 4 feet, it shows costumed Mardi Gras revelers, most of whom were neighbors. The panel still exists and the current owners of the house diligently care for it, but past conservation efforts were poor. Sealants used to cover the fresco caused moisture to become trapped inside the painting. A time-consuming process of removing the efflorescent plaster, while retaining as much of the original paint as pos-

sible, is necessary to save the mural. Proper conservation is ongoing as resources allow.

Albrizio remained committed to the idea of the artist as a socially conscious leader.[1] It is remarkable that he was able to interest major factions in fresco decoration as late as 1949 (the Waterman cycle) and 1954 (the Union Passenger Terminal). Fresco had long been out of favor as an interior embellishment. Albrizio, however, had several advantages in selling his projects. One, he was passionate about the need for art in public areas, and, two, he was trained in the discipline of architecture. He could speak in terms that builders and architects understood and could supply detailed drawings with architectural notations. He understood the limitations, and sometimes advantages, of the structure, and he was sensitive to the massive scale of the commission. Murals were his medium.

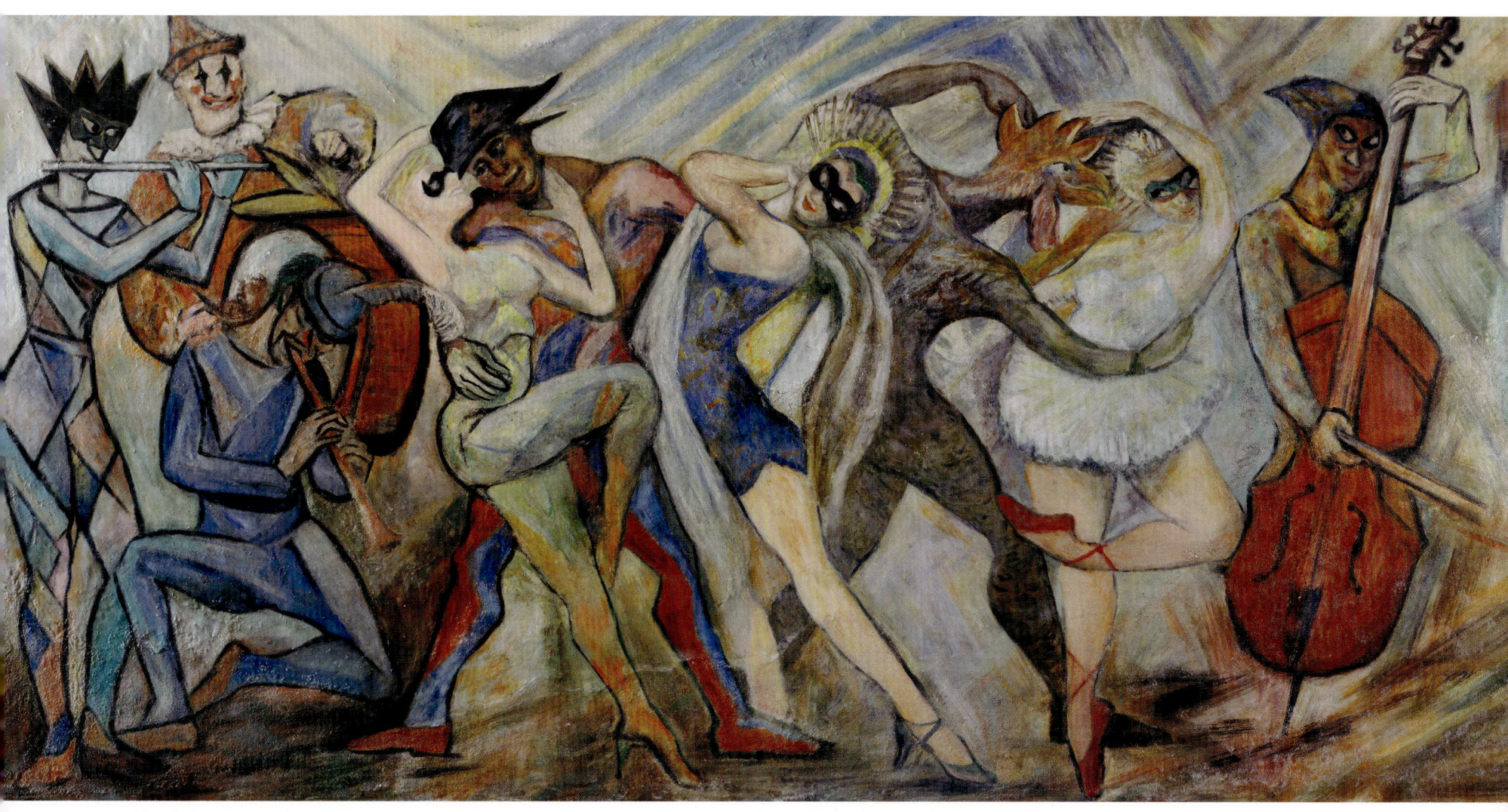

Plate 85. *Revelry,* c. 1965, fresco, c. 3 x 4 feet, private residence, New Orleans. Courtesy of Jeff and Celia Collins. Photo by Patrick Barnes.

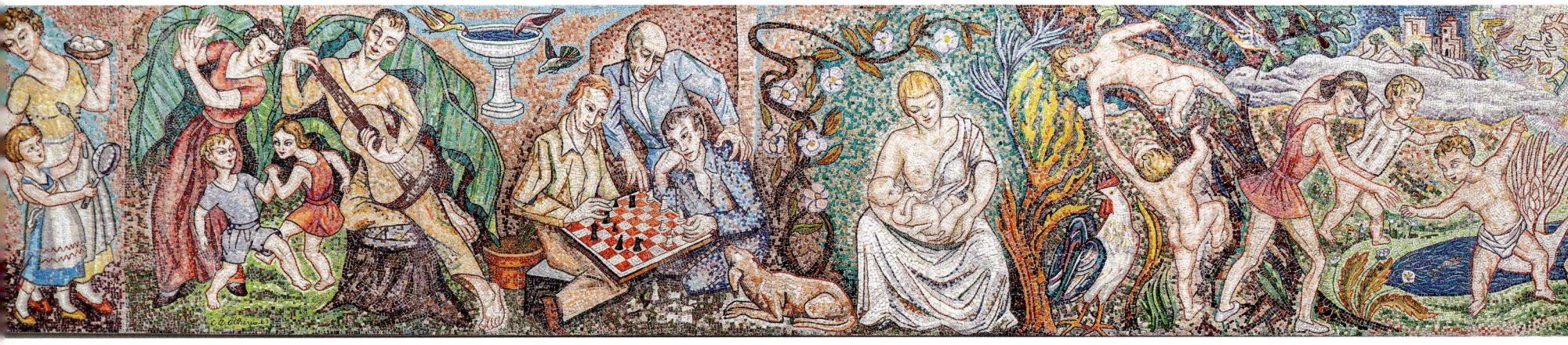

Plate 86.

Family Life, 1964, mosaic, Louisiana State Museum, Baton Rouge. Originally installed at the Algiers Mental Health Center, Algiers, LA. Courtesy Louisiana State Museum. Photo by Tim Mueller.

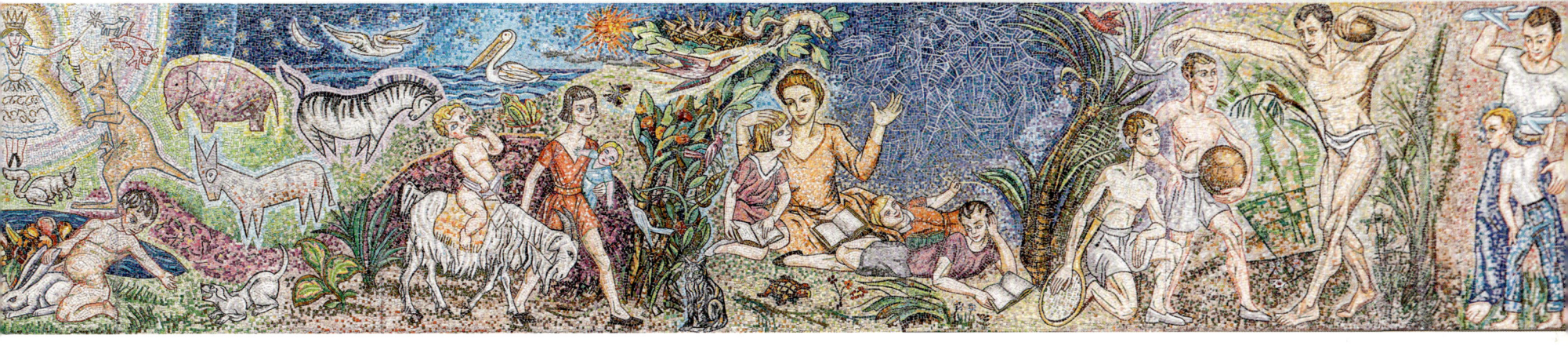

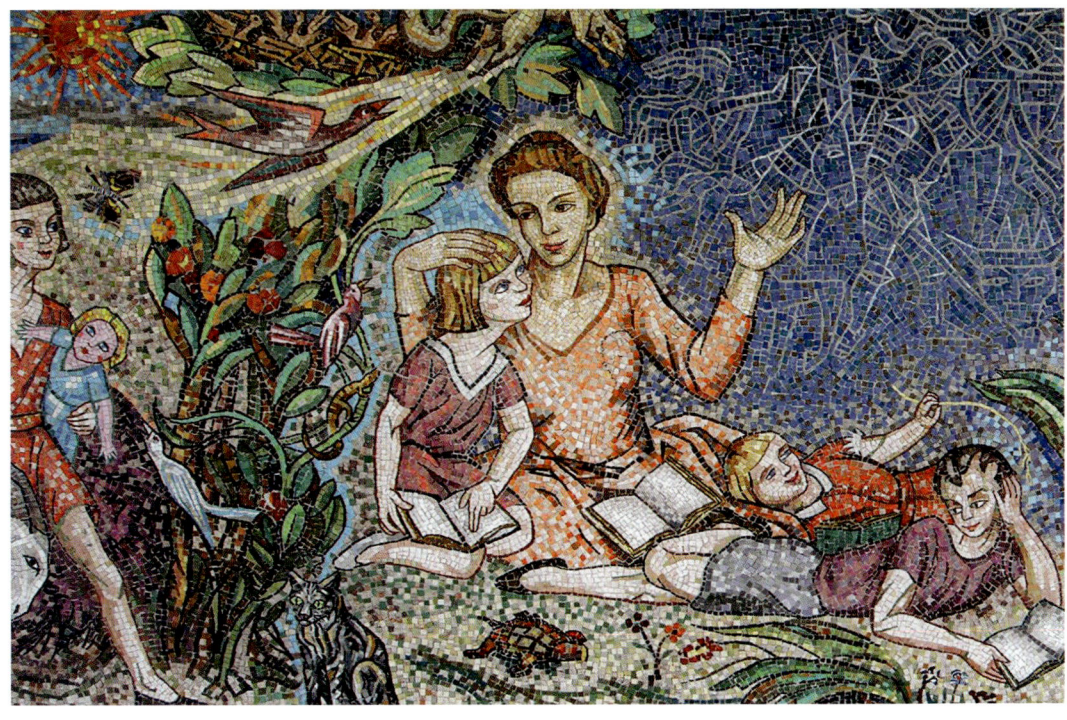

Plate 87.
Detail of *Family Life*.
Courtesy Louisiana
State Museum.
Photo by Tim Mueller.

By the 1950s, mosaic murals had gained popularity as an art form allied to modern architecture. Even though characterized by simplicity of form and lack of detail and decoration, modernist-style architecture occasionally used strategically placed materials to add visual interest or texture. Mosaics worked well with the sleek, clean, often synthetic new building material of the era as well as with the blank wall spaces.

In 1955, Albrizio traveled to Mexico to study the technique of mosaic art and to examine the mosaic murals of Diego Rivera and Juan O'Gorman in University City, the location of the National Autonomous University of Mexico, completed in 1954. He was enthralled by the Mexican culture and felt that "the relation of the people to their soil" was the secret of the creativity and character of the Mexican people.[2] His interest in Mexican mosaics expanded to a love of Mexican artifacts and sketches of the people and countryside.

In 1954, before his first trip to Mexico, Albrizio received a commission to create his first mosaic mural. The Louisiana State Capitol was undergoing remodeling under the auspices of Governor Robert Kennon, and a mosaic panel was desired to decorate the entrance of the governor's reception room. Coincidentally, the panel would cover the spot where Huey Long had been assassinated by gunfire in 1935. By the time details were settled, Earl K. Long had become governor, and he objected to obliterating the bullet holes associated with his brother's death. The project was halted, and the proposed mural, *Law, Order, and Government,* was reassigned

to the Louisiana Supreme Court Building in New Orleans. "I suffered over the change at first," Albrizio remarked. "I had to perform some serious surgery on the mosaic to make it fit in the space here in the court building. But I probably am the only one that will know the difference."[3] The installation was finally realized in September of 1957.[4] After Hurricane Katrina, damage to the building necessitated removal and relocation of the mural to its current location at the 19th Judicial District Court Building in Baton Rouge.

Albrizio went on to pursue mosaic art as avidly as he had fresco painting. He completed a small panel for the First National Bank in Houma, Louisiana, and then an impressive panel for the courthouse in Gretna, Louisiana. Both were done in 1957. He then returned to Mexico for further study.

In 1958, he completed a mosaic mural for the courthouse in Mobile, Alabama, as well as a small mosaic panel for the city's YWCA. That same year he traveled to Venice to study the many exquisite mosaics there and to gather from the famed glassmaking foundries of Murano materials for future projects. He purchased different types of glass, such as enameled, gold, and milk, for use as tesserae, the pieces that make up a mosaic. His next mosaic, *Family Life,* for the Algiers Mental Health Center in Algiers, Louisiana, took five artisans approximately five months to fabricate under Albrizio's direction in Venice. Once completed, the panel was cut, meticulously packed in sections, and shipped to New Orleans. It was anchored to an exterior wall of the facility in 1964.[5] The building was irreparably damaged by Hurricane Katrina in 2005, though the mosaic was not

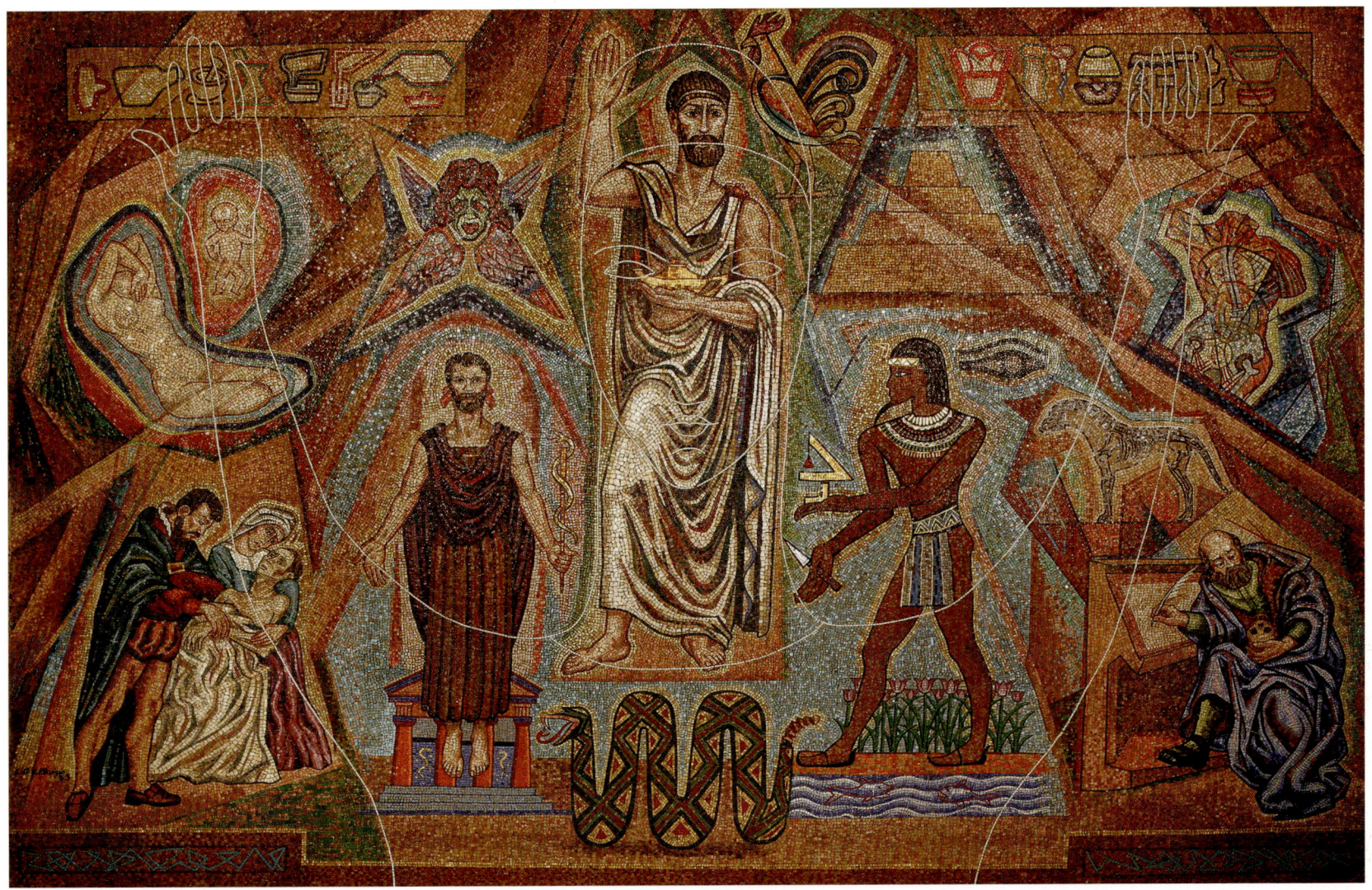

Plate 88.

The History of Medicine, 1965, mosaic, 22 × 24 feet, University of South Alabama Medical Center, Mobile. Originally installed in the Mobile General Hospital. Courtesy University of South Alabama.

harmed. It has now been permanently relocated to the Capitol Park Museum in Baton Rouge (plates 86–87).

In 1965, Albrizio completed *The History of Medicine* for the Mobile General Hospital. The mosaic mural gives viewers in a single glance the sweep of medical history from Hippocrates to Imhotep to the modern surgeon (plate 88). It is now located in the lobby of the University of South Alabama Medical Center in Mobile.

A final trip to Italy in 1964 allowed Albrizio to work on the last murals of his career. Two enormous mosaics—*Mardi Gras* and *The Circus*—for the Mobile Municipal Auditorium took him to Venice. During an extended stay, he worked on the murals, visited cousins in Rome, and spent Christmas with relatives in Trani, the hometown of his parents.[6] He looked forward to returning to the United States in the early part of 1965 only to be delayed by a longshoremen's strike upon his arrival. Unable to dock in New Orleans, the SS *Monfiore* was directed to Galveston, where it sat waiting to be unloaded. Dozens of vessels clogged the port, and Albrizio watched days become weeks as he sat alone on board, refusing to leave his mosaics and supplies unattended.

In 1965, Albrizio returned to easel painting due to successive strokes and ill health. In the private space of his studio, he created countless canvases, ranging from still lifes to dream worlds.[7] Albrizio's ceaseless energy and inspiration had provided him many years of creative satisfaction and artistic accomplishment. Art was so much a part of him that even during his last days he painted an acrylic mural on the corridor walls of the nursing facility where he stayed. Albrizio died in Baton Rouge in early January of 1973 at the age of 78. He was buried in Westbury, New York, in the Cemetery of the Holy Rood close to his family.

* * *

The legacy of Conrad Albrizio is unique. He was a New Yorker by birth, but he chose to live in the South. As early as 1936 he stated, "The south should supply a rich nucleus for what will ultimately constitute the true American Art," and like many converts, his passion was deep.[8]

Albrizio's training as an architectural draftsman gave him an excellent understanding of structural principles and building design. He could easily converse with architects when planning his murals and was comfortable with the large-scale mural format. He worked in fresco long into the 1950s and then changed to mosaic murals when fresco was deemed an unsuitable complement to modern architecture. Mosaics became his preferred medium until 1965, when he returned to easel painting.

Although his early executions of fresco painting are awkward and reflect the challenges of working in the medium, Albrizio quickly matured into a more sophisticated fresco painter. By the time he painted the Waterman cycle in 1949 and the Union Passenger Terminal in 1954, he was a consummate fresco artist able to control his brush to paint as he commanded.

If we critically judge the artist, as we must do in a study of his work, we can conclude that Albrizio's contribution to southern art is remarkable. His murals are unique, and the noble technique of fresco that he employed is an important artistic legacy. The quality of his paintings varies; while some works are masterful, especially his easel paintings from the 1930s (see *Jordan,* plate 30), others seem to struggle to find an expressive form, such as his painting *Duality*.

Because of the nature of the media, Albrizio's frescoes and mosaics will endure, carrying forward long and revered artistic practices. A record of southern life, they speak of the subjects Albrizio chose as well as the artist himself. The details they immortalize become more precious over time. Art is extraordinary because there is so much beneath the surface. "I paint because I often have no words," says Albrizio. "I can feel with a brush."[9]

Acknowledgments

MY DEEPEST THANKS FOR THE support and encouragement of the staff of LSU Press for seeing this project to its fruition. My sincerest gratitude goes to Margaret Lovecraft, acquisitions editor, and Catherine L. Kadair, senior editor, for their many talents and endless patience during this protracted undertaking.

For assistance in the tedious task of research, I would like to thank Paula Taylor, who spent many hours at her computer emailing various repositories and museums on my behalf. I am also grateful to Evan D'Antoni for assistance with computer woes and Valerie Andrews for sorting out formatting and typing problems. Thanks to fellow museum curator Turry Flucker, whose expertise on midcentury New Orleans and civil rights expanded my knowledge of the era when the New Orleans Union Passenger Terminal murals were painted. Thanks also to curator Wayne Phillips at the Louisiana State Museum for his assistance in photographing the grid drawings. It was a complicated task.

Gathering the many illustrations in this book was a daunting task. Thanks to photographers Patrick Barnes, Brad Smith, Brian Lewis, Bevil Knapp, Jim Zietz, Eddy Perez, Chad Riley, Jackson Hill, and Tim Mueller, as well as the many other anonymous photographers connected with museums and repositories who often go unnoticed. Your work is art as well.

Last but not least, I would like to thank the institutions and private owners who allowed their works to be reproduced. A special thank you to members of the Albrizio family, especially Anne Albrizio Orvin (now deceased), niece of the artist, who generously shared her time and personal effects of the artist, allowing me to understand the man more fully.

Notes

PREFACE

1. Conversation with Dorothy French, friend of the artist, May 1988.
2. Ibid.
3. Jack Hastings, letter to the author, February 24, 1984, in the author's possession.

1.
EDUCATION OF THE ARTIST

1. Interview with Janice R. Sachse, friend of the artist, 17 April 1978.
2. Jack Hastings, letter to the author, 12 Aug. 1985, in the author's possession.
3. Interview with David Cicalese, relative of Conrad Albrizio, New York City, May 2012.
4. *Lives: New Orleans Artists,* WPA Project, p. 000012. Isaac Delgado Museum of Art, n.d., in New Orleans Museum of Art Library, New Orleans.
5. Anne Albrizio Orvin, niece of Conrad Albrizio, letter to the author, 15 Aug. 1978, in the author's possession.
6. "Noted BR Artist Conrad Albrizio Is Dead at 78," *Baton Rouge State-Times,* 8 Jan. 1978.
7. Interview with Cicalese.
8. John Shelton Reed, *Dixie Bohemia: A French Quarter Circle in the 1920s* (Baton Rouge: LSU Press, 2012), 1–4.
9. "Noted BR Artist Conrad Albrizio Is Dead at 78."
10. Conrad A. Albrizio, letter to Dr. J. M. Smith, Louisiana State University, 23 May 1935, in Conrad Albrizio Papers, MSS 3349, Louisiana and Lower Mississippi Valley Collections, LSU Libraries, Baton Rouge (hereafter Albrizio Papers, LLMVC).
11. Virginia Taylor, "Return of an Artist," *New Orleans Times-Picayune/States Magazine,* 15 Feb. 1948, 26.
12. Albrizio, letter to Smith.
13. Taylor, "Return of an Artist," 26.
14. "Majorcan Landscape Exhibited by Arts and Crafts Club," *New Orleans States,* 24 Oct. 1925.
15. Untitled article, *New Orleans Times-Picayune,* 13 Oct. 1925, n.p., in Vertical Files (Artists), Humanities Division, Howard-Tilton Memorial Library, Tulane University, New Orleans.
16. Taylor, "Return of an Artist," 26.
17. Albrizio, letter to Smith.
18. Ibid.
19. Untitled article, *New Orleans Times-Picayune,* 31 Mar. 1940, in Louisiana Room, LSU Libraries' Special Collections.
20. *Lives,* 000014.

2.
THE LOUISIANA STATE CAPITOL FRESCOES

1. *Lives,* 000014.
2. Conversation with David Cicalese, 7 May 2017.
3. "History of Louisiana State University," unpublished report, LSU Libraries' Special Collections.

4. "Louisiana's New Capitol, Masterpiece of Cut Stone and Bronze, Opens May 16," *New Orleans Times-Picayune*, 8 May 1932.

5. John C. Ferguson, "New State Capitol," in *knowlouisiana.org/Encyclopedia of Louisiana*, ed. David Johnson, Louisiana Endowment for the Humanities, 1 Feb 2011.

6. "New Orleans Artists to Do Work on New State Capitol," *New Orleans Item-Tribune*, 21 June 1931.

7. Vincent F. Kubly, *The Louisiana Capitol: Its Art and Architecture* (Gretna: Pelican Pub. Co., 1977), 9.

8. In 1955, during a major renovation, it was noted that the four murals in the governor's reception room had cracked. Albrizio estimated the repair costs to be around $13,000. Due to this expense and to the fact that fresco painting was not as fashionable in 1955 as it had been in 1931, it was agreed that the works would be destroyed and remodeling proceed. Another panel, originally in the Court of Appeals room, was destroyed in 1966–67. See Kubly, *Louisiana Capitol*, 141. The one remaining panel, originally in the Supreme Court room, now decorates the governor's pressroom (ibid., 67).

9. Orene Simmons, "Lost Art of Fresco Is Used in Reception Room of Governor at Capitol," in Albrizio Papers, LLMVC.

10. Kubly, *Louisiana Capitol*, 66.

11. Ibid., 67.

3.
THE INFLUENCE OF THE MEXICAN MURALISTS

1. *Lives*, 00013.

2. Alma M. Reed, *The Mexican Muralists* (New York: Crown Publishers, 1960), 50.

3. Leah Dickerman and Anna Indych-López, *Diego Rivera: Murals for the Museum of Modern Art* (New York: Museum of Modern Art, 2011), 41–43.

4. Ibid.

5. Ibid.

6. William F. McDonald, *Federal Relief Administration and the Arts: The Origins and Administrative History of the Arts Projects of the Works Progress Administration* (Columbus: Ohio State University Press, 1969), 369.

4.
A NEW DEAL FOR ALBRIZIO

1. McDonald, *Federal Relief Administration and the Arts*, 368–69.

2. "Louisiana Artist Appointed to Staff," Unidentified newspaper clipping, 1936, Humanities Division, Howard-Tilton Memorial Library.

3. Ibid.

4. Conrad A. Albrizio, letter to Inslee A. Hopper, assistant superintendent, Section of Painting and Sculpture, 29 June 1936, Washington, DC, General Services Administration, National Archives and Records Service, Washington, DC (hereafter GSA, NA).

5. Members of the review committee for the Section of Painting and Sculpture were chosen not only for their qualities of leadership and political acumen, but for their training in the arts as well. Such individuals as Olin Downs, Edward Bruce, and Edward Rowan commonly served on these competition juries. Their credentials are impressive. Downs worked in both PWAP and the Section. He also served as chief of the Treasury Relief Art Project. He won two section competitions, executing post office murals in Rhinebeck and Hyde Park, New York. He attended Harvard and studied painting at Yale for two years. See Francis V. O'Connor, ed., *The New Deal Art Projects: An Anthology of Memoirs* (Washington, DC: Smithsonian Institution, 1972), 10. Rowan served as assistant director of PWAP and later as superintendent of the Section. He was former director of the Little Gallery in Cedar Rapids, Iowa. See Richard D. McKinzie, *The New Deal for Artists* (Princeton, NJ: Princeton University Press, 1973), 22.

6. U.S. Treasury Dept., Procurement Division, Section of Painting and Sculpture, contract with Conrad A. Albrizio, 18 July 1936, GSA, NA.

7. Inslee A. Hopper, letter to Conrad A. Albrizio, 16 May 1936, GSA, NA.

8. U.S. Treasury Dept., contract with Albrizio, 18 July 1936.

9. Conrad A. Albrizio, letter to Edward B. Rowan, 20 July 1936, GSA, NA.

10. Albrizio, letter to Rowan, 11 Aug. 1936, GSA, NA.

11. Albrizio, letter to Rowan, 26 Aug. 1936, GSA, NA.

12. Albrizio, letter to Rowan, 17 Sept. 1936, GSA, NA.

13. Rowan, letter to Albrizio, 18 May 1937, GSA, NA.

14. Edward B. Rowan, letter to Maxon H. Holloway, curator, Museum of Art, 27 Apr. 1937, Montgomery, AL, GSA, NA.

15. U.S. Treasury Dept., Procurement Division, Section of Painting and Sculpture, contract with Conrad A. Albrizio, 14 Jan. 1938, GSA, NA.

16. Albrizio, letter to Rowan, 1 July 1937, GSA, NA.

17. Rowan, letter to Albrizio, 13 July 1937, GSA, NA.

18. Robert Mitchell, "The Battle of the Beehive Furnace Mural," *Alabama Heritage,* Spring 1987, 34.

19. Ibid., 36.

20. Ibid.

21. Ibid., 37.

5.
PUBLIC WORKS UNDER THE FEDERAL EMERGENCY RELIEF ACT

1. Documents and Records, Louisiana State Exhibit Building, Shreveport, LA.

2. McDonald, *Federal Relief Administration and the Arts,* 25–27.

3. "Polishing the Jewel of the Ark-La-Tex," *Shreveport Magazine,* June 1978, 48.

4. Georgia L. Wilson, "Albrizio Exhibit on Mural Painting to Be on Display through Saturday," *Baton Rouge State-Times,* 29 Apr. 1940.

5. "Conrad Albrizio Begins Work on Murals in State Office Building," *Baton Rouge Morning Advocate,* n.d., in Louisiana Room, LSU Libraries' Special Collections.

6. "State Gets New Murals," *New Orleans Item-Tribune,* 23 Oct. 1938.

7. Ibid.

8. Ibid.

9. Untitled newspaper article, *New Orleans Item,* 6 July 1940, Howard-Tilton Memorial Library.

10. Ibid.

11. Thomas Hart Benton, *An American in Art: A Professional and Technical Autobiography* (Lawrence: University Press of Kansas, 1969), 58–59.

12. Thomas H. Benton, letter to Conrad A. Albrizio, 5 Aug. 1935, Albrizio Papers, LLMVC.

13. Stephen Polcari, "Jackson Pollock and Thomas Hart Benton," *Arts,* Mar. 1979, 121–23.

14. Richard Megraw, "Xavier Gonzalez," in *knowlouisiana.org/Encyclopedia of Louisiana,* ed. David Johnson, Louisiana Endowment for the Humanities, 13 Jan. 2011.

6.
THE END OF THE 1930S AND INTO THE 1940S

1. Untitled newspaper article, *New Orleans Times-Picayune/States,* 21 Nov. 1937, Howard-Tilton Memorial Library.

2. Douglas M. Gruse, "The Art of Social Consciousness," *LSU Magazine,* Spring 1990, 41–44.

3. Ibid.

4. Ibid.

5. "History of Louisiana State University."

6. Gruse, "Art of Social Consciousness."

7. Ibid., 41.

8. Ibid., 43.

9. Conrad A. Albrizio, papers from the Iberia Parish Clerk of Court, Iberia Parish Courthouse, New Iberia, LA.

10. Harris Jackson, "Art Should Awaken People, Incite Them, Says Albrizio," *Baton Rouge Morning Advocate,* 21 Apr. 1940.

11. "Conrad Albrizio's Louisiana Paintings to Be Exhibited in Allen Hall April 5–19," *Daily Reveille* (LSU), 2 Apr. 1943.

12. Taylor, "Return of an Artist."

13. *MKR's Art Weekly: Gallery Guide to New York and Vicinity,* No. 8, 4–11 Mar. 1946, 4, Albrizio Papers, LLMVC.

14. Untitled and undated article, *Baton Rouge State-Times,* in Albrizio Papers, LLMVC.

7.

THE MURALS OF THE WATERMAN STEAMSHIP CORPORATION, MOBILE, ALABAMA

1. John Will, "Waterman Building's Formal Opening Set March 3–4," *Mobile Press-Register,* 26 Feb. 1950.

2. "Man Designing Murals Here to Speak at Artist Meeting," *Mobile Press-Register,* 17 Oct. 1948.

3. John Fay, "Waterman Lobby Murals Draw National Attention," *Mobile Press-Register,* 26 Feb. 1950.

4. Jack Hastings, letter to the author, 13 Sept. 1978, in the author's possession.

5. Ibid.

6. Albrizio Papers, LLMVC.

7. Marie A. Reed, "Mural Painting Draws Attention of Mobilians," *Mobile Press-Register,* 23 Feb. 1947.

8. Matthew Baigell, *The American Scene: American Painting of the 1930's* (New York: Praeger, 1974), 90.

9. Albrizio Papers, LLMVC.

10. Hastings, letter to the author.

11. Personal interview with D. T. Coates, Building Manager, Guaranty National Bank Building, May 1978, Mobile, AL.

12. Hastings, letter to the author.

13. Ibid.

14. Kathy Jumper, "Beyond Its Time," *Mobile Press-Register,* 24 Oct. 1999.

15. Conrad A. Albrizio, letter to Imogene Inge Albrizio, 4 June 1958, en route from the United States to Italy, Albrizio Papers, LLMVC.

16. Albrizio Papers, LLMVC.

17. Albrizio, letter to Imogene Inge Albrizio.

18. Albrizio Papers, LLMVC.

19. Newton Mayall, Margaret Mayall, and Jerome Wyckoff, *The Sky Observer's Guide: A Handbook for Amateur Astronomers* (New York: St. Martin's Press, 1959), 18–21.

20. "Ethyl Silicate Murals," *Art Digest,* 16 Oct. 1950, 14.

21. E. B. Newton, Carbide and Carbon Chemicals Corporation, letter to Conrad A. Albrizio, 29 Nov. 1948, in Albrizio Papers, LLMVC.

22. John Fay, "Mural Painting Here Making Art History, Attracting Onlookers," *Mobile Press-Register,* 2 Jan. 1949.

8.

THE MURALS OF THE NEW ORLEANS UNION PASSENGER TERMINAL

1. Taylor, "Return of an Artist," 26.

2. "SAM Out to Save Albrizio Mural," *Scope,* Jan. 1976, 1, 4.

3. "Southern History in Fresco," *New Orleans Times-Picayune/States,* 11 Apr. 1954.

4. Bill Rivers, "The History of the South in Pictures," *Baton Rouge Morning Advocate,* 26 Dec. 1954.

5. "Southern History in Fresco," 14.

6. Rowland Stockk, "The Murals of the NOUPT," *L and N Employees' Magazine,* March 1956, 20.

7. "Southern History in Fresco," 14.

8. Rivers, "History of the South in Pictures."

9. Edwin Adams Davis, *Louisiana: A Narrative History* (Baton Rouge: Claitor's Publishing, 1971), 27–28.

10. Albrizio, *Mural Paintings in the New Orleans Union Passenger Terminal,* 1955, New Orleans (booklet written by the artist), in possession of the author.

11. "Painter of UPT Murals to Be Honored for Work," unidentified newspaper article, in Albrizio Papers, LLMVC.

12. Davis, *Narrative History,* 52–54, 61–62.

13. Albrizio, *Mural Paintings.*

14. Ibid.

15. Davis, *Narrative History,* 80.

16. Conversation with Anne Albrizio Orvin, 27 Oct. 1985, New York City.

17. Margaret Rose Vendryes, *Barthé: A Life in Sculpture* (Jackson: University Press of Mississippi, 2008), 22.

18. Albrizio, *Mural Paintings.*

19. Davis, *Narrative History,* 60, 92.

20. Ibid., 58, 59.

21. Ibid., 72.

22. Albrizio, *Mural Paintings.*

23. Ibid.

24. Stockk, "Murals of the NOUPT," 20.

25. Edwin Adams Davis, *Louisiana, the Pelican State* (Baton Rouge: LSU Press, 1961), 109.

26. Davis, *Narrative History,* 122.

27. Albrizio, *Mural Paintings.*

28. Davis, *Narrative History,* 159–64.

29. Albrizio, *Mural Paintings.*

30. Davis, *Narrative History,* 177–86.

31. Albrizio, *Mural Paintings.*

32. Ibid.

33. Davis, *Narrative History,* 235.

34. Ibid.

35. Ibid. 247–51.

36. Albrizio, *Mural Paintings.*

37. Ibid.

38. Davis, *Pelican State,* 239.

39. Albrizio, *Mural Paintings.*

40. Ralph Mayer, *The Artist's Handbook of Materials and Techniques,* 3rd ed. (New York: Viking, 1970), 324–29.

41. "Southern History in Fresco," 14.

42. Ibid., 16.

9.
BEYOND THE FRESCOES

1. M. Reed, "Mural Painting Draws Attention of Mobilians."

2. Alma M. Reed, "Mexican Art Inspires New Orleans Muralist," *News Weekly* (Mexico, D.F.), 16 Oct. 1955.

3. Iris Turner, "New Supreme Court Gets Mosaic Made for Capitol," *New Orleans States,* 7 Sept. 1957.

4. "17-Foot Mosaic Is Being Placed in Court Building," *New Orleans Times-Picayune,* 8 Sept. 1957.

5. "Mosaics and Mental Health," *Dixie Roto Magazine (New Orleans Times-Picayune),* 19 Jan. 1964.

6. Conrad A. Albrizio, letter to Dorothy French, Dec. 1964, in possession of the author.

7. Janice R. Sachse, letter to the author, 15 Aug. 1978, in possession of the author.

8. "Louisiana Artist Appointed to Staff," newspaper clipping, 1936.

9. Conversation with Anne Albrizio Orvin, 27 Oct. 1985, New York City.

Selected Bibliography

BOOKS

Baigell, Matthew. *The American Scene: American Painting of the 1930's*. New York: Prager, 1974.

Benton, Thomas Hart. *An American in Art: A Professional and Technical Autobiography*. Lawrence: University Press of Kansas, 1969.

Bruce, Edward, and Forbes Watson. *Art in Federal Buildings, Volume 1: Mural Designs, 1934–1936*. Washington, DC: Art in Federal Buildings Inc., 1936.

Charlot, Jean. *The Mexican Mural Renaissance, 1920–1925*. New Haven: Yale University Press, 1963.

Cheney, Martha Candler. *Modern Art in America*. New York: McGraw-Hill, 1939.

Davis, Edwin Adams. *Louisiana: A Narrative History*. Baton Rouge: Claitor's, 1971.

———. *Louisiana, the Pelican State*. Baton Rouge: LSU Press, 1961.

Dickerman, Leah, and Anna Indych-López. *Diego Rivera: Murals for the Museum of Modern Art*. New York: Museum of Modern Art, 2011.

Dickerson, Albert I., ed. *The Orozco Frescoes at Dartmouth*. Hanover, NH: Dartmouth College Publications, 1934.

Fundaburk, Emma Lila, and Thomas G. Davenport, comps. *Art in Public Places in the United States*. Bowling Green, OH: Bowling Green University Popular Press, 1975.

Heller, Nancy, and Julia Williams. *The Regionalists*. New York: Watson-Guptill Publications, 1976.

Helmberger, Werner, and Matthias Staschull. *Tiepolo's World: The Ceiling Fresco in the Staircase Hall of the Würzburg Residence*. Trans. Sue Bollans, eds. Irmgard Killing and Michael Robertson. Munich: Bayerische Schlösserverwaltung, 2008.

Hunter, Sam. *American Art of the 20th Century: Painting, Sculpture, Architecture*. New York: Harry N. Abrams, 1974.

Kubly, Vincent F. *The Louisiana Capitol: Its Art and Architecture*. Gretna, LA: Pelican Pub. Co., 1977.

Marling, Karal Ann. *Wall-to-Wall America: A Cultural History of Post-Office Murals in the Great Depression.* Minneapolis: University of Minnesota Press, 1982.

Mayall, Newton, Margaret Mayall, and Jerome Wyckoff. *The Sky Observer's Guide: A Handbook for Amateur Astronomers.* New York: St. Martin's Press, 1959.

Mayer, Ralph. *The Artist's Handbook of Materials and Techniques.* 3rd ed. New York: Viking, 1970, 324–29.

McDonald, William F. *Federal Relief Administration and the Arts: The Origins and Administrative History of the Arts Projects of the Works Progress Administration.* Columbus: Ohio State University Press, 1969.

McKinzie, Richard D. *The New Deal for Artists.* Princeton, NJ: Princeton University Press, 1973.

Meltzer, Milton. *Violins and Shovels: The WPA Arts Projects.* New York: Delacorte Press, 1976.

O'Connor, Francis V., ed. *Art for the Millions: Essays from the 1930s by Artists and Administrators of the WPA Federal Art Project.* Boston: New York Graphic Society, 1974.

———. *Federal Support for the Visual Arts: The New Deal and Now.* Greenwich, CT: New York Graphic Society, 1969.

———, ed. *The New Deal Art Projects: An Anthology of Memoirs.* Washington, DC: Smithsonian Institution, 1972.

Olcott, William Tyler. *A Field Book of the Stars.* New York: G. P. Putnam, 1935.

Reed, Alma M. *José Clemente Orozco.* New York: Delphic Studios, 1932.

———. *The Mexican Muralists.* New York: Crown Publishers, 1960.

———. *Orozco.* New York: Oxford University Press, 1956.

Reed, John Shelton. *Dixie Bohemia: A French Quarter Circle in the 1920s.* Baton Rouge: LSU Press, 2012.

Secker, Hans F. *Diego Rivera.* Dresden: Verlag der Kunst, 1957.

Tibol, Raquel. *Siqueiros, introductor de realidades.* Mexico: Universidad Nacional Autónoma de Mexico, 1961.

Wagner, Ann Prentice. *1934: A New Deal for Artists.* Washington, DC: Smithsonian American Art Museum, 2009.

Wolfe, Bertram D. *Diego Rivera: His Life and Times.* New York: Alfred A. Knopf, 1939.

PERIODICALS

"Art Project Cut." *Art Digest,* July 1937, 16.

Baldwin, C. R. "Shahn's Bronx Post Office Murals: The Perils of Public Art." *Art in America,* May 1977, pp. 15–16+.

Benson, E. M. "Art on Parole." *American Magazine of Art,* Nov. 1936, pp. 694–709+.

Biddle, George. "Mural Painting in America." *American Magazine of Art,* July 1934, pp. 361–71.

Bloom, J. "Changing Walls: Art for the People and the People as Artists." *Architectural Forum,* May 1973, pp. 20–27.

"Boon to Frescoers: Chemical Formula Permits Artist to Work on a Fresco up to 56 Hours." *Art Digest,* 1 Oct. 1937, p. 12.

Boswell, P. "Government and Art." *Art Digest,* 15 Dec. 1937, p. 3.

———. "Mural Painting." *Art Digest,* 1 Oct. 1934, pp. 3–4.

Boswell, P., and E. J. Kahn. "Artist Plus Architect." *Art Digest,* 1 Jan. 1939, pp. 3+.

Bulliet, C. J. "New Horizons in American Art." *Art Digest,* 15 Oct. 1936, p. 23.

Cahell, H. "Mural America." *Architectural Record,* Sept. 1937, pp. 63–68.

Callahan, K. "Mural Freedom." *Art Digest,* Aug. 1932, p. 17.

Charlot, Jean. "Murals for Tomorrow." *Art News,* July 1945, pp. 20–23.

Clute, E. "Old Techniques for New Walls." *Architectural Forum,* Aug. 1931, pp. 201–2.

Cornwell, D. "Art of Mural Painting." *Design,* Feb. 1950, pp. 8–9+.

"Critics Evaluate Federal Murals at the Whitney Museum." *Art Digest,* 15 Mar. 1940, pp. 3, 8–9+.

Davidson, M. "Government as a Patron of Art." *Art News,* 10 Oct. 1936, pp. 10–12.

———. "WPA Art Marches On; Federal Patronage Justifies Itself." *Art News,* 30 Oct. 1937, p. 11.

"End." *Art Digest,* 15 Feb. 1944, p. 7.

"Exhibition, Passedoit Gallery." *Art News,* March 1946, p. 56.

Fitzgerald, C. J. "Two Mural Projects." *American Artist,* Feb. 1960, pp. 32–37+.

"Fresco Revival." *Art Digest,* 15 May 1932, p. 20.

Garnsey, J. "Thoughts on American Mural Painting." *Architectural Forum,* Jan. 1947, p. 47.

Geist, S. "Prelude: The 1930s." *Arts,* Sept. 1956, pp. 49–55.

Grafly, P. "Mural Painting." *Art Digest,* 15 May 1932, p. 11.

Holbrook, H. "Fresco Painting Technique." *Design,* June 1952, pp. 211+.

"Is a WPA Mural Inviolate—or Whitewashable?" *Art Digest,* Aug. 1943, p. 18.

"Leaf Raking?" *Art Digest,* 15 Oct. 1937, pp. 12–13.

Lichtenauer, J. Mortimer. "A Mural Painter's Attitude toward the Old and New in Art." *American Magazine of Art,* Oct. 1929, pp. 565–68.

Lowe, J. "New Murals for U.S. Communities; Walls Socialized by WPA Artists." *Art News,* 4 June 1938, pp. 15+.

Mahoney, J. O. "Whose Wall Is It?" *Design,* Feb. 1947, p. 18.

Marling, K. A. "William M. Milliken and Federal Art Patronage of the Depression Decade." *Cleveland Museum Bulletin,* Oct. 1974, pp. 360–70.

Mayer, Ralph. "On the Material Side: Fresco Painting." *Art Digest,* 1 Jan. 1950, pp. 16+.

McCausland, E. "Mural Designs for Federal Buildings: Whitney Museum." *Parnassus,* Mar. 1940, pp. 32+.

McCoy, G. "Poverty, Politics and Artists, 1930–1935." *Art in America,* Aug. 1965, pp. 88–107.

McMahon, A. "May the Artist Live?" *Parnassus,* Oct. 1933, pp. 1–4.

Millier, A. "Advocates Federal Art Program When Relief Need Wanes." *Art Digest,* 15 Oct. 1937, p. 12.

———. "Murals and Men." *Art Digest,* Sept. 1935, p. 6.

"More Thoughts on Murals." *Art News,* 11 May 1935, p. 12.

"Mural, Waterman Building, Mobile, Alabama." *Art Digest,* 15 Oct. 1950, p. 14.

"Mural Painting." *Art News.* 14 Oct. 1933, p. 10.

"Mural Project Is Announced; Work of Embellishing Public Buildings." *Art News,* 27 Apr. 1935, p. 17.

"Murals, Citizenship, and Labels." *American Magazine of Art,* Jan. 1935, pp. 53–55.

"Murals, Murals Everywhere: New York Project." *Art Digest,* June 1935, p. 10.

"Murals, Murals in Every Post Office, but What Do They Express?" *Art Digest,* Sept. 1935, pp. 7–8.

"Murals by the Day." *Arts and Decoration,* Feb. 1934, pp. 46–47.

"Murals of the New Waterman Building in Mobile, Alabama." *Art Digest,* 15 Apr. 1949, p. 24.

"Mural Tempest." *Art Digest,* 15 Feb. 1932, p. 5.

"Orozco Murals." *Art Digest,* Sept. 1935, p. 6.

Ozenfant, A. "Requirements for a Mural Art." *Magazine of Art,* Feb. 1945, pp. 42–45+.

Polcari, Stephen. "Jackson Pollock and Thomas Hart Benton." *Arts,* Mar. 1979, pp. 120–24.

"Polishing the Jewel of the Ark-La-Tex." *Shreveport Magazine,* June 1978, pp. 20, 47–48.

"Project Murals Avoid Sweetness and Light." *Art Digest,* June 1938, p. 15.

Reed, A. T. "WPA—RIP!" *Art Digest,* 15 Mar. 1944, p. 28.

"Relief for Artists." *Art Digest,* Sept. 1935, p. 11.

"State Showcase." *Shreveport Magazine,* Feb. 1952, pp. 13–15.

"Testing Pigments for Use in Fresco Painting." *Technical Studies,* July 1941, p. 56.

"Two Years of WPA." *Art Digest,* 1 Mar. 1938, p. 9.

"Vital Expressionism at Passedoit Galleries." *Art Digest,* Mar. 1946, p. 17.

"What Is a Mural? National Society of Mural Painters' Exhibition, Whitney Museum." *Art Digest,* 15 Nov. 1940, p. 21.

"Whitney Museum Rests the Case." *Art Digest,* 1 Apr. 1944, pp. 14+.

Wiley, Hugh. "Art, Artists and Architecture: Walls and Murals." *Architectural Record,* Aug. 1956, pp. 167–70.

"WPA Advisory Group to Raise the Artistic Level." *Art Digest,* 15 Nov. 1940, p. 15.

"WPA Honorably Discharged." *Art Digest,* 15 Dec. 1942, p. 3.

THESES

Brown, Sue Eleanor. "Execution of an Exterior Mural in Fresco." Master's thesis, Louisiana State University, 1940.

Henderson, Roy B. "Execution of a Mural in Fresco." Master's thesis, Louisiana State University, 1939.

Watkins, Ben Porter. "Execution of an Exterior Mural in Fresco." Master's thesis, Louisiana State University, 1940.

Woolfolk, Anne. "Execution of a Mural in Fresco." Master's thesis, Louisiana State University, 1941.

NEWSPAPERS

Baton Rouge Morning Advocate
Baton Rouge State-Times
Daily Reveille (LSU)
Mobile Press
Mobile Press-Register
New Orleans Item
New Orleans Item-Tribune
New Orleans Progress
New Orleans States

New Orleans Times-Picayune
New Orleans Tribune
New York Herald-Tribune
News Weekly (Mexico, D.F.)
Shreveport Journal
Shreveport Times

EXHIBITS

Museum of Modern Art, New York, NY. *Diego Rivera.* 1931.
———. *New Horizons in American Art.* 1936.

UNPUBLISHED MATERIALS AND PUBLIC RECORDS

Amoco Industries, New Orleans, LA
    Files and records.
DeRidder, LA, Post Office, DeRidder, LA

Records and contracts.
Donald, Froom, and Rogers, Architects, Mobile, AL
    Files and records.
General Services Administration, National Archives and Rec-
    ords Services, Washington, DC
    Contracts and letters.
Howard-Tilton Memorial Library, Tulane University, New
    Orleans, LA
    Humanities Division. Vertical files (Artists).
    Louisiana Room. Vertical files.
Iberia Parish Courthouse, New Iberia, LA
    Records of the Clerk of Court.
Louisiana State Exhibit Building, Shreveport, LA
    Documents and records.
LSU Libraries. Louisiana and Lower Mississippi Valley Col-
    lections, Hill Memorial Library, Louisiana State Univer-
    sity, Baton Rouge, LA
    Conrad A. Albrizio Papers. MSS 3349.

"History of Louisiana State University." Unpublished
    report.
    Vertical files. Louisiana Room.
Mobile Historical Society, Mobile, AL
    Vertical files.
New Orleans Museum of Art Library, New Orleans, LA
    Lives: New Orleans Artists, WPA Project, p. 000012.
    Isaac Delgado Museum of Art, n.d.
New Orleans Union Passenger Terminal, New Orleans, LA
    Files and records.
New York Public Library, New York, NY
Russellville, AL, Post Office, Russellville, AL
    Records and contracts.
Shreveport Memorial Library, Shreveport, LA
    Vertical files.
Waterman Steamship Corporation, Mobile, AL
    Files and records.

Index